Life Without Death?

NILS O. JACOBSON, M.D.
Life Without Death?

ON PARAPSYCHOLOGY, MYSTICISM, AND THE QUESTION OF SURVIVAL

Translated from the Swedish by
Sheila La Farge

DELACORTE PRESS / SEYMOUR LAWRENCE

Originally published by Zindermans Förlag,
Gothenburg, Sweden,
under the title *Liv efter döden?*

Copyright © 1971 by Nils-Olof Jacobson
English translation copyright © 1973, 1974 by Dell Publishing Co., Inc.
Manufactured in the United States of America
First printing

Design by Jerry Tillett

LIBRARY OF CONGRESS CATALOGING IN PUBLICATION DATA

Jacobson, Nils-Olof, 1937–
Life without death?

Translation of Liv efter doden?
Includes bibliographical references.
1. Psychical research.   2. Future life.   I. Title.
BF1038.S7J313   133.9′013   73–12714
ISBN: 0-440-04801-X

Contents

Foreword

This book has two purposes. On the one hand, it offers an introduction to that branch of science known as parapsychology, with a survey of some of its current areas of research and findings to date. On the other hand, it attempts to step off from the results of these researches to discuss a question which concerned earlier parapsychologists but which seems to preoccupy only a small number of them now—namely, the question of what happens to human consciousness at death. That is: Can some kind of experience be thought to continue after the death of the body? If the answer should be yes, then what might that experience turn out to be like?

I have tried to present this material in such a way as to make it accessible to readers without any special knowledge or training in parapsychology, psychology, or psychiatry. The reader who is familiar with these subjects is asked to make allowances for definitions and explanations which are obvious and elementary to him. So as not to overburden my approach with technical terms, experiments have been described as succinctly as possible. Readers with a particular interest may pursue references to original source material listed in the bibliography.

Part One outlines the subject in question. Part Two provides a short survey defining parapsychology and what it is concerned with. The most important so-called paranormal phenomena are described by examples from both experimental work and spontaneous personal experiences. Part Three contains examples of paranormal phenomena which are difficult to study in controlled experimental conditions but which are of the greatest importance to a discussion of what happens at death. Part Four takes up questions surrounding the relationship between the brain and consciousness. This discussion attempts to clarify the paranormal experience by relating it to various different states of consciousness, for example, psychedelic and mystical experiences. Finally, Part Five provides examples from psychology and other sources which could be thought to tell us something about what life after death (if it does exist) would be like.

I have tried to avoid unnecessary foreign words. Of course, certain technical terms cannot be avoided. These are defined in the text notes and in the glossary. Numbers in the text refer to the bibliography and notes at the end of the book. I should also point out that when I use a phrase such as "telepathic" or "precognitive," it does not mean that I consider the experience being described to be a proven case of telepathy or precognition. But I would burden my text unnecessarily if I continually repeated phrases like "presumably telepathic" or "allegedly precognitive," and therefore such reservations must be understood from the start.

I am grateful to the Martinus Institute, the Parapsychology Foundation and the American Society for Psychical Research for permission to quote from copyrighted material.

I wish to express my deep gratitude to my subjects and all the others who have worked with me so that this book could be written. A special thanks to Helene Reeder for good advice, without which there would have been no book, and thanks, also, to Lillemor Lönnqvist and Olof Rydén for invaluable practical help and positive criticism.

NILS O. JACOBSON, M.D.
Lund, Sweden
December 1970

Part One

THE PROBLEM OF DEATH

1

Four Ways of Looking at Death

The whole of life is but keeping away the thoughts of death.
SAMUEL JOHNSON

What happens when a person dies? Perhaps this is neither a weighty nor an important question. But it often arises at the time of a sudden death in the family or your circle of friends and may even precipitate a personal crisis. The loss and void left by someone's death can lead to an intense need to know whether that person still exists somewhere, in some manner of being. This need may persist even after you have worked through sorrow and adapted yourself to the new situation, even when your life appears to have returned to normal.

The question also surfaces sometimes in public debate, becomes the subject of several articles and then disappears again. People are never eager to talk about death. There is, of course, so much else to discuss, and, moreover, science apparently demonstrated a long time ago that nothing can exist after death [1].*

But "science" has in fact demonstrated nothing. A definite answer has yet to be found; the question remains open, unsettled. For this reason, it might be helpful to put down the various existing possibilities, to try to reach one's own point of view, and then see what the consequences of that point of view may be.

Let us draw a straight line to symbolize our life span between a star to represent birth and a cross for death. All we know for certain is that we experience an existence for a while on the physical plane, a time of individual consciousness between birth and death.

* Figures within brackets refer to the bibliography and notes, which begin on p. 295.

3

We can then take one of four different positions:

1. | ★_____ **+** |

We can maintain that nothing exists except that which we know for certain. No one has been able to prove that an individual consciousness continues beyond death. Our life span is a brief, bright flash of consciousness in the darkness. Before birth it did not exist, and death ends everything.

2. ? ★_____ **+** ?

We can maintain that it is meaningless to concern ourselves with this question, since in any case we are unable to know anything about it.

3. | ★_____ **+** ?

We can believe what we're taught from the pulpit: our life begins at birth (or perhaps at conception), but continues on into eternity, because, a certain time after death, resurrection will occur. The alternatives of this later existence, one an agreeable future life and the other a disagreeable one, depend on our behavior during our earthly existence.

4. ? ★_____ **+** _ _ _ _ _ _ ?

We can, finally, consider the possibility that our individual consciousness in some way still exists after the process called death. This possibility is still only a hypothesis, a theory; we have no sure proof of it. But a rich body of evidence, human observations and experiences, does exist which suggests that it could be true. This evidence will be touched on later in more detail. Here we must content ourselves with presenting the hypothesis. For the moment we will also not consider the question of individual consciousness before birth.

Now let us look at the four possibilities. The second alternative may be dismissed, since we are concerned with the question precisely because it does interest us and we do find it meaningful. The third possibility must also be put aside, for this is in fact a dogma, an article of religious belief requiring faith, which at the same time does not allow for any personal speculation or theorizing. We are able to believe, to accept it impassively or to deny it, depending on our attitude toward the dogma of which this tenet is a part.

So there remain only the two alternatives: 1—death signifies the end of my individual consciousness, and 4—my individual consciousness continues after death. (Here we will not discuss the various forms of "collective consciousness," of which we can scarcely have any conception. Nor will we concern ourselves with the theory that only certain special human beings are able to live beyond death.) Both alternatives, 1 and 4, are hypotheses, unproved assumptions. Alternative 1 is in accord with the materialistic point of view which is prevalent at present. Consequently, it is easy to find material to support this hypothesis. Documents of personal experience which support alternative 4 are less widely known, and therefore those who champion this hypothesis too gullibly are readily dismissed as unrealistic, enthusiastic fanatics. But we can find support for both alternatives, and both have honest and intelligent spokesmen. It may seem unimportant which we choose. Perhaps in the end we will return to hypothesis 2 and decide that it is meaningless to mull over the question any further.

But let us see what consequences each of these alternatives would have for us *if one or the other were true.* If my consciousness ends with death, then it makes absolutely no difference which theory I hold while I live—I would, after all, never get to know if I had been right or wrong. But if I do find that I have some form of individual consciousness despite the fact that I am what is called dead, then this consciousness will be experiencing something. And so it could be that my experiences might become richer and more pleasant if I were prepared in advance for the possibility of being able to experience beyond death. In other words, by preparing myself for the continuation of consciousness after death, perhaps I could at the same time increase the possibility of a more pleasurable existence after death than I would face if I were totally unprepared. And if this should prove wrong and the preparations were in vain, because consciousness ceased—what would it matter? I would never know that it was wrong.

Furthermore, the idea that our individual consciousnesses continue beyond death might bring a certain value and meaning to our experience of life here and now. Life could become richer for one person, and sorrow easier to bear for another; a third might behave more humanely toward his fellow man than he would if he followed another way of thinking. It could be seen as part of a way of life that would open wider perspectives to existence. Here an adversary will cry out, "Opiate of the people!" No. A mature, deliberate belief, not blind, but truly grounded in the conviction that consciousness continues after death, need not draw our attention away from what should concern us here and now as private individuals and members of a community. A concept like this, on the contrary, might well bring a wider perspective to our present responsibilities and increase our potential for fulfilling some of them.

But before we examine in greater detail the material that bears upon the choice between alternatives 1 and 4, we must consider another question. Are our five senses—sight, hearing, smell, taste and touch—the only channels through which we can receive knowledge of conditions outside our own bodies? Are there not other means? This is the question which parapsychology strives to answer, and therefore the second part of this book deals with that branch of science and the phenomena it investigates.

Part Two

PARANORMAL PHENOMENA AND PARAPSYCHOLOGY

2

What Is Parapsychology?

Let us now, before the restricted view of the laboratory worker gains too firm a hold, try to realize how wide our subject is. We should try once more to see it through the eyes of Frederic Myers as a subject which lies at the meeting place of religion, philosophy and science, whose business it is to grasp all that can be grasped of the nature of human personality.   G. N. M. TYRRELL

Our capacity to adapt ourselves to conditions we cannot alter (e.g., to use umbrellas when it is raining) and to act rationally to change certain other circumstances (e.g., to pick up something we have just dropped) involves among other things a certain perception of how existence is structured. Through experience we have learned that things normally function in a definite set way. This realization entails certain principles which appear so obvious to us that we scarcely think of them. The following demonstrate these principles [1].

1. We cannot know what another person is thinking, feeling or experiencing (or thought, felt and experienced) if he does not communicate this through speech, writing, pictures, facial expressions or movements—that is, through some sort of signal which can be received by our sensory organs.

2. We cannot know what he experiences before he has experienced it. In other words, we cannot know anything about events which have not already happened.

3. We cannot make an object behave in a certain way (e.g., make a die fall with the six face up) by thinking in a certain way.

But sometimes occurrences seem to contradict some of these principles, as in, for example, the case of the woman who experienced the following:

1. One day, after lunch, I came rushing into the office I shared with Miss A and Miss B. Now a strange woman was standing there talking with them. I noticed a terrible smell of gas, and blurted out, "What a horrible smell of gas! Open the windows and let's air it out. Who's committed suicide here?"

Three sheet-white faces turned toward me and Miss A staggered and reeled. The strange woman dragged me aside and gave me hell. When I came back into the room, terribly embarrassed, I saw Miss A was crying. The police had just phoned to tell her that her sister had managed to kill herself in her apartment on the other side of town. Gased to death, unclear whether it had been an accident or suicide.

So then, here we have a woman who entered a room where she worked and noticed a strong smell of gas though no gas was really there at all. She experienced a sensory illusion, a perception without any foundation in external reality. This is, actually, neither unusual nor remarkable—we have all had the experience at one time or other that one of our sensory organs seems to have tricked us. What makes this event remarkable is, of course, the correlation between her perception and the situation concerning the three other women. It seems as if, in some way other than through her sensory organs, she had learned what those three were thinking about, as if this information had made itself known to her consciousness precisely as a perception of gas.

Paranormal Phenomena

This occurrence is an example of experiences which do not fit into the picture of how we normally receive information from the outside world. These experiences are therefore usually called *paranormal* (the prefix "para-" means "beyond"). I believe that the majority of readers can recall some such experience they have had themselves or know of from their circle of acquaintances. People speak of premonitions, forebodings, and dreams which come true, of clairvoyance, mind reading, and thought transference. These phenomena are sometimes called *extrasensory* or *supernatural*. These labels, however, are misleading; since nature encompasses everything that exists, there cannot actually be anything supernatural! The expression *occult* is sometimes used for paranormal phenomena but it refers specifically to all those phenomena related to magic and secret doctrines.

Paranormal phenomena are called supernatural because they cannot be explained by the so-called laws of nature. But this need not necessarily mean that these phenomena go against the laws of nature. A more accurate explanation is that our knowledge of the laws of nature is still incomplete. With total knowledge we would be able to explain paranormal phenomena as well, and in that case they would no longer be paranormal or supernatural.

The branch of science that investigates paranormal phenomena is called *parapsychology*. In reference books a definition like the following will be found: "Parapsychology (metapsychology), the study of extrasensory psychical phenomena, the so-called occult phenomena, and man's contact with them. Related to this is spiritism. . . . [2]" This is to some extent inaccurate. Spiritism is a persuasion of belief, a faith; parapsychology is a branch of science, an area of research that investigates certain phenomena, namely, the paranormal, with commonly accepted conventional scientific methods. Researchers in the field are therefore known as parapsychologists.

Which phenomena, then, are paranormal? The answer to this question depends on what attitude the person answering has toward parapsychology. If he is opposed to it, he will probably consider that there are no paranormal phenomena. According to him, such things are due to sensory illusions, misconceptions, wrong readings of statistics, self-deception or fraud. For all those occurrences which have been called paranormal, he argues that there are completely natural explanations. But a person acquainted with parapsychological literature, or one who has made experiments in the area himself, is more disposed to consider that there really are paranormal phenomena. The more important phenomena that are considered paranormal will be listed here, as if they were confirmed facts, and then later each phenomenon will be discussed individually.

Clairvoyance: knowledge of objects and facts without the intermediary help of the ordinary senses, provided that telepathy is not involved.

Telepathy or thought transference: knowledge of thoughts, feelings and events received from another person without the use of the ordinary senses.

Clairvoyance gives knowledge of the state of material things and circumstances, while telepathy brings information about the mental state of another person's consciousness. Both of these phenomena concern conditions in the *present*.

Precognition: If the information applies to states which have not yet taken place, that is, events and circumstances in the future, the phenomenon is called instead *precognition*.

Retrocognition: Similarly, should the information refer to states in the past, the phenomenon is called *retrocognition* (the prefix "pre-" means "before," "ahead," and "retro-" means "behind," and "cognition" means "knowledge").

It is difficult to distinguish between telepathy and clairvoyance in regard to both pre- and retro-cognition, and, in fact, the term clairvoyance is used mostly in reference to information that concerns circumstances at the present moment. The concept is summarized in Figure 1.

FIGURE 1

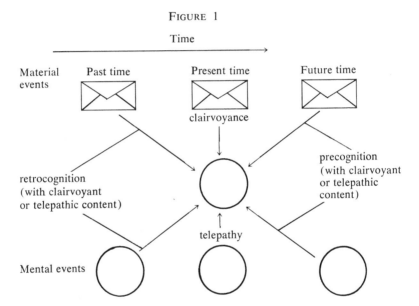

Psychometry is an unfortunate choice for a term but is nevertheless widely used and difficult to replace. It designates the ability to receive information, with the help of an object, about people and circumstances which have been, or continue to be, associated with that object.

Psychokinesis, also called *telekinesis,* is the ability to affect objects and the material course of events mentally, for example, to cause dice which have been thrown by a machine to fall in a certain way. Psychokinesis is often abbreviated PK.

Clairvoyance, telepathy, pre- and retro-cognition are known collectively by the term *extrasensory perception,* abbreviated as ESP. In German it is called *Aussersinnlicher Wahrnehmung* or ASW and the equivalent Swedish term is *utomsinnlig varseblivning* or *förnimmelse.* The term *psi* is also used when referring to more generally described paranormal phenomena (*psi* is the first letter of the Greek word for psychic). From now on here, for the sake of simplicity, we will use the most common abbreviations, ESP for extrasensory perception and PK for psychokinesis. ESP and PK together are called psi-phenomena, or simply, psi.

What Is the Paranormal?

Parapsychologists follow two main lines of inquiry in their study of paranormal phenomena: on the one hand, the investigation of spontaneous experiences, and on the other, systematic and controlled laboratory experiments following and conforming to standard scientific principles.

Especially when spontaneous experiences are involved, according to Broad [1], certain set questions must always be posed:

1. Did the phenomenon really occur? Did the woman in Case 1 really have the experience which was described, or was the whole thing fantasized or dreamed? Were the other three women questioned? Were the immediate circumstances and surroundings accurately described?

2. If the event has been accurately reported, is it truly paranormal? Is it contrary to any of the principles mentioned on page 9? Perhaps the woman in our case has an unusual ability to draw conclusions consciously or unconsciously from other people's behavior and appearance? Or might she perhaps have unusually keen hearing, so that she could have heard snatches of their conversation in the corridor?

3. If the event has passed both these tests, then we must ask if nevertheless it could not be explained by some known biological fact or law in physics. Or could it have been pure coincidence? Was it merely an unusual coincidence that the woman received her smell sensation and associated it with suicide just at that very moment when her colleague was telephoned by the police?

Only if the event has passed all these tests have we good grounds for considering that it really is paranormal. Then the task of the parapsychologist is to place this occurrence in relation to other similar phenomena and attempt to find some explanation for it. Can it be explained with the help of existent theories and hypotheses or must we invent new ones? Could its significance be clarified by laboratory experiments?

In principle, the same questions must also be posed when considering reports of experiments, but then we must also ask if we can really rely on the experimenters; if experimental procedures were properly, fully, and accurately written down; if properly scientific procedures were strictly observed; if the statistical results were correct, etc. Of course, these questions apply to all scientific operations, not only to parapsychology.

Parapsychology and Statistics

Let us consider a simple experiment. Someone places a number of postcard-sized cards—green on one side, white on the other, and absolutely smooth—in completely opaque envelopes, one card in each. The envelopes have no markings of any sort on either side and are all identical. A stack of envelopes is given to the experimenter (E) who does not know in which envelopes the green sides are uppermost. E places the pile of envelopes in front of the subject (S) who then guesses with each envelope in turn whether the green or the white side faces up. After a previously determined number of attempts, the envelopes are opened and the right number of guesses is counted. This is in principle the same as tossing for heads or tails: each time you have a 50-percent chance of guessing correctly. Therefore, out of 100 guesses, you might expect to have 50 correct, according to the laws of chance. Now, if S guesses correctly 55 times instead of the expected 50, then with the help of statistical methods, you can measure the likelihood that this or a better result depended purely on chance. In this case, it would be 32 percent or 0.32, which means that such a result can be expected on the average 32 times out of 100 such series of 100 guesses each.

Usually two assumptions or hypotheses are involved in judging the results of such experiments. The first, known as the null hypothesis, assumes that the results depend on chance. The second hypothesis maintains that some factor other than chance is involved. But this result, 55 correct guesses out of 100, would also be arrived at 32 times out of 100 purely by chance. Therefore in this case we cannot rule out the null hypothesis. Some factor other than chance was probably not involved. The result was not *significant*. There are certain arbitrarily chosen limits designated beyond which, in most scientific studies, we reject the null hypothesis and consider that some factor other than chance is involved. If, for example, the probability is 5 percent that a certain result depends on chance, then we say that the result is significant on a 5-percent level of probability. This means that with random distribution, a person would only get a certain result 5 times out of 100, and this would, to a certain extent, support the possibility that in the experiment in question some factor other than chance was involved. If the probability (probability is often designated by the letter p) that a certain result depended on chance is only 1 percent, then there is even stronger support for the assumption that some factor other than chance was involved.

Now let S guess 1,000 cards instead of 100. He continues to have 55 percent correct, that is 550 correct guesses, instead of the 50 percent expected at chance level. The probability of this result being due to chance is only 0.0016, or p equals 0.0016. This result would only occur randomly 16 times out of 10,000 attempts of 1,000 trials each. Therefore we can say that this result is significant at the 1-percent (or less) level, and the null hypothesis can be dismissed. In other words, probably some factor other than chance was involved. If the experiment is made so that S cannot, with the help of his senses, get to know anything of the way the cards are facing, *and if* ESP does exist, then it is highly probable that ESP was involved in this experiment. If we go on to imagine that S guesses correctly 55 percent of 10,000 guesses, than p is so insignificant that the usual statistical tables do not include it, that is, p less than 10^{-22}.

Thus, using the same scoring percentage, if one increases the number of guesses and still obtains the same results, there is ever diminishing reason to assume that the result is simple random probability. But the question remains unanswered: is this just something improbable which has, nevertheless, happened, or is it the result of some factor, for example, ESP?

Statistics have been a battling ground throughout the whole history of parapsychology. Opponents have accused parapsychologists of inaccurate and misleading statistics and explanations resulting from them. But methods have been refined, and people have in general agreed that methods considered reliable according to usual scientific procedures are also used and respected in parapsychology. When p is 5 percent or less, the result, in psychology and medicine, for example is usually considered to support the hypothesis proposed, and when

p is 1 percent or less, the support is significant. But when this applies to demonstrating the occurrence of paranormal phenomena, agreement and acceptance are not always general. A very much lower p value is often expected, and though indeed this has been achieved in many experiments, it has not always succeeded in convincing the skeptics.

The result of our hypothetical experiment of 1,000 or 10,000 guesses, if the experiment was set up and carried out in such a way that cheating and sensory cues can be ruled out, could mean that S might be able to perceive clairvoyantly which side of the card was uppermost. (It could also be contended that he perceived the card using precognition, that is, perceived the situation of the card being taken out of the envelope! We could then, by certain strategies, reduce this possibility.) But clairvoyance, telepathy, and precognition are only working names for those unknown factors which so strikingly distinguish certain experimental results from those expected with random distribution. The phenomenon is not explained simply by calling it clairvoyance.

Many studies are being made now of the statistical factors in ESP experimentation. Changes in the scoring percentage while the experiments are being carried out are being investigated. Differences have been found in various groups of subjects, not in the total score of hits, but in divergences from the average performance, and so forth. These investigations will not be dealt with here; those who are interested are referred to articles in, for example, the *Journal of Parapsychology*. In descriptions of experiments in the following pages, p factors will sometimes be mentioned to illustrate the results arrived at, but otherwise statistics will not be discussed further.

The Evolution of Parapsychology—Several Classic Experiments

Man's curiosity about the phenomena which parapsychology investigates is age-old. The earliest known written description of a parapsychological experiment recounts how, in about 500 B.C., King Croesus sent messengers to seven different oracles to ask what he was doing on a certain day. He chose the most improbable thing he could conceive of: he boiled a tortoise and a lamb in a brass caldron. But the Oracle at Delphi was still able to say what the king had been doing [3].

Then a long time passed until, in the latter half of the nineteenth century, an interest in systematic parapsychology was awakened. The history of parapsychology has been very well described by, among others, Tyrrell [7] and Heywood [8]. Here it need only be said that in 1882 several highly respected and prominent men of science in England founded the Society for Psychical Research (SPR) and the American equivalent was founded in 1885, the American Society for Psychical Research (ASPR). Initially, people seemed most interested in spontaneous experiences of a paranormal nature. Hundreds of such occurrences were researched, and witnesses cross-examined in detail. Over the years a very comprehensive, extensive corpus of well-examined spontaneous experiences has been collected in the publications of SPR and ASPR. During the twentieth century, the burden of investigation has shifted more toward laboratory experimentation, and only a small number of parapsychologists are now concerned primarily with spontaneous experiences. At the same time, parapsychology has gradually got a foot in the door of a good number of universities and high schools, primarily in the United States but also in Europe. There, methodical investigations are carried out, and doctoral dissertations in parapsychology are accepted at a number of universities. It is true there are only several dozen researchers who work with parapsychology full time, but at least a hundred devote a substantial part of their work to parapsychology.

An international organization of investigators of the subject, the Parapsychological Association, was founded in 1957. Its admission in 1969 into the American Association for the Advancement of Science can be taken as a definite acknowledgment of parapsychology as a science—after ninety years.

In Sweden, the interest in parapsychology seems to have been greater among the general public than within the scientific community. One reason may be that it has not been profitable for an academic reputation to be involved in parapsychology. On the contrary, to show interest in such work has required a certain courage, especially if the researcher leans to the opinion that some genuine paranormal phenomena do exist.

Several doctors, Poul Bjerre [4], Gerard Odencrants, and, especially, John Björkhem [5], have nevertheless undertaken to study spontaneous experiences of parapsychological interest. They have also been studying the possibilities of causing and observing paranormal phenomena under hypnosis. The engineer, Håkon Forwald, has made extensive experiments in psychokinesis (more about this in Chapter 6). Otherwise, qualified experimental work has been carried out almost exclusively at Lund University under the direction of the psychologist Martin Johnson. His contribution, among others, has been to help illustrate the relationship between the ability to demonstrate ESP and other measurable personality factors, which we will return to in Chapter 7.

In surveying the field briefly, we can mention three phases in experimental work. The first comprised research that attempted to confirm the existence of ESP. During the next phase, methods of experimentation were varied in an attempt to ascertain which factor might be involved: clairvoyance, telepathy, or precognition. Experiments from both these phases up until the Fifties are described by, among others, Tyrrell [7], Heywood [8], and Pratt [12]. Here only a few examples will be mentioned:

Up until 1930, a considerable number of scientific researchers made ESP experiments and got results, but for various reasons—primarily lack of funds—the promising experiments could not be continued [3]. It was J. B. Rhine who, starting in 1927, carried out more systematic long-term research at Duke University in Durham, North Carolina. He began with card-guessing experiments using the so-called Zener cards, which have often been part of experimental parapsychology. These are five cards each with a different image on one side: a circle, a wavy line, a square, a star or a cross. The first experiments were carried out under primitive conditions. The "sender" and the "receiver" sat on either side of a screen, so that they were unable to see one another. The sender took up one card at a time from the shuffled deck (which usually contains twenty-five cards, five of each picture) and the receiver noted down his guesses as to which card it was. Then, gradually, conditions were improved and made more elegant, and in 1933 experiments were set up to show that ESP could be demonstrated under infallible experimental conditions and from a distance. Formerly, experiments had always been carried out with the sender and the receiver in the same room [13].

An assistant of Dr. Rhine, J. G. Pratt, sat in one room, acting as the sender. A student, H. Pearce, acting as the receiver, was in another building 90 meters away. (In one series Pearce was in a building 200 meters away.) Once each minute Pratt put down one card from a mixed deck of twenty-five cards, with the back side up. He did not look at the face side. Meanwhile, once every minute, Pearce wrote down his guess. Since there were five different cards at each guess, the probability of guessing correctly was 20 percent. In all, 1,850 guesses were made (in four series under somewhat different conditions), and Pearce had 558 correct guesses against an anticipated 370. The probability of arriving at his results according to chance was less than $p = 10^{-22}$.

During the Forties the English mathematician S. G. Soal carried out thousands of card-guessing experiments under well-controlled conditions. He got significant results with only two subjects, Basil Shackleton and Gloria Stewart, but their results were all the more remarkable. It appeared that Shackleton guessed correctly a high number of times for the card which came *after* the one the sender had just looked at, so that the results indicated precognition [14]. In an experiment of over 6,000 guesses, Shackleton got so many hits over the expected chance level that p was less than 10^{-35}. Mrs. Stewart had equally great success with the card which the sender had just looked at. In her case "pure" telepathic experiments were also made. Here a code system was used, which the experimenter and the sender had learned by heart before without writing it down or giving any other indication (which might have been picked up clairvoyantly) and with the help of which a normal card-guessing experiment from the receiver's viewpoint could be made. Only the appropriate number was communicated in code from experimenter to sender. There was, therefore, no way the receiver could have been able to perceive through clairvoyance or precognition. In that experiment, too, Mrs. Stewart got better than chance results. Other variations of "pure" telepathic experiments also gave significant results [15].

As early as 1935, Tyrrell constructed an ingenious machine for ESP experiments [16]. Five light bulbs were set in small light-sealed boxes. The machine chose randomly which bulb to light, and the subject guessed by lifting the lid of the box in which he thought the bulb was lit. The number of hits and misses was registered automatically, and the machine could be adjusted to other conditions so that telepathy could be ruled out. Some of Tyrrell's results with this machine seem to indicate "pure" clairvoyance most clearly, others precognition.

These and many other experiments up until the Fifties have accordingly confirmed the conviction of many that certain people can actually receive information about the surrounding world without the use of their known senses. Experiments have been made under strict conditions which seem to rule out the possibility of "normal" explanations, and they have given results which diverge so greatly from what would have been probable according to chance, that it seems impossible that the results could be due to pure coincidence. Coincidence seems even less likely if you take into account that certain subjects repeat their highly successful guessing in experiment after experiment, while others continue to receive only random results in otherwise identical conditions. Nor have critics of this work gone swiftly to the attack with the assertion that either the experiments or the statistical totalling must have been incorrectly carried out. No, for want of weak points in method or statistics, critics have often asserted that the results were probably the product of conscious, deliberate deception by the experimenter and subject, in collusion with one another. The criticism of parapsychology will be treated further in Chapter 7.

Such work has strongly indicated that ESP exists. (According to the opinion of some, it constitutes conclusive proof). On the other hand, it has proved increasingly difficult to categorize ESP factors such as clairvoyance, telepathy, or precognition, even though results were obtained which basically asserted that one and only one of these factors was indicated.

In the third phase of parapsychological research, which continues today, there is less interest in attempting to distinguish the various types of ESP. The focus is rather on general ESP (GESP). Since earlier experiments have shown that the phenomenon exists, people are now more interested in how the ESP ability is related to other personality characteristics. Can we presuppose that people with certain characteristics will have better results in ESP experiments than others? Can we in some way facilitate or learn ESP? These are now the main questions, and the following provides an introduction to current inquiries and experimentation.

Laboratory Experimentation and Spontaneous Cases

Parapsychology also includes the investigation of spontaneous experiences. The following chapter is illustrated with examples of these. A very rich assortment of such case descriptions has been published, many of which have been well researched and verified so that they advance the claims for a paranormal experience as defined on page 10. I could have selected cases only from published collections, but have preferred also to present experiences which have been told to me directly by the person who had the experience (here called the percipient). Such cases are identified in this book by numbers.

These firsthand descriptions are not designed to "demonstrate" something, rather, primarily, they are meant to illustrate how phenomena that are considered paranormal can be experienced in everyday life.

Then the question arises, how can I be sure that these stories are true, that is to say, do they fulfill Broad's first requirement, mentioned above. In several, but not all of the cases, the story has been verified by other people. Even then, of course, I might have been the unfortunate victim of a conspiracy of several people who had gotten together to trick me with a good story. An even greater uncertainty surrounds those cases where no confirmation of the story can be found, for example, because the person who could have been able to give evidence is dead.

The time factor also increases the uncertainty. A suspected paranormal experience ought to be written down immediately, if possible, in every detail and witnessed by an outsider; with any passage of time, the possibility of faulty memory and after-the-fact reconstruction will, of course, increase. On the other hand, we are also dealing here with unusual experiences, often heavily loaded emotionally, which stamp a more intense impression on the memory than ordinary everyday events. Older cases are in no way more "sensational" than recent ones.

So that an experience of, for example, plausible telepathic contact may be considered verified, it is necessary that (1) a person has said or done something which signifies knowledge that another person (usually in another place) is in a certain situation which he could not normally know of or deduce from the facts he does know and (2) that another person certifies that he heard the statement or saw the behavior *before* any confirmation came that the situation really was such as had been described. A conceivable example: A woman says to her husband in the morning: "Last night I dreamed that Mom fell and broke her leg. She was wearing a green coat which I have never seen." Later that day came the message that her mother, somewhere else, had fallen and broken her leg during the night, and it is possible to verify that she had been wearing a recently purchased green coat. For various reasons, it was not possible to verify most of my numbered cases in this way. They are repeated here, as has been said, not so much because they claim to prove something, but as typical examples of experiences which researchers and others consider to be paranormal. Similar cases, including many which are written up and well verified, are to be found by the hundreds in parapsychological publications.

It must also be noted that some such experiences are by their very nature completely subjective and therefore *cannot* be verified by an outsider. These include, for example, out-of-the-body experiences (Chapter 8) and the mystical experience (Chapter 17). Such experiences can, nevertheless, be studied. By collecting a large number of cases, we can outline general characteristics and distinguish various types. We can predict that if an experience evolved under certain conditions and circumstances, then it is probable that certain qualities will characterize the story rather than certain others. We can compare cases from different cultures and different times. Such studies, defining and comparing large numbers of cases, support the conviction that the percipients did not fantasize, but described an actual experience.

It is still possible that some of the stories cited here are pure and simple fabrications. But it seems to me highly improbable that this should be the case in all or even most of them. I have reason to believe that the majority of my percipients really did experience what they reported. The people mentioned here are (with few exceptions) not familiar with the parapsychological literature and therefore they are ignorant of the sort of experiences generally reported. They could scarcely have lied in the hope of receiving some sort of remunerative advantage from their story, whether esteem, publicity or money. It was clearly specified from the start that none would be forthcoming. Instead, the following is a common reaction: "It is good to be able to tell this to someone who is interested. Every time I have tried to before, people either laughed at me or said I was crazy, and so I learned to keep quiet about it. But I know that it is really true." Several percipients also experienced considerable relief when they heard that other people had similar experiences, and that such things need not in any way be considered an indication of mental illness.

As a rule, the accounts are given in the percipient's own words, with some necessary editing. For reasons of space, the edited parts are marked ". . .". Since the majority of percipients wish to remain anonymous, fictitious names or initials have been used.

The reader may consider that I have reproduced too many spontaneous cases and chosen too few experiments or theories. I have tried to choose experiments which illustrate ESP's conceivable working mechanism or nature. But, for the most part, parapsychology still proves to be in the first scientific stage: the descriptive. Attempts at theory are diverse and numerous, which indicates that no one theory is widely accepted. If a commonly acceptable theory existed, it would be sufficient to present a small number of experiments and spontaneous cases to illustrate it.

Several parapsychologists consider that the study of spontaneous cases is now a past stage and concentrate only on laboratory experimentation. But the risk then is that we pose completely artificial questions and get answers that are so artificial they only apply to the laboratory. We must never lose contact with the phenomena which made us pose the questions in the first place. Therefore I consider it necessary to cite a number of spontaneous cases in order to illustrate the great variety of what seem to be paranormal experiences in everyday life.

The expression "what seem to be paranormal experiences" implies no doubting on my part of the good intention and the honest opinions of those people who have described such experiences. But it is easy to misinterpret the development of events and construe more from them than the facts lead one to see. The psychology of giving evidence provides many examples of this. To give a common example, two people can begin to talk at the same time about the same thing, but this does not necessarily mean that telepathy is involved.

The following chapter is based first of all on work published during the last ten to fifteen years [17]. This does not mean that earlier material is less interesting. The value of written, well-studied cases or well-executed experiments does not diminish simply because of the passage of years. But work in parapsychology up to the Forties has already been described in several books [4–17].

Some critics have considered that the whole case for parapsychology stands or falls with certain "classic" experiments made several decades ago. Such an attitude is mistaken. During the Sixties important research has been done, and a whole new area has been opened up for parapsychological work. Moreover, people are now beginning to aim for a "cross-disciplinary" working method, in which results from, on the one hand, parapsychology and on the other, e.g., psychology, psychoanalysis, physiology, and medicine mutually enrich each other. This approach is still only in its infancy. But an indication of this development is that parapsychological work is being published now more often in medical and psychological journals [18].

In Chapters 3 through 5 phenomena are separately described which most closely indicate clairvoyance, telepathy, or precognition.

This arrangement was chosen only in an effort to present a clear and lucid survey. In actuality, such a precise categorizing of ESP cannot be done. Clairvoyance, telepathy, and precognition are so named only to try to put a label on the phenomena we are studying. A subsequent chapter deals with psychokinesis, and Part Two closes with a survey of the debate surrounding parapsychology.

3

Clairvoyance and Psychometry

The Experiment with Pavel Stepanek

Around 1960 the Czech physicist Milan Ryzl attempted to train subjects to find objects clairvoyantly while under hypnosis. A librarian in his thirties, Pavel Stepanek, "trained" first under hypnosis and then in a wakened state, participated in experiments similar to those described on page 18. Cards, green on one side, white on the other, were placed in separate, completely opaque envelopes. In some experiments other colors were used. The point was to guess which side, green or white, faced up, in a well-shuffled pile of envelopes. From the very start, the series was successful and significant ($p = 10^{-9}$), and Stepanek continued to give positive results in series after series [1]. He proved to be a subject unique in the history of experimental parapsychology. Shackleton and Mrs. Stewart were effective and gave results considerably above random expectation (technically, they would thus be known as high-scoring subjects) for several years, but no subject has been active as long as Stepanek. In series after series, under monotonous, tedious, and exhausting conditions, with different senders, he got significant results (with ups and downs) year after year [2].

Ryzl's training seems therefore to have been effective: during the series of experiments made between 1961 and 1964, Stepanek could guess the cards correctly on an average of 8 percent above the expected 50 percent. This does not sound like much, but with thousands of guesses, the p value becomes very small. On the other hand, it seemed that this training had at the same time caused Stepanek's ability to become limited to the first situation he learned. As soon as the arrangement was changed and experiments with other materials were attempted, failures occurred. Stepanek worked willingly, but the results were only those of random probability.

To cancel out the possibility of sensory cues, the envelopes had been placed in outer paper covers (here called covers A). J. G. Pratt, who at that time was the person working most regularly with Stepanek, found during 1963–1964 that Stepanek could no longer guess the cards with his former high percentage. Instead it seemed that his impression of green came from the covers A. When certain covers were presented to him, he guessed white much more often than for others, regardless of which side of the card was uppermost, and when working with other covers, he would guess green [3]. But the explanation appeared simple, since he could actually see the covers. It must have been easy for him, consciously or unconsciously, to have some little trace or difference stick in his mind. Still, it was noteworthy that he could connect both sides of the cover into one entity—he never had occasion to handle them and never examined both sides of the same cover at one time. Nevertheless, he seemed able to focus his attention on certain covers.

Pratt suspected that Stepanek could distinguish between the different covers through ESP. In order to test this suspicion, Pratt made outer covers, here referred to as covers B, of thin but completely opaque cardboard of the same sort as covers A, each cover B containing one cover A, one envelope, and an enclosed card. In this way, covers A were not visible at all to Stepanek, yet he still continued to say "green" significantly more often for certain of the covers and "white" for certain others [4].

These experiments indicated that Stepanek's ESP "crept out." He first received his impression from the hidden card and possibly from the envelope, and then later from cover A—but only from some of them. Most of them were "all the same" and he called these green or white quite randomly. But his attention had focused on some of them, which, for example, were later called white a high percentage of times—and which he continued to call white even when they had been hidden within covers B and therefore could hardly have been identified any other way than through ESP. Example: one cover A which was used, hidden in five series of experiments between 1967 and 1968, was called white most of the time throughout the whole series [5], the random probability of such guessing in this case (green versus white guesses for the whole cover) being down to 10^{-10}. In eight of the series, p was less than 10^{-5}.

But why does ESP leak or creep out? Why had Stepanek lost his ability to guess the original, primary object, the card? Perhaps a critic will say the explanation is simple: it had never been a question of ESP but only of sensory cues, and these are naturally easier to pick up the less covered an object is. It is also true that, at least to date, Stepanek has not been successful when the object has been in another room or behind a screen. He seems to be dependent on contact with the object's cover. But the arrangement of the experiments appears to exclude every plausible sensory cue; a cover of cardboard usually hides the card just as well as a screen would. There is still no definite explanation of what happens, but Pratt [6] has a working hypothesis: during an experimental series, in which the outer covers are used many times, Stepanek gradually develops a habit of associating certain individual covers with "green" or "white" (a so-called stimulus response association). When, later, these covers are hidden, this very habit of associating a certain object with a certain word becomes the "bearer" of his ESP. His "habitual answer" can therefore continue even though the object may now only be identified through ESP.

Pratt received corroboration for this view by observing what happened when he introduced covers B. They were openly shown in a run of experiments, and the focusing effect came as expected. To determine whether ESP really was involved the covers B had to be hidden within something else. Pratt chose large padded covers called Jiffy Bags, designed to send books, etc., through the mail, here referred to as covers C. A series of experiments [6] made in 1968 demonstrated that the focusing effect also began to show up with covers C, with p down to less than 2×10^{-9}. If Stepanek's ESP continues to creep outward in this way, the next step will be to hide covers C in portfolios, then these inside suitcases. . . .

From the autumn of 1968 to the present, Stepanek has not shown the same degree of focusing as earlier, and experiments to "go back in" to regain his former high percentage of hits with the cards have not succeeded. Still, during this period, significant results have been obtained, and the work was continuing in 1970 when I wrote this. To date, Stepanek is the only subject who has been investigated from the aspect of the focusing-effect phenomenon. It would be of great interest to see if others, working as he has, would reveal the same phenomenon. It would bring considerable support for Pratt's hypothesis that habitual association of word and object is the "bearer" of ESP.

Psi-traces

Other attempts have also been made to explain the source of the focusing effect. One hypothesis is that the physical object in some way takes up an impression of, or is "impregnated" by the events or the people it comes into contact with. Roll [7] talks about the "psi-field" which surrounds an object and which changes under the influence of different events. Such (to date totally hypothetical) alterations in an object or some other medium or "field" which surrounds it, alterations which take up and include information about events, are called "psi-traces." These psi-traces would then be perceived through ESP. This theory could be illustrated by the results of two British researchers, West and Fisk, from an experiment in which they sent sealed cards to the subjects [8]. West found that he got poor results when he met his subjects personally. But then the number of hits was also lower for West's cards than when the subjects guessed the cards that Fisk had handled! This happened despite the fact that the subjects did not know that West was taking part in the experiment, and West did not know when his cards were being handled. It would seem that he left an adverse psi-trace, unfavorable for ESP, on the cards which he handled.

What Is a Medium?

Next we come to the phenomenon called psychometry. This occurs with people called *mediums,* a term we must define.

Paranormal phenomena are uncommon in our culture. Most people only experience a few such isolated occurrences during their lifetime. But there are those who often experience occurrences that might be considered paranormal. They impress those around them by demonstrating, again and again, knowledge of situations and events which they "normally" would not be able to know about. Such people are called *psychic.* The term "sensitive" is also used. For a person to be called psychic, the phenomena he experiences or produces need not be either confirmed or proved. It only means that he gives this impression to those around him. The word *medium* signifies a person who is psychic (the Dutch word "paragnost" is also used). But a medium can also mean someone who more or less professionally, usually within the spiritualist movement, receives people in what are called seances and during these seances imparts information that is considered paranormal. It is believed within that movement that a medium acts as an intermediary linking the physical world with the so-called spirit world in which the dead are thought to exist. Depending on the medium's working methods, one would then refer to a *clairvoyant medium,* who primarily describes visual or auditory impressions without any particular means of help, or to a *psychometric medium,* who prefers to use an object to establish "contact" with the source of information. The clairvoyant "sees" something. He experiences a sensory impression but is generally aware of the fact that it does not come to him through his physical, visual sense. If the impression was received through hearing, the term used is *clairaudience,* but this is a rather rare phenomenon. There are also *physical mediums,* who are thought to produce physical phenomena such as knockings, rappings, materializations, and so forth. Clairvoyant and psychometric mediums are sometimes called *mental mediums,* to distinguish them from physical mediums. A medium may work in a totally awakened state or in a trance, which is probably a self-induced hypnotic state. The activity and operations of mediums are discussed in greater detail in Chapter 10.

Psychometry, Object Association

In a psychometric seance, a medium is usually given an object, which he then handles as he wishes. Some mediums wish to touch the object themselves; others can work just as well if the object is enclosed in paper or material. The objects chosen usually do not give the medium much of a clue in themselves—for example, a stone, or a commonplace object like a watch or a pen. The medium then expresses associations received from the object. The term psychometry is misleading because the medium does not "measure the spirit" at all. The term refers rather to ordinary psychological tests. The British use another expression: "token object test." A term which expresses what takes place is *object association.*

2. During a seance in Uppsala in the autumn of 1968, the medium T. E. received a little stone from Mr. O. B. The medium's statement, which was taped, was worded: "Something like a

temple, a wall. Not Italy, but a country on the Mediterranean.
A sort of mountain plateau. When one stands there one can see
the ocean in the distance, far away. The country has something
to do with France, belongs to it in some way. One has a feeling
in this place that here I am right in the midst of ancient times.
The present culture is the fourth in that land. [Then talk of
other things, approaching travels for O. B., and so forth. Back
to the stone:] Here comes something about a camel. Hasn't
there been a danger of fire here? And battle, I hear the clang
of weapons and cries and shouts and horses. [Talk of other
things; the tape is indistinct. Then:] In this place kings and
emperors have been proclaimed. And an emperor—this is very
long ago—passed over [died] here, he was butchered, some way.
Antelopes. You can check the name, it comes so strongly. I
only see his body, not the head. His right hand was wounded
or withered."

O. B. had been to Tunisia during the summer with his wife,
which the medium did not know. They visited El Djem, a famous
monument with an amphitheater from Roman times. O. B. took
two small stones from there, one from the wall itself, one from the
ground outside. One of these, O. B. could not remember which, the
medium had been given. The stone did not look striking, it could
just as well have been picked up locally, in Sweden. Let us sort out
the medium's statements:

STATEMENT:	VERIFICATION:
1. Not Italy, but a land on the Mediterranean.	Correct.
2. The land has something to do with France, belongs to it in some way.	Correct. Tunisia was a French protectorate from 1881 to 1956.
3. The present culture is the fourth in that land.	Correct. A brochure handed out by the Tunisian tourist bureau records four cultures: Carthaginian, Roman before Christ, Roman during the Christian era, and Arabic-Islamic from A.D. 647.
4. Here comes something about a camel.	Correct. There are camels in that country.
5. A sort of mountain plateau.	Partly correct. A mountain plateau is nearby but is not the distinguishing feature of the place.

6. When one stands there, one sees the ocean far away in the distance.	From the amphitheater one cannot see the ocean, but one probably can from the mountain top. Unclear which was meant.
7. Something like a temple, a wall.	Correct.
8. Here one is right in the midst of ancient times.	Correct.
9. Here have been battles, the clang of weapons, shouts, and horses.	Correct.
10. Hasn't there been a danger of fire?	Possibly, but not specifically associated with the place.
11. Here kings and emperors have been proclaimed.	Unknown.
12. Long ago an emperor died here, butchered in some way.	Unknown.
13. His name was Antelopes.	Unknown.
14. His right hand was wounded or withered.	Unknown.

Statements like these are not unusual from psychometric mediums. General and specific information are all mixed up together. Statements 1, 5, 6, 7, and 8 could be correct for many places around the Mediterranean, but a normal explanation for them would require that the medium know that a ruin from Roman times existed in just that location. Statements 2, 3, and 4, on the other hand, preclude most countries north of the Mediterranean. The most specific statements, 11–14, despite extensive research and questioning of historians, have been neither substantiated nor denied. If they could be verified as well as the others, the case would, of course, be more convincing. From what could be heard on the tape, and according to O. B., the medium never received any indication from O. B. that he was guessing correctly. The only statement that could be classed as a leading question is number 10. But O. B. did not know the answer to this and only answered, "It is possible." It seems to be highly probable that the medium received all this information in a paranormal way. Telepathy cannot be ruled out in statements 1–9, which contain facts known to O. B. and his wife. Statements 11–14 would contradict this if they could be verified, and would argue strongly for "pure" psychometry, or retrocognition.

During psychometry, the medium seems first of all to experience directly conscious activities which are or have been associated with the object. The stronger the emotional weight of the situation the object is associated with, the stronger these "psi-traces" obviously become, and thus the chances are increased that the medium will experience something of them. But the medium cannot choose what will be experienced or received, what traces will be followed. Some comments illustrate the experience from the medium's point of view:

> When I take an object it is mostly silent. But sometimes it behaves like when you listen to a record . . . you listen with a mind "outside" your ordinary mind, and the hand which holds the object acts like the pickup arm. In itself the object is something which has been recorded on. . . . In a tape recorder the old track is erased when you record something new. But in an object there is no erasure. Everything can be absorbed there, and a cacophony can pour out of it right at you. But from this cacophony suddenly a stronger theme can be received by the brain. One experiences an occurrence in the midst of the static, but it could be anything, weird, strange. One suddenly experiences a sensation of unease, sorrow, anxiety. One gets an intense feeling that one just has to grab that object and give it to a person who is very sympathetic, but whom one doesn't know. Each time one takes an object just about the same thing happens. One really doesn't know how to explain it, but not long ago someone talked about "this here thing I got from my son, we'd been arguing and he bought it for me to patch up our quarrel."
>
> But perhaps it wasn't one particular communication that the scientist who handed the object to the medium wanted to get back, but another—perhaps he had placed the object in a plane which had flown over the straights of Malacca during a thunderstorm, but that event was too weak for the object to pick it up . . . it was lost in the cacophony. The scientist was disappointed, the medium disconcerted. Very often the medium has to pose questions when she relates the feelings and tries to dress up these feelings in words, to the irritation of the scientist.

The medium in Case 2 experienced visual and auditory impressions of events and relationships associated with the object. The medium whom we have just quoted instead described experiences of feelings and thoughts, without pictures or other sensory impressions. As we can see, impulses which can be interpreted as telepathy and precognition are experienced in these different ways.

People can also be objects of a psychometric experience, exemplified by the following case:

3. In 1965 I met the medium G. A. During one of the first occasions we talked together she asked if I had been to Florence. I answered in the affirmative. "I seldom receive anything about former incarnations," she said, "but I am receiving that you lived in Florence in the fifteenth century. Moreover you are sitting in a painting in the Uffizi Palace. There is a mother with two or three children in the picture. An artist of that period painted his family. You are one of his children."

I could scarcely believe my ears . . . on my first visit to Florence nine years earlier, during a visit to that gallery, I had stopped in front of a painting by a famous medieval [sic] artist. I could not draw myself away from the painting. The thought never entered my mind that one of the children could be myself. I just stood and meditated in front of the painting . . . examined every detail.

At that time I had not yet thought through my personal opinion of the concept of reincarnation . . . but as a joke I said to my sister, "Here I once lived in a former life."—The effect of the medium's statement became more powerful when she described at the same time an experience I had had in the Baptistery, how I had responded to Donatello's famous sculpture of Mary Magdalene in a remarkable way.

Experiences like this one are often taken as indices of reincarnation, and the person referring to them considers that it "gives a certain definite instance verifying that reincarnation really exists." But a simpler and more probable explanation is either telepathy or object association: the medium experienced the individual as a psychometric object and can recount details from his life, just as other mediums can narrate details from an object's history. The object's "psi-traces" correspond to the person's "memory-traces" which the medium experiences. This conceivable way of working is of great significance for the interpretation of many phenomena in the spiritualist context: see more on that in Chapter 10. But the case tells us nothing about reincarnation. As Chapter 13 will show, support for that theory must be sought from entirely different experiences.

Clairvoyants, Dowsers, Skin Sight

In connection with notorious criminal cases, newspaper articles often appear about "clairvoyants" (by which they usually mean, more precisely, psychometric mediums) who have helped the police find missing persons, dead or alive. In several well-examined cases, mediums do seem actually to have given accurate information and clues and helped to unravel the mystery [9]. But all too often these articles in newspapers are sensation-mongering, exaggerated or built upon misunderstandings. The case of Kyllikki Saari in 1953 was much written about. A Finnish girl disappeared and was later found dead. It was commonly accepted that she had been murdered, but this was not proved. A Swedish psychometric medium had, according to newspaper articles and her own statements, described the place of the accident, and the corpse was supposedly discovered by following up her suggestions [10]. But in reality the medium's information did not further the investigation of the case, which remains unsolved [11].

It is often difficult to draw a clear line between psychometric and telepathic clairvoyance. In Case 3 the information can be explained as psychometry of a living person by the reading of "psi-traces." But usually similar cases are explained as telepathy: the medium has unconsciously gained access to the subject's thoughts and memory and received the information telepathically. Why the medium received precisely that information and nothing else, still remains to be explained. Usually only when telepathy can be ruled out can the results be considered to depend on clairvoyance or "pure" psychometry. A more detailed description of telepathy will be the subject of the next chapter, but first two phenomena of a possible paranormal nature must be mentioned.

The first is dowsing, that is, the art of finding water with a branch which a person holds in front of him. When held by psychic individuals, the branch is "pulled" downward when the person passes over water. The phenomenon's authenticity is widely disputed; despite the fact that hundreds of articles with scientific claims have been written, the dispute persists as to whether the phenomenon even occurs at all. But those who have found water personally with the help of a dowser do not doubt it. Experiments have shown that the "dowsing reflex" appears in association with measurable changes in other outward circumstances: the magnetic field, electrostatic charges, infrared waves, and electrical power lines under ground. The geologist Tromp [12], who has studied the correlation of the phenomenon with other biological and geological conditions, considers that it is not clairvoyance but rather a purely physiological phenomenon based on some hitherto unknown "supersensory" mechanism in the human body.

The other phenomenon is the ability to "see" with the fingers and to distinguish colors while one's eyes are completely covered. This is called *dermo-optic perception* or *skin sight*. Researchers mention that this may not actually be a paranormal phenomenon but rather a sensitivity to the differences of waves from "something" in the surface of different colors. This "something" is thought to be infrared waves [13].

4

Telepathy

Walking down a street, you start thinking about a friend you haven't seen for a long time and rarely think of. Then you bump into him at the next street corner: a pure coincidence. But sometimes we receive information about other people and their situation in what appears to be a paranormal way: so many details prove correct that the explanation of pure coincidence actually seems rather far-fetched. In collections of alleged paranormal experiences, such telepathic cases are therefore among the most common. Some examples:

4. My husband is a fisherman. On one night I'll try to describe, three of my sons were out with him. I woke with a strong feeling of anxiety, I didn't know what about, suffering deeply inside myself. My thoughts were drawn to the boat. I thought about my sixteen-year-old son Roland. I started to pray a long time, finally it calmed down and I fell asleep. That night the boat was on its way home from the North Sea. Roland was at the helm, he had the watch with his elder brother. It was foggy and the visibility was poor. He saw two lights sweep past, thought they were from lighthouses over in Norway—but no, a big Russian boat bore down across their course. With all his might he turned the tiller and swung the boat aside, the Russians cut across just after their boat's stern. He ran into the chart room and told his brother, and then they saw the Russians' whole prow loom through the window. They were that near death, everyone on board. It was a big boat.

5. On this particular afternoon I had a very hard time concentrating on my work, and as soon as the last patient that day went out the door, I left everything right where it was and

rushed home. Had to catch the last bus into town, didn't know why, only that I had to. Felt a little foolish sitting there in the bus, but gradually it became clear. I suddenly knew whom I had to visit.

I also knew that I had to hurry, and I ran when the bus let me off. Went down a street I don't usually take and met my friend there. Can't explain why I took a street I never go on and which, besides, is longer than my usual way—but if I hadn't done that I wouldn't have found her. She was standing on the edge of the sidewalk trying to start her motorbike, very drunk.

She grabbed me and clung to me, saying over and over, "How come you happened by just now?" Then gradually I learned that her despair about her very depressing life had overwhelmed her that day and she had decided to drive her motorbike out onto the frozen ocean. It was March: the ice would have broken.

6. *Vendla:* My friend Anna had a tape recording of a trumpet melody which for some reason had stuck in my mind [this happened in what seems to have been a paranormal way, see Chapter 12]. I had last heard it played in the autumn. On December twelfth, sitting at work, I suddenly got a signal in my ear, exactly like when you turn on the radio. It was the trumpet melody from the tape. I looked at the clock, it was 1:50, and I said out loud, "Anna, what is it?" The music came back again now and then, hour after hour. It sought me out. I grew pale; my boss noticed it, too. I told him about the tape recording and he told me I really ought to telephone her, but you don't phone a person who needs you just to say that you don't have time to come. I was supposed to work that evening, too, but by seven o'clock I was so tired and upset that I took work home with me instead, but couldn't do much of it and just went to bed. The next morning I took the unfinished work and left it at the office, bought a hyacinth and walked over to Anna's. I rang the doorbell, she opened the door in a complete state of breakdown, with a box of tablets in her hand, about to take them. We talked at length, for several hours, and it relieved her.

Anna: On the twelfth, at 1:50, I was on my way to Vendla's home but turned back, thought that there was no point going to see people in this state, better to drive home again and think the whole thing over. [Didn't know she was working that day.] If I couldn't figure things out clearly myself, I would put an end to it all. I knew, of course, this would be wrong to do to my relatives, and really I didn't usually think about suicide. But everything had been too much for me just around that time, and it had become obvious to me that I was psychic and this was very difficult for me. But then my husband came home and nothing happened that evening and I finally fell asleep. But if Vendla hadn't come that next morning just when she did I really probably would have taken all those sleeping pills. I did have a box of a hundred in my hand. I'd arranged everything in the house, everything was neat and tidy, all that was left was to go to sleep, and I'd decided to take all the tablets to make sure of it.

7. I was lying ill in my parents' home after a crisis I'd experienced of a mixture of Nietzsche, Strindberg, and the spiritual and religious life. I was lying on the sofa . . . my thoughts turned to my sister, who lived with her family on the other side of town. Suddenly I saw their kitchen window and the chopped firewood piled up outside under the window. Her two boys were running around playing in front of the pile of wood, and suddenly I saw the wood teeter out from against the wall and threaten to crash right down on the boys. But it just avoided them. I jumped up from the sofa . . . told my mother what I'd seen. The next day my sister came to visit and told how the wood pile had tumbled, just as I'd seen it, and time was also the same. We talked about it for ages. It was weird.

The telepathic experience [1], as seen in these examples, is often connected with strong and intense feelings for, or experiences of, the person who is called the "sender," while the "receiver" as a rule is occupied with something completely ordinary and mundane. The terms sender and receiver give an impression that the process is related to that of radio transmission, which is not at all certain. Therefore we will use the words *percipient* (he who has the experience) for the receiver, and *agent* for the sender, the person about whom the percipient experiences something.

Thus, in Case 4 the mother is the percipient and the son the agent. But couldn't it perhaps have been a simple coincidence? It's natural enough for a fisherman's wife lying in bed at night to awaken, anxious about her loved ones out in their boat, especially if the weather is bad. The percipient agreed that she did easily become anxious, but, on the other hand, she very rarely woke up like that in the middle of the night with such a strong emotion of alarm. Something that can be called a true telepathic connection is also possible, as her alarm subsided after a while when the time of the danger had passed. Perhaps she became calm not only as a result of her prayers.

Case 5 is even less easily explained as an example of coincidence.

The percipient had never experienced anything similar in connection with that friend, and the friend didn't usually make preparations for suicide. The indefinite anxiety forced the percipient to behave in a way that at first seemed meaningless. But "gradually it became clear and I suddenly knew whom I had to visit. I also knew that I had to hurry." In itself the experience gave no indication of what sort of crisis the agent was facing—it only said that there was a danger in store for the agent.

The agent in Case 6, Anna, was also not one of those who often contemplate committing suicide. On the contrary, her friends considered her to be a strong, receptive, sympathetic person to whom one could always turn with one's problems. But then why didn't Vendla go home to Anna that evening? She explained this by saying that her anxiety had subsided, it no longer felt so acute, and she was completely worn out by the events of the day. It also did seem that Anna had thought over her problem until her husband returned home, whereupon she had a lot to do and nothing came of it, and then she ultimately went to sleep. But on the following morning doubts overcame her once again in full force.

Case 7 is an example of how it is often difficult to draw sharp distinctions between clairvoyance and telepathy. The experience could perhaps be taken as a clairvoyant perception of the threat of an accident, but it is more likely telepathy, released by the boys' fear at the moment the wood fell.

Impressions connected with death, above all, but also with accidents or sudden illness of a close friend or relative are among the most commonly reported spontaneous paranormal cases:

8. We had just finished eating lunch. . . . I was sitting on the floor by the stove in Papa's studio. Suddenly I felt a mild summer breeze sweep through the room, although the windows were closed. Someone patted my cheek and my grandmother said, "Now I am leaving."—I experienced this as something indescribably beautiful and good. I loved my grandmother very deeply.

A little later I talked about what had happened to my parents, who were also in the studio. Mother sniffed, and father, to whom such things were not completely foreign, said it was one of the risks of dieting.

We didn't have a telephone then. The next day we got a message that grandmother had died just at that time.

9. I was going to a country school and asked the rector if I could be allowed out on my father's sixty-fifth birthday to help mother, who was old and needed a hand. But I was given a curt no. My aunt and I traveled home to my parents over Saturday and Sunday, but I had to start back as early as three on Sunday, so that mother was without help on the most difficult day. I cried at the station, and my aunt told me that one does not get everything one wishes for in this life.

That evening in bed in school, I dreamed that mother went down the stairs into the cellar and her pocket flashlight went out. She tripped over an iron rod, fell down, and lay still. I stood looking on, screaming to high heaven. I heard voices from the room above, but my screams were not heard. I tried to lift mother, but was unable to, she was unconscious and had an ugly wound on her leg. Then I heard steps on the cellar stairs and invisible people came and bustled around mother. I felt people were there but I couldn't see them. I realized they were not living people, they were other powers. Then I traveled with dizzying speed from the cellar to the school where with a shriek I rose up in my bed. My roommate managed to calm me: just a bad dream.

When I was home again a couple of weeks later, I thought of telling about the dream, but mother forestalled me and I saw the bandage on her leg. She had gone down after liquor—her pocket flashlight went out and she hit herself so terribly that there was blood and she was unconscious a while. She didn't come to until she was standing in the kitchen again, bleeding heavily. Despite her suffering, she managed to serve her guests as if nothing had happened. I really had left her in the lurch.

The death of household pets also gives rise to telepathic impressions, but it is significantly less common:

10. During the spring, Ping became ill. Ping was our beloved housepet, a guinea pig. He was very old then; we'd had him eight years and he was full grown when we got him. He had a definite personality.

Ping improved and went along as usual when Mom and my brother traveled to Värmland for the summer. I stayed in Stockholm.

One evening while I sat watching a long TV film, I heard the sound of a guinea pig on the TV, which didn't belong in the film. I recognized Ping's "voice" and knew what had happened. That evening my brother phoned from Karlstad and told me that

Ping had not been well when he drove from home several hours earlier. Then when he came home later that night, Ping had indeed gone to his fathers.

Even these few cases demonstrate how telepathic impressions vary: from an indefinite anxiety, which gradually becomes more focused on a certain person and can force the percipient to take definite steps, to a detailed sensory impression. But any one of the sensory organs may bring the signal to the consciousness, even smell, as is shown in Case 1.

These cases are examples of the three most common types of telepathic impressions:

1. A dream (Case 9).

2. A visual picture, an auditory impression, or any other sensory impression, more or less detailed, experienced in a wakened state (Cases 1,6,7,8,10).

3. An "imageless" impression experienced in a wakened state; the experience is characterized not primarily by sensory impressions but rather by an anxiety more difficult to describe, an emotion or certainty which moves the agent (Cases 4 and 5). In Chapter 7, examples will be given of two further types which can be included more precisely as variants of group 3, namely, (4) physical symptoms, e.g., pain and (5) physiological actions which can be recorded by instruments without the percipient being conscious of them.

The telepathic experience can therefore vary from a detailed sensory impression to a bodily reaction which doesn't reach into consciousness at all. Dreams are the most common of groups 1 through 3, while the frequency of the remaining types varies with different material [20].

The experience can also be so intense that the agent is perceived as if vividly present in bodily form, nearby in space, but then we would no longer refer to a telepathic impression but rather to an apparition. Moreover, certain researchers maintain that telepathy is not an adequate explanation for such an experience. This will be treated in greater detail in Chapter 9.

Another form of telepathic impression occurs when someone "comes the first time":

11. My father drove off in a coach to the local community meeting, and we sat there waiting for him to return home. The first time it happened I was surprised: I heard them come,

drive into the coachhouse, and father helped the coachman ungird the horses—but then he never came in! Then I turned and it felt completely natural to say, "Now they've come the first time, we can put on water for tea, for they'll be here in fifteen minutes!" I was never afraid of this, it was completely natural.

As a rule, the agent and the percipient in these cases are closely related, and the impression is conveyed through hearing. One wonders how often such premonitions turn out to be false and the agent doesn't come at all. But here it is not a question of someone thinking of a person on a few isolated occasions, with a feeling that he is approaching which then turns out to be true. Instead an auditory impression occurs a short while before the agent's arrival, even if he comes at completely irregular times. Occasionally this sort of phenomenon causes considerable trouble:

12. When I went off to school I didn't know there was anything strange about me except that I was interested in the "unknown." I had a friend who lived with her mother in a neat little cottage. Her mother and I clicked immediately—she was big, warmhearted, and dark like a gypsy. But soon she began to say, "I know exactly when you're coming, because then there'll be a commotion in the cupboard, and the cup you usually drink out of clatters or a spoon hops out of the drawers. Or else I drop everything I have in my hands. Then a short time passes and you come storming along!"
I never thought too much about it. But when I moved to Stockholm and lived at Mrs. F's, she began to complain bitterly. "Now, Elsa, you just must stop this nonsense or you'll have to leave. You come before you actually show up, the lock in the door clicks. You come in and take off your coat; rummage around in the hall. Then you walk past me and into your room— and I follow you to ask if you'd like some coffee, and I don't find a soul there! Stop all this or you'll drive me crazy!" It didn't stop. I got more warnings and talkings to and then eventually I moved.

Here it appears that we also have a case of spontaneous recurrent psychokinesis of a type which will be described in greater detail in Chapter 6. Instigators of such occurrences are apt to be young people in their teens.

Telepathy in the Laboratory

Some researchers, the psychologist T. Moss in particular, try to re-create in the laboratory the sort of intensely emotional situations which are usually involved in spontaneous telepathic experiences. In such researches the agent is placed in a soundproof room and the percipient in another room [2]. Music is played for the agent and slides shown which are thought to create a certain mood. One of the motifs was the murder of President Kennedy (the test was conducted with American subjects nine months after his murder). The percipient lay relaxed on a couch and was then instructed to report all impressions or associations that came into his consciousness. The agent was likewise to describe impressions received from the pictures. Both accounts were recorded at the same time on tape and each transcribed tape was given a code number and then handed over to outsiders to study. Each pair of one agent and one percipient worked on six episodes, planned to re-create different emotional states. There were, therefore, six pairs of accounts from each pair of agent and percipient. The experimental group comprised thirty pairs in all, and there were also two control groups where significant results would primarily indicate precognition of clairvoyance. The appraisers' task was to read the six double runs from each pair and, on the basis of similarities of emotional states and choice of words, match the agent's run with the one recorded by the percipient when he described his experience of the same episode. The statistical analysis showed that the appraisers succeeded much better when working with material from the experimental group than with material from the control groups. Support was found for the hypothesis that the connection between the agent and the percipient's account of the same episode was stronger than what could be expected from random distribution. There was also cause to assume that information of the agent's experiences really had been received by the percipient.

In a subsequent experiment the conditions for the agent were similar [3]. The percipient, as in the first test, was asked to recount his impressions and associations. There were three pairs of episodes with pictures and music, pairs chosen to give the greatest possible contrast. One pair contained, on the one hand, paintings with the theme of the Madonna and Child by medieval and Renaissance artists to the accompaniment of "Silent Night," this was intended to create a mood of peace and calm, solemnity or devotion. The contrast was represented by a series of self-portraits of Vincent Van Gogh accompanied by Ravel's *La Valse,* abruptly interrupted by a man's voice which, with increasing intensity, shouted "Van Gogh!" The purpose here was to give the agent feelings of chaos and confusion. At the beginning of the experiment it was decided randomly which of the two paired series would be shown to the agent. The percipient in his room was to recount his impressions, but this time he was shown two slides simultaneously, one from each series of pairs. He was then to choose which picture corresponded to the series the agent had seen.

There were 144 subjects, divided into three groups of 24 pairs each: an ESP group which believed in ESP and considered they had had such experiences themselves, a ?-group which was doubtful about ESP, and a no-group which denied that ESP exists. In the ESP group, 19 out of the 24 percipients had two or three hits out of three possibilities of guessing which picture the agent had seen, compared with 13 in the ?-group and 9 in the no-group. The results were significant for the ESP group ($p = 0.003$) but not for either of the other groups.

Moss had the impression that pairs which included an artist (this meant writers, musicians, painters, etc.) succeeded better than others. Therefore she grouped them in pairs. Twenty-six pairs were made up of one or two artists. In 24 of these pairs the percipient had two or three hits, which is significant ($p = 0.000005$). In the remaining 46 pairs only 17 percipients had at least two hits, which would have been expected by random distribution [4].

In spontaneous cases, the distance between agent and percipient can be very great. To reproduce this phenomenon, Moss made a test with a group of agents in Los Angeles, one in New York, and another in Sussex, England [5]. At certain previously determined times the agents in Los Angeles were to experience "emotional episodes" using the same method as in earlier tests, and the three groups of percipients tried to receive impressions at the same time. They were to recount their spontaneous associations and choose which of two slides shown them simultaneously corresponded to the one shown the agents. A total of 57 percipients took part and 39 had two or three hits, which is significant with $p = 0.003$. The results for each group were significant for Los Angeles, nearly significant for Sussex, but not for New York, with $p = 0.018$, 0.089, and 0.30 respectively. In some of the tests, control episodes were shown to the agents without the percipients' knowledge. These pictures included just pictures of letters, numbers, and meaningless lines. The percipients were then asked to choose between two contrasting slides which had no connection with any of the other episodes. The percipients got no significant results for these control episodes, which meant that they chose randomly between two pictures shown them, thus also indicating the chance factor.

The percipients' associations from the episodes were remarkable. When the Los Angeles agents saw a run of pictures which showed various kinds of "water sports" (surfing, canoeing, sailing, diving, etc.) to the accompaniment of Debussy's *La Mer,* six of the percipients in Sussex reported the following:

1. "I can hear water rushing, and feel the spray against my face. I think of a waterfall nearby."
2. "Tropical beach lagoon. Surf gently coming in. . . . Woman wearing bikini, man briefs, golden sand. Travel poster effect."
3. "A ship's shadow, an old ship of the *Mayflower* type, shining in the orange sun."
4. "Distant view of Greenwich river bank, with dramatically colored sunset . . . view of green grass running from the river side to the summer house."
5. "Cool green water . . . and a waterfall."
6. "In the valley, a calm, wide, deep stream and overhanging willow tree."

Experiments with Dreams

Spontaneous ESP experiences often occur during sleep. The percipient wakes out of a dream which appears unusually clear, palpable, and lifelike, which he seems able to remember in detail (e.g., Case 9). He "knows" that something has happened to the agent. Sometimes he has seen very vividly and completely clearly what has happened to the agent and then later by post or telephone he receives confirmation of the fact. The course of events can also be portrayed symbolically.

Naturally we would like to study dreams experimentally in the laboratory, and now that too is possible. Subjects go to sleep in the laboratory. During the night their EEG is recorded. Their eye movements are also recorded during sleep. It is known that a curve of a certain shape (which, among other things, is characterized by rapid eye movements, REM) can be distinguished during periods of lively dreaming, the so-called REM-sleep. Dream tests are being undertaken in many places and with many different objectives, among other purposes, to test sleep remedies.

At the Maimonides Medical Center in Brooklyn, New York, the Dream Laboratory is used to research telepathic dreams. A person who has otherwise nothing to do with the tests selects a large number of art reproductions of postcard size and places them in envelopes which are sealed. The agent is alone in a room with a randomly selected chosen envelope. He opens it and spends the night concentrating on this "target picture," tries in every way to project himself into the theme. The percipient sleeps in the laboratory and has a local telephone contact with the test leader, who does not know which picture the agent has received to look at. After the EEG has indicated REM-sleep for a while, the percipient is awakened and talks about his dream and all accompanying associations into a tape recorder. In the morning he also gets to make a direct guess of what might have been the target picture for the night's dreams. The descriptions are written out verbatim.

As an example, here are selections from a dream account one night when the randomly chosen picture was a painting by George Bellows, *Dempsey and Firpo,* showing a boxing match in Madison Square Garden [7]:

> Something about Madison Square Garden and a boxing fight. . . . I had to go to Madison Square Garden to pick up tickets to a boxing fight, and there were a lot of tough punks—people connected with the fight—around the place. . . . There were all these wrestling and boxing posters around, and a bunch of kookie-looking people—most of them sort of looked like they could have been wrestlers, or old fighters, or something—in line wanting to get tickets to these events and I went upstairs and went to this thing called the Boxing Club or something where you get tickets.

A series of tests might include, for example, eight night dreams with one or several percipients and different target pictures each night. The eight accounts and the pictures are then sent to an outside appraiser who studies similarities in the content of dreams and pictures. This can be done in various ways depending on which aspects one is most interested in. The appraiser gives each dream a score number in relation to each picture and, finally, using these as a guide, he reports for each dream night which picture, or which of several, seemed to him most probably the target picture for that night. Of the runs which have so far been published, the results have been significant in the majority, that is to say, the appraisers have been able to pair the correct picture with its dream account more often than could have been expected according to pure chance. Even in those series which have not given clearly significant results, certain individual dream nights have revealed striking resemblances between dream and target image. Starting in the autumn of 1969 a total of 134 dream nights have been studied to date, and the results under varied conditions have been judged as 97 "hits" and 37 "misses" [8–10]."

In a run of 74 dream nights, it was shown unexpectedly that men seemed to succeed better than women as percipients in these tests [11]. In these latter tests the agent, who was placed in another part of New York, was not just given a picture, but in fact was literally bombarded with images of a certain theme. Then, in the morning, the percipient, along with the experimenter, chose, on the basis of his own dream accounts, which of the six possible themes had been the theme of those pictures shown to the agent during that night [12, 13].

The Maimonides Dream Laboratory represents a promising line of development in modern parapsychology. Other dream laboratories have started similar work. These results have also contributed to an increased interest in altered states of consciousness and their significance for ESP [13]. This will be discussed in greater detail in Chapter 15.

Psychoanalysis and Telepathy

But why do some people receive telepathic experiences and not others? Does everyone have the ability to receive signals but do only a few allow these to come into their consciousness? Does everyone have telepathic dreams without knowing it? Psychoanalysts have concerned themselves with this problem. Freud published several reports of probable telepathic dreams [14]. Indeed, psychoanalysis involves a lengthy and emotionally laden relationship between analyst and patient, and the analyst's overview of the patient's emotionally laden situations gives him the possibility of studying those situations in which telepathic contact could be thought to occur between himself and the patient. Two examples told by Emilio Servadio [14]:

> A patient recounted a dream in which a married couple celebrated their eighth wedding anniversary. The patient was unable

to associate this with anything from his own life. But the analyst herself recalled that the previous day she had been more than permissibly distracted listening to the patient talk and instead was preoccupied with mental preparations for her own wedding anniversary! It was a completely private occasion which the patient could not possibly have known about.

Another patient dreamed that blood was flowing from his fingertip. Asked to associate with this dream, he answered that he remembered an occasion several years earlier when a blood test had been taken from that finger. The patient could scarcely have known that on the day before the dream night the analyst had gone for the first time in a long while to a laboratory to have a blood test and it was taken from a finger.

It is as if patients who report these dreams want to say, "I know that you have private problems, but right now try to pay a little less attention to them and a little more to my own analysis!" Several similar cases have been published, some obviously more complex. Schwarz [15] describes a technique for discerning such telepathic occurrences encountered during psychotherapy. He recorded 1,443 such occurrences during the years 1955–1956. In all, he treated 2,013 patients during this time. From his personal experience he even doubted that there would be any reason for further treatment of the patient if telepathic occurrences had not happened rather early on in the analysis.

Still, cases like these do not constitute a proof of the existence of telepathy. The relationship between analyst and patient allows for many possibilities of common associations and coincidences of other causes. Even if the explanation of telepathy seems absolutely definite to the analyst, he cannot make it plausible for others without very extensive descriptions of the psychodynamic situation of the occurrence. These experiences are primarily valuable when seeking an explanation for *why* telepathy occurs. Certain psychoanalysts have written a good deal about the psychodynamic situation which promotes or favors the source of telepathic communication, but I cannot go into that in greater detail here [14–16]. They propose that telepathy is a normal psychic mechanism which operates when certain psychodynamic needs are emphasized, a mechanism which therefore fulfills certain definite functions for the individual. The following case may illustrate such "need-fulfilling" telepathic communication:

13. *Lasse:* When I got to know my wife, she was together with another man. So my job was to compete with him, and it wasn't

going very well, I thought. I lived in a rented room, didn't know what she was up to, and what's more hadn't declared my feelings for her openly, so I guessed I couldn't hope for very much in any case. One night about 2:30, I suddenly woke up with terror in my soul. I had experienced intercourse between her and the other man, vividly and completely; perceived it. It was so painful, so close, and so intense; I experienced it just as if I were in the same room with them. I lay there squirming like a worm in my bed; it wasn't at all just an imaginary experience.

Eva: I felt rather caught between these two men and didn't really know which I should stay with. That night, just when I was actually having sex with the other man, but it was a disharmonious, disagreeable situation, I cried out deep within me, "Lasse, Lasse, help me!" or something like that—so my thoughts were more with Lasse than with the man I was sleeping with. The next day Lasse phoned to say he was having a very hard time concentrating on his lectures that day and he told me about the experience. We met that evening and talked out the whole thing together and that conversation helped bring us closer.

Certainly it is easy to take this as a pure coincidence—it is really not at all unusual for young lovers to have envious imaginings about each other. But the relationship hadn't yet reached a stage in which Lasse had taken up the challenge with his rival seriously; on the conscious plane, he'd rather resigned himself for the time being. He denied that he'd had similar dreams before or even fantasized about her. Perhaps he had unconsciously perceived that Eva had begun to waver in her relationship with the other man. He had no definite personal recollection of hearing Eva call out his name, which, according to her, he had said in their conversation the following evening. In any case, this dream, with its probable telepathic contents, became the direct cause for a conversation which led to clarifying their relationship and solving the problem with the other man. Since then the couple have experienced many coincidences which they consider telepathic.

The Russian researcher Vasiliev is known for his experiments with inducing hypnotism telepathically [18]. The close contact which a psychoanalyst has with his patients can encourage similar experiments [19]:

The psychoanalyst R. Weiler treated a certain Mrs. C by suggestion under hypnosis to help her undergo complicated dental surgery. Subsequently she had difficulty sleeping, which was also helped by hypnosis. Eight months later the sleeping difficulty returned during a period of stress. Mrs. C had very regular habits, always set her alarm clock for 6 A.M. to be sure of getting to work on time, and to be sure that she would on no account oversleep, no matter how tired she was or how little she had slept during the night. She lived on the other side of town from the doctor.

Dr. W was concerned about her condition, and, thinking through her case one night before he fell asleep, he decided to resume the sleep-treatment hypnosis the following day. In his thoughts he went through the hypnosis technique which he had used with her before, when Mrs. C had previously been ill. A suggestion was included to sleep peacefully, undisturbed by all outside sounds, until 7:30. He usually induced hypnosis by gently stroking her forehead.

The next day Mrs. C phoned him and told how she had slept well for the first time in several nights. She dreamed that she had felt Dr. W's hand over her forehead and that she had then fallen asleep. She slept past the alarm, woke at 7:30, and arrived late to work, something which had never happened to her before. She felt much better and hypnosis did not have to be used.

Dr. W related nothing about his part in the incident. Some months later he felt the desire to try an experiment to consciously induce hypnosis by telepathy. Late in the evening he went through the procedure alone, imagining himself laying his hands on Mrs. C's forehead. He gave the same suggestions in his thoughts as he had on the previous occasion, but changed the time of waking to 7:00. Several days later Mrs. C told him that she had again dreamed that he was near and had rested his hand on her forehead and that she had fallen asleep. She slept through the alarm (which hadn't happened since the former hypnosis) and woke at 7:00.

Dr. W emphasized that he had never had any success with formal telepathic experiments, either as agent or percipient. "I have experimented no further, as I have an obsession against exposing my patients to conditions or circumstances I don't understand, and which I feel are not under my control."

Does Telepathy Exist?

Telepathy is the most probable explanation of the results in the above-mentioned tests of emotionally laden situations or dreams, if one accepts the existence of ESP. But it could also be maintained that the subjects perceived the target pictures clairvoyantly, or, through precognition, perceived the later verification of the information. Even if these possibilities seem highly unlikely and even though we try to eliminate them by various procedures, they cannot be totally ruled out. Telepathy is the form of ESP which is most difficult to isolate experimentally. To do this we must have target objects which exist only in someone's consciousness, not written down anywhere. And the accounts should not be completely written down after the experiment either; only the number of hits and misses should be noted. Only two experiments have been published in which clairvoyance and precognition have been ruled out in this way and in which the results—which were significant—consequently speak for "pure" telepathy unequivocally [21]. In spontaneous instances as well, the situations are often "mixed," but many cases correspond more closely to "pure" telepathy, e.g., Cases 5, 6, 8, and Dr. Weiler's case.

As has been mentioned, the dividing of ESP into these categories is no longer as important as it was formerly. We are now more interested in studying the factors involved in ESP as a whole. Telepathy could be considered the paranormal phenomenon most accepted outside of parapsychology. Certainly contributing to this is the fact that so many have themselves had experiences which have been interpreted as telepathy: these are among the most commonly reported spontaneous paranormal occurrences. Telepathy seems to happen "naturally" and obviously, in a way completely different from clairvoyance.

It is more difficult to imagine how we can know about an event that has not yet happened. But there are experiences which do indicate this, as the next chapter will show.

5

Precognition

Experiments with Precognition

Toward the end of the Thirties, the British researcher W. Carington made ESP experiments using drawings. His percipients were asked to make sketches of what they thought a certain drawing looked like, a drawing which he made and then kept to himself. He made new drawings each day, and similarities between these and the percipients' drawings were studied by outside observers. It was found that certain percipients tended to produce drawings which did not resemble that day's drawings but rather resembled those selected for the previous day or chosen for the following day [1].

When Carington realized that S. G. Soal had not obtained significant results from his thousands of card-guessing experiments, he advised him to investigate whether some of his subjects might have made correct guesses for the cards which came *after* the cards they were supposed to be guessing at the time. Soal went through his results once again and it was then that he noticed that Mr. Shackleton, in particular, had guessed the cards correctly ahead of time much more often than what would have been expected according to chance. New experiments gave the remarkably significant results mentioned in Chapter 2. Shackleton continued to guess cards ahead of time, even when he could not have known by telepathy or clairvoyance which card was to be the target for the next guess, since the target card had not been chosen until after he had already made his guess.

The experiment indicated that Shackleton really had knowledge of what card would be chosen. But mightn't it have been the *experi-*

ment leader who had ESP and used it in making his choice of the target object to correspond with Shackleton's guess? No, other experiments in which the selection of the target object was made completely mechanically proved to give similar results.

In striking experiments, H. Schmidt used electrons, which gave off radioactive strontium-90 [2, 3]. He placed a small quantity of strontium near a Geiger-Müller tube, so that an average of ten electrons were registered per second. According to quantum physics it is impossible to predict when the next electron will be registered. The subjects were to guess the appearance of the next electron, using an apparatus which registered the appearance in connection with a four-circuit breaker, each circuit of which was changed a million times a second with the help of an electric pulse generator. The apparatus had four buttons to press and four corresponding lights. When a button was depressed, nothing happened until the appearance of the next electron was registered by the meter. In that instant the contact between the pulse generator and the circuit breaker was broken so that the latter switched off one of the four circuits in which the electron was when it was registered. The corresponding lamp lit up. If the subject had depressed the correct button, the circuit breaker registered a hit; the number of guesses was counted automatically. Three subjects chosen from the preliminary experiments made altogether a total of 63,000 guesses and got 4.4 percent more hits above chance. This does not sound like much, but with such a large number of guesses, the probability that the results depended on chance alone was less than 1 in 500 million.

In subsequent experiments, the subjects either tried to guess correctly, or tried to press the *wrong* button. A total of 20,000 guesses were made. The first 10,672 which were aimed at getting a high number of hits, 7.1 percent more hits were produced than those expected according to chance, and the remainder, aiming for low scores, gave 9.1 percent fewer hits than chance (p less than 10^{-10}). According to Schmidt, these experiments indicate that the subjects really could foresee the occurrences in the electronic apparatus. Schmidt's experiments have been repeated by others with significant results [2].

Experiments in the Maimonides Dream Laboratory have also given results that indicate precognition. Certain percipients have given accounts of dreams which correspond to the pictures that were later chosen for the night *after* the dream [4].

True Dreams, Premonitions, and Apparitions

Usually in large collections of spontaneous paranormal experiences, 30 to 50 percent of the experiences give information about future events in the form of "premonitions," visions, or, most common of all, "true dreams." The character of the experiences can vary in the same way as telepathic impressions (page 41). Thus, they may be dreams; visions or other sensory imagery; more diffuse experiences of unease, feelings, or impressions; or bodily discomfort.

A simple premonition can be taken as an example of this:

> 14. I have premonitions occasionally about things which come true almost immediately, but this was something special and went like this: tomorrow morning a young lady E will come to pay a bill for her grandfather. Her mother will come along with her but stay down on the path in the garden while E comes up into the backyard and carries out her errand. The event happened exactly as the premonition came to me.

The details here are no more than those coincidence might cause, especially if E often does business with the percipient. But the information may be more detailed:

> 15. I was working late one evening, alone in the room. Suddenly I heard myself say, "Idealia wins the last race!" I was startled and wondered if it had got so bad that I was talking out loud to myself now, but then went on working and didn't think about it any more. Couldn't remember any horse named Idealia.
>
> A couple of times a year I used to drive out to the trotting races and look at the horses. Several weeks after that evening, I drove there and bet a few five-crown notes with bad results. Then the eighth race was over and I was looking for a possible winner in the last race and that was when I saw a horse called Idealia listed as starting there. It was listed in the papers as an outsider. No one thought of it as a favorite, and I knew nothing about it. I remembered my premonition, but scarcely trusted it. In any case, I bet a ten on it, not counting on the tip so much that I dared take on the winners. But Idealia was the clear winner ahead of the tipped favorites and gave twenty-five crowns on the place.

The most common content of a premonition is, however, misfortune of some sort, which as a rule hits someone in the percipient's closest circle. Premonitions of this sort can come in symbolic form (the same percipient as in Case 15):

16. I was out on the bathing beach with my wife and her sister, in the bright sunshine. Suddenly I saw an ordinary hospital bed, made up but empty, its real size and physically very vivid, palpable. It appeared up out of the sand behind my sister-in-law. This happened to me before I became familiar with parapsychological literature. I got scared and felt completely icy, didn't dare say anything to anyone, really didn't know what it meant. The vision lasted at the most fifteen seconds. No one suspected at the time that my sister-in-law was ill, but shortly afterward she became very ill and entered a hospital and then recovered.

Less common are dreams foretelling the dreamer's own death. C. G. Jung was particularly interested in such dreams. He narrates, for example, a series dreamt by an eight-year-old girl [5]. She attached so much importance to them that she wrote them down and gave the collection to her father as a Christmas present when she was ten. He was deeply moved by them but couldn't understand them at all. They included images the source of which was completely mysterious to him, although he himself was a psychiatrist. Nine out of the twelve dreams were about annihilation and recovery, death and resurrection, in imagery characteristically "archetypical." Jung became distressed when he read the dreams; they indicated an impending catastrophe. The girl died of an infection when she was eleven. Her impending death had cast its shadow "backward in time" over her life and her dreams.

True dreams are usually fulfilled in rather a short time, but the fulfillment can be delayed several years:

17. It was Christmas night 1933 and I was fifteen years old. . . . At two o'clock I woke full of terror and alarm after having dreamed the following: I sat at a big table by a gable window with Mother and Elin, a girl eight years older than I. Actually I had not seen Elin since I was eleven; she had gone away to earn her living. Now in this dream she was sitting in my home and she was a real lady. Her red hair hung down loose over her

shoulders and she was wearing a green dress which had a row of small cloth-covered buttons on the arms and back. We were having a very pleasant time, laughing and drinking coffee, it was summer. . . . Then I saw my neighbor through the window. He was German; he walked over to the flagpole, raised the flag and then an enormous flag flapped out over the blue sky, bigger and bigger until the sky was darkened. It wasn't the Swedish flag, but one with a strange cross. Then when the flag spread out over the sky, the cross opened and a host of people, war vehicles and war planes swarmed in the sky, a stream of blood ran down over the earth. I arose stiff with terror while I pointed, look, look, look! Elin also got up and looked, then she said, "There's going to be a terrible war in Europe, but before then I will be dead." Then she clutched her breast and fell to the ground. Out of her mouth came a stream of blood, and just when I leaned over her, I woke up. I was soaking with sweaty terror. I was fifteen and it was absolutely clear to me that the dream was true, a vision of the future which would be a great burden for me to bear.

Then three years passed . . . I had a position in Malmö. I didn't know anyone there and was rather lonely. One day on the street . . . I noticed a woman in a green dress with long red hair a little way ahead of me. I hurried, thinking it was Elin—the red hair, the green dress, the dream I'd never forgotten—I walked very fast, came nearer to her and then I noticed on her dress a row of little cloth-covered buttons on the back and on the arms, just as I had seen them in my dream. I shouted. . . . she didn't recognize me at first, but then she was happy to see me again. I kept quiet about the dream, convinced that was what I should do. [She had bought the green dress recently.]

Then a wonderful period of time followed. . . . Elin had many friends who became mine too, but my joy was mixed with sorrow that this time would not last forever. Elin had a hacking cough but she laughed away suggestions that she should consult a doctor . . . then a year later she entered a sanatorium . . . In 1938, in August, Elin was well enough to go home. I felt an anxious sort of joy. The flag I had seen in my dream now appeared everywhere in the press. At the end of August I got the news that Elin had died suddenly of a lung hemorrhage, and a year later war broke out in Europe.

Another form of precognition concerns a certain place rather than a certain event. Someone has, for example, visited a certain place in a dream which he later finds again in reality. J. B. Priestley [6] discusses a man who dreamed "an innumerable number of times" over a ten-year period of a certain city which he had never actually visited. He approached it from different directions in the dreams, sometimes by sea, sometimes by rail. Gradually he got a rather thorough knowledge of the whole city, and especially of a certain street. He tried to find out which his dream city was, but had no success until he visited Danzig (Gdansk) for the first time in 1948. Then "without the slightest doubt" he realized that the city in his dreams was Danzig—but in the dreams it looked as it had before the war. After that, he stopped dreaming about the city. Priestley himself had an intensely strong dream experience of a certain view of the Grand Canyon in America two years before he visited the place for the first time. A further example may be included for illustration:

18. I am nine years old, live in a city, and my best friend is called Marianne. So far as I know she had no grandmother. A dream:

Marianne and I get to go along with Marianne's mother to her grandmother to fetch newly made buttermilk. She lives in a remote herdsman's shack near the summer pasturage, and we have to walk first a long way through the woods. I'm not used to big woods and look around carefully so I'll be able to find my way back. I think it's beautiful, the big dark firs, the birch grove we walk through, the meadow with long soft grass which looks like flaxen hair, the paths covered with pine needles. We turn off onto a still narrower path winding between stones and bushes, we jump over a little brook and arrive at a low red cottage in a clearing in the forest. The cottage is on an incline with the stream down in the valley and a little hillock on the other side. Granny says that people used to stand up there when they called the cows home in the evening. Down below, tall junipers are growing. We walk in and are offered wild raspberries, which grow on the slope outside the house, and cold buttermilk, which Granny fetches from the cellar under the cottage. It's really good. The cottage has a kitchen and a tiny little back room. Marianne and I go in there while the adults talk in the kitchen. We find a loose stone in a tiled stove in the room there. We think it's exciting and imagine that a treasure has been hidden behind it. We pick it out, but find nothing. I've just learned about runic writing in school, and with a good many giggles we write our names on a slip of paper which we place behind the stone.

About three years pass. We have moved out into the country and my best friend is now called Kerstin [she didn't have a granny either]. A dream:

Exactly the same dream returns, but now it is Kerstin's grand-mother we're to visit in the herdsman's cottage. We walk through the same woods (I remember my way and I am not so afraid of getting lost) and come to the same cottage. We're given cold buttermilk and wild raspberries, which we eat on the same white wooden plank table in the kitchen. Kerstin and I walk into the back room, find a loose stone in the tile stove, think perhaps a treasure has been hidden behind it some time before. We pick out the stone; it's terribly exciting, and when we catch sight of a little piece of paper behind the stone we nearly burst with ex-citement. Runic writing is on it so it must be very ancient! We try to make out the runes, we only remember a few of them now—but enough so I can soon remember with deep disappoint-ment that I was the one who wrote on that slip of paper the last time I was there!

Still a few years later. We have moved again and now live near a forest where my elder sister and I walk on Sundays. One day we set off in a new direction, and after a while I suddenly recognize where I am (we had never been there before): the white birch trunks among the dark pines, the soft grass, the path which forks and forks again. I know that soon the stream will come that we have to jump over and then the cottage. Then my sister wants to turn back; I'm disappointed at first but then re-lieved because I'd rather go on alone. The next day I return and it feels like a very solemn occasion. Everything fits: the stream (which however is smaller now), the overgrown grazing pasture (but more overgrown than I remembered), the pines (taller now), the hillock, and the high junipers, several straggling rasp-berry bushes on the slope—but no cottage. I'm crestfallen. After a while I find a deep hole in the earth with an improvised stairs down the shallower side. The cellar! Several foundation stones also turn up lying around. I'm happy again; it fits. I question the oldest inhabitant of the village later who tells me that a herds-man's cottage had once stood there.

Often over the years I've visited that old, remote, abandoned cowherd's valley and always experienced an unusually strong feeling of security just being there.

You could say that paths through a forest are all so much alike that this need not be anything more than pure coincidence, in which some details just happened to be similar both in the dream and reality. But while following the winding path up to the cottage, the dreamer gave further details (which for considerations of space will not be gone into here) which made it seem to me that she had dreamed about this very path and not just any other. For forest paths can also be distinctly dissimilar.

Priestley attempts two explanations for the dreams about Danzig. One is that the dreams were precognition but were based upon a book, a film, or a play about Danzig rather than the city itself. The other is that the dreams were caused by telepathic impulses from some inhabitant in that city, received through "telepathic wrong connections" such as one occasionally experiences listening into someone else's conversation on the telephone. Thus, the dreamer was living the life of someone else in Danzig. But neither of these explanations appears to fit the dreams about the herdsman's cottage satisfactorily. No book about that exists, nor does any inhabitant who might have been sending out telepathic impulses—in fact, the cottage had been deserted for a long time, a long time prior to the dreams. In Chapter 13 another conceivable explanation will be considered for these dreams.

Is Everything Predetermined?

People who have told about their dreams sometimes experience these occurrences as a frightening premonition, as an indication that everything is predetermined:

19. After having studied the phenomenon of true dreams for some time, I began making notes every morning as soon as I awoke and wrote down as many details as I could remember from my dreams during the night. By following the advice given by Professor Dunne [6] in his book *An Experiment with Time,* by concentrating on how I felt in the split second upon waking, I found it much easier to remember dreams in detail, even when I felt at first as though I hadn't dreamed a thing.

Some dreams perfectly obviously consisted of fragments from made-up experiences, often very imaginative. Others were more or less disguised symbols for primary urges. But mixed in with these surrealistic tales were dreams which later proved true, and more and more of these accumulated. I think that my consciously directed intention to get true dreams eventually worked upon my subconscious and loosened the barriers there.

Certain dreams contained elements both from the past and the future and were also affected by the promptings of an instinctive level. In one dream I stood in line behind a girl waiting for coffee in a lunchroom where I worked. She had on only a rose-colored corset, and said, while she munched a pastry, that her dress had split. On waking I thought the dream belonged to the past, because we'd had pastries in the lunchroom the previous day. But later that day I stood in line behind the girl waiting for coffee [there were no pastries] and suddenly, moving out of the line, she cried out, "Damn it, my corset burst!"

The inescapable things in some of these dreams frightened me. I mulled over the possibility that the dream was plausible but that there could be an alternative "present moment of time." By altering little things, one ought to be able to slip into another temporal world track, but I never succeeded. Here is a frightening example:

I was working at the X photo studio. Among other things, I worked on developing and printing bridal pictures. One night I dreamed I was standing down in the basement darkroom and had just lifted the little rolls of film with bridal pictures out of their canisters in the fixing bath. I held them up to the safety light and was terrified to see that the films were black and overdeveloped. Then I heard footsteps in the outer room and *felt intensely that I had experienced this very thing before.* Miss Bengtsson, the manageress, walked into the darkroom, stood behind me, and I heard her say clearly, "What is it now?" Then she started shouting in rage and one of the things she said was, "How could you, Mr. Lindström, a professional, do something like this!"

I wrote the dream down very carefully, but thought it couldn't possibly happen, because I used a timer when developing, tested the temperature, and never left the process while it was going on. Moreover, the darkroom door was kept locked, and no one could enter unless I opened it first.

The very next Saturday I was standing there developing that day's bridal pictures. I put the cover on the can, set the timer, and then remembered that I had reproduction work in the other darkroom. Well, I had more than five minutes, so I walked out and studied the order. While I did that someone knocked on the door. I opened it. It was the caretaker, who used to chat with me quite often. We started talking and went on that way until I froze with the thought of the films in the developer.

I dashed into the darkroom, slammed the door but didn't lock it, and turned off the lights. I pulled off the lid and rushed the film into the fixing bath. Then a couple of nervous minutes passed before I could turn on the safety light and lift out the first roll. The film was very dark. And just then a clattering sound approached through the outer room and I stood there as if frozen to the spot. I felt as if I'd experienced all this before;

yes, I had: I'd dreamed it! Then in walked Miss Bengtsson, and her words were the very ones I had written down.

It was awful. Even when I was completely determined to change fate, it took its ineluctable course. There was no escape because the dreams drew all the elements together into a logical chain of cause and effect. If, for example, I'd been able to treat the films with a reducer and thus avoid being balled out, then the dream would have included that.

I dreamed ahead of time about the whole experience of a woman suffering from diabetes who fell into an insulin shock because she'd taken her injections but also spent the whole day skiing. What if I'd warned her the day before and told her to take less insulin or eat more? I said nothing. The dream had been about her falling into a coma from too much insulin and when I dreamed it, I'd already started resigning myself in my battle against fate. I didn't bother to warn her, and probably she would have neglected my warning anyway. She knew her diabetic complications better than I.

. . . After several years I started working against my future-sensing organ and finally I could live like other people again. But still I can occasionally wake in the morning remembering a dream with that special vibration which tells me that it's going to happen, and I'm never happy about it because it mostly deals with unpleasantness. Unfortunately, I don't know any method for filtering out unpleasantness so as to dream only about happy things. So my future sense lies fallow.

But all true dreams need not be precognitive. Stevenson [7] cites a case: a Japanese man dreamed one night that a tidal wave covered his village. He woke and warned his neighbors who took the dream seriously and managed to get themselves to safety before the tidal wave broke over the village later that day. But in such a case, a change in the winds which precede a tidal wave by several hours may have been picked up subconsciously by the dreamer and caused the dream. In Case 16, the percipient, normally or paranormally, experienced the latent illness of his sister-in-law, and the perception became conscious as a visual illusion of a hospital bed. Similarly, in Case 17, the dreamer unconsciously received information of Elin's latent illness and the violent outlook of certain foreign politics. In other words, Stevenson means: information which has come to the attention of the percipient in a paranormal way, can (if that really has happened) work upon the unconscious and become the source of what appears to be a precognitive dream, which simply reveals those conclusions which the percipient unconsciously drew from the information. (On the other hand, the detailed picture of Elin's dress can scarcely be explained in this way, this instead is probably "real" precognition.) The girl's vision of the coming war may be compared with C. G. Jung's visions before the First World War [8]:

> Toward the autumn of 1913 the pressure which I had felt was in me seemed to be moving outward, as though it were something in the air. The atmosphere actually seemed to be darker than it had been. It was as though the sense of oppression no longer sprang exclusively from a psychic situation, but from concrete reality. This feeling grew more and more intense.
>
> In October, while I was alone on a journey, I was suddenly seized by an overpowering vision: I saw a monstrous vision covering all the northern and low-lying lands between the North Sea and the Alps. When it came up to Switzerland, I saw that the mountains grew higher and higher to protect our country. I realized that a frightful catastrophe was in progress. I saw the mighty yellow waves, the floating rubble of a civilization, and the drowning bodies of countless thousands. Then the whole sea turned to blood. This vision lasted about one hour. I was perplexed and nauseated, and ashamed of my weakness.
>
> Two weeks passed; then the vision recurred, under the same conditions, even more vividly than before, and the blood was more emphasized. An inner voice spoke. "Look at it well; it is wholly real, and it will be so. You cannot doubt it."
>
> That winter someone asked me what I thought were the political prospects of the world in the near future. I replied that I had no thoughts on the matter, but that I saw rivers of blood. The visions would not let me be.
>
> I asked myself whether these visions pointed to a revolution, but could not really imagine anything of the sort. And so I drew the conclusion that they had to do with me myself, and decided that I was threatened by a psychosis. The idea of war did not occur to me at all.

Jung's description suggests that he received his original information from the surrounding "psychical atmosphere," and the visions became a symbolic image of that material. On the conscious plane he did not relate them to an impending war.

But if true precognition exists—and many parapsychologists believe that both laboratory experiments as well as researched cases of spontaneous experiences indicate that it does—how can it be explained? If it is possible to predict the future, then what happens to our free will?

Let us imagine a scene: An explorer glides swiftly in his boat down a winding river through rolling countryside. He cannot see that a group of cannibals are waiting behind a bend in the river to attack him. But someone on the lookout from a high hill by the river can see both him and the cannibals, can foresee that if nothing intervenes to cause him to beach on the other bank and disappear from there, he'll be eaten up. With every passing moment his decision not to interrupt the journey diminishes further his possibilities of escaping, until he has rounded the bend and caught sight of the cannibals' fire —but then it is too late. In a similar way, someone with sufficiently pertinent and profound knowledge of a person's disposition, wishes, and needs, together with the decisions he has already made, can foresee his future actions. The more intimate that knowledge is, the more can be foreseen. Just as a person's genetic makeup can be thought to build an invisible "program" for development in regard to illness and health, so there may also exist in the unconscious a "program" for future conscious life. With sufficiently deep knowledge of this, gained through normal or paranormal means, one could draw conclusions which the unconscious mind might ponder and express in the form of what appears to be a precognitive dream [7].

But there still remain cases of what appears to be real precognition (that is to say, those cases which cannot be derived from paranormal information in the present). These do not fit into our ordinary perception of time. Philosophers have taken up the problem. Broad [9] comes to the conclusion that real precognition is a logical absurdity and as such simply cannot exist. Others, like Garnett [10] have imagined a "medium" or a field linking all events, the psychic as well as the material. This field could be seen to include "programs" for future events. You can feed into a computer calculations concerning the building of a bridge, and that machine can give out a list of formulae and tables which a trained person could translate into a picture of the bridge. But even though the design is complete, the bridge itself need not necessarily be absolutely similar to the design: the design may be altered, some details changed, even though the plan of construction was completed a long while ago. Garnett's field contains, one could say, the present state of the universe plus a design or model, limited in time and space, for its future state. In that field or medium, associations between a mental and material course of events can be anticipated, that is to say, details in the model can be discovered through ESP and become consciously known as symbolic or realistic experiences or dreams. But the model is not definitely binding, it can be altered through active human intervention.

There are also cases in which the very experience of the future has caused the percipient to take the necessary steps to prevent its occurrence. Philosophers have spoken of "the paradox of intervention [11]." Consider if, for example, someone who foresaw that President Kennedy would be assassinated in Dallas warned the President and really persuaded him to change his plans. Thus the murder would not have happened—at least not right then. But in that case, no one could possibly have said whether the premonitions were true precognition or not. More precisely, we would only be able to say that it was *not* precognition, since the foreseen event did not actually occur. As a rule, we cannot demonstrate after the fact that events turned out as a direct consequence of the percipient's intervention. Still, in some cases the intervention can change a course of events which otherwise would have occurred. Krippner cites as an example [4]:

> A woman woke her husband one night to describe a terrifying dream. She saw a large ornamental chandelier above the child's bed fall and crush the child to death. The clock in the room read 4:35. Her husband laughed at her anxiety when she took the child into her own bed, but he did not laugh two hours later when a crash was heard from the child's room and the time was 4:35. The chandelier had fallen down into the empty child's bed.

In this case, Garnett's field theory suggests a pattern for the future state of the chandelier (which at the time of the dream was about to fall), of the child in the bed, and of the clock. So, then, the field contains both mental and material aspects possible in association with the physical events surrounding the chandelier's crash and the mental events in the mother leading up to the dream. Since these associations became conscious, she could perceive the pattern and alter it in some way, namely, in respect to the child's death which otherwise would have been the result.

The occurrence of real precognition, therefore, need not result in the acceptance of a completely fatalistic view of life. There is always an opportunity for someone to intervene to alter the situation which needs to be changed.

Could we conceive of the possibility of working to effect a future outcome practically, for example, for economic gain? Case 15 indicates that it can be done, and several earlier cases are known. Schwarz [12] mentions a woman patient who won bets on horses in sixty-four races for two seasons. O'Neill recounts how he picked out sixty-seven winners over several months [13]. He developed a technique of dreaming about the winning horses' names in symbolic form. But he also found that he eventually became increasingly nervous and anxious—he had thrust aside the dream's natural function as a "safety valve" in order to use it to receive information about horses, and in the end he was forced to stop these tests completely, to keep his psychic health. There have also been attempts to apply ESP to roulette playing [14].

Can Precognition Prevent Catastrophes?

Usually precognition involves separate individuals, the percipient himself and someone close to him. But sometimes events are foreseen for complete strangers, or catastrophes which befall many people. And occasionally a whole group of percipients have had experiences related to the same catastrophe. We may wonder how many premonitions of catastrophes never turn out to happen, and how many alleged experiences were indeed genuine and received *before* the catastrophe.

After the great mine disaster at Aberfan in Wales on October 21, 1966, in which 144 people perished, reports were collected from people who considered that they had had premonitions of the disaster [7, 15]. Of seventy-six reports received, thirty-four could be considered credible, and twenty-four could be verified in so far as the percipient actually had talked to another person about the premonition before the catastrophe. Twenty-five of the experiences were dreams. Eighteen of the thirty-four came within four days before the accident, eight within two weeks, and the remaining cases were earlier. If each of these premonitions had been studied before the disaster, perhaps they might not have been considered to indicate that particular catastrophe, but taken all together, considering the close time span, they do give the impression of being related. Their distribution in time may also indicate that these precognitions were the result of an unconscious use of information, from which one could predict that something would happen. As time passed, this information was received more clearly in more vivid detail and caused experiences for more and more people, normally or paranormally, while at the same time the disaster itself became more and more "unavoidable."

It could be objected that the risks of a catastrophe like the one in Aberfan were so obvious that they could be seen by anyone. The risks therefore might have been picked up just under the threshold of consciousness (subliminally) and then later might have taken the forms of impressions in dreams and visions. But most of the percipients did not live near Aberfan and had no direct knowledge of the conditions there. Several percipients experienced psychic and physical discomfort before the catastrophe which emphasized their premonitions; more of this in Chapter 7.

Among other things, this aspect of the Aberfan disaster stimulated the interest in a more systematic gathering of material pertaining to premonitions. There are now special centers which receive reports from people who consider that they have had premonitions of coming events [16]. The offices analyze these reports and look for similar characteristics in them. Perhaps eventually it will be possible to use these reports as a kind of warning system. If many premonitions were to come on a certain theme, for example, a catastrophe of a certain sort, perhaps people or authorities could be on their guard, watching for risks, so that the necessary steps could be taken to avoid an accident.

We have discussed clairvoyance, telepathy, and precognition, which together make up what is known as extrasensory perception, or ESP. We call ESP the psi-phenomenon's sensory, perceiving aspect. But psi also has an active, motor aspect. This is psychokinesis, which is the subject of the next chapter.

6

Psychokinesis

The Rosenheim Case

In November 1967, the Bavarian newspapers told of remarkable occurrences in the Adams law office in the town of Rosenheim. Overhead neon lights unexpectedly went out time and again, and the electricians discovered that some of them had come unscrewed in their sockets. Sharp knockings were heard; the four telephones in the office would ring simultaneously; conversations were interrupted, broken off; telephone bills shot up, though no one was using the phones more than usual. Faulty wiring was suspected. Employees from the electrical company installed a voltage recorder in the office to check variations in the supply of current. The metering instruments sometimes registered inexplicable discharges (which were recorded by a needle on paper) as well as other phenomena. On November 20, 1967, at 7:30 A.M., "a light fixture in the boss's office fell to the floor and broke, following a sharp bang." But the fuses didn't blow. The meter measuring electrical current registered two maximal discharges of about 50 amps. All this was inexplicable, especially the fact that the fuses didn't blow out. Fluorescent tubes were replaced with ordinary incandescent light bulbs "because of the danger of falling fluorescent tubes." But the light bulbs exploded in inexplicable ways. The ceiling lights swayed, but the swaying could not be related to anything happening in the room above. The municipal electrical company found nothing wrong with the supply of electrical current, but, at the lawyer's request, the office was cut off from the municipal electrical mains and received its current from a special generator to guarantee an "undisturbed" supply of electrical current. The lawyer reported "malicious damage" to the police, and the police investigated without discovering any culprit.

The occurrences became widely known throughout Germany; a TV program was made. Professor Hans Bender of the Parapsychological Institute at Freiburg came to Rosenheim on December 1, 1967, to start investigations [1].

It was found that the mysterious events occurred only during office hours. They seemed to have something to do with a nineteen-year-old girl, Annemarie Ur, who worked in the office. Whenever she walked through the office, "the lamps started swinging behind her, light bulbs exploded, and the fragments flew in her direction."

Of course, possible explanations of the occurrences were sought. Two physicists, one from the Max Planck Institute in Munich, connected the meter for electrical current to an oscillograph and then went systematically through all conceivable physical causes for the voltage-recorder deflections. It was found that the recorder's writing arm gave a strong reaction at the time of the abnormal events despite the fact that no alternation in the strength of the electrical current could be ascertained. Even when the meter was connected to a 1.5-volt battery, it registered strongly. Did this mean there was something wrong with the instrument? The following factors were studied: changes in tension in the wiring, HF tension, the condenser's load capacity, the electrostatic charge, the outer static electromagnetic field, infrared or ultra sound, strong vibrations, faults in the metering apparatus; someone's incompetent work on the machine. All these investigations gave negative results and the conclusion reached was that no conceivable physical explanation could be given for the fact that the instrument's writing arm gave strong or maximal readings at the same time as the other abnormal events occurred. It seemed, therefore, as if the behavior of the instrument depended on a mechanical power which worked the writing arm itself. Sometimes the evidence was so strong that there were deep gashes in the paper [2].

The telephones were removed and a single test instrument to meter conversations was installed. It appeared that Miss Ur's number showed up as being engaged sometimes four or five times a minute, certain days up to fifty times in succession. The telephone company had systematically tested every conceivable reason for the complaints and arrived at the conclusion that the conversations must have been initiated from the office. The staff denied the accusations and insisted that the metering instrument had registered conversations when no one was talking. Then, on one occasion, when an outside official was present, the meter was seen to register twenty calls in ten minutes despite the fact that no one was using the phone.

The phenomenon continued throughout December, and a constant contact was maintained between Freiburg and Rosenheim even though, for economic reasons, a regular investigator could not remain there. After the Christmas season, Annemarie was on holiday but still came into the office quite often. She sided with Adams, the lawyer, against the town gossip, which maintained that his son caused the disturbances.

Between the fifth and the seventeenth of January 1968, the phenomenon culminated. Before the very eyes of a physicist, a heavy storage filing cabinet weighing 175 kilos (400 lbs.) moved 30 cm from the wall. A new phenomenon occurred: paintings on the walls rotated vertically as much as 360 degrees around the hooks they hung from. This could be documented on videotape. When Annemarie stopped her job in January to start work with another lawyer, the disturbances ceased and quiet returned to Adams' office. Then, in her own home, similar phenomena occurred for a short while, and some were also reported initially at her new place of employment, but soon all was peaceful again.

Poltergeists and RSPK

The events in Rosenheim are unusual but not unique. About five hundred such cases have been reported in Europe as well as America [3, 4]. The unique aspect of the Rosenheim case (and several later cases [5]) is rather that such a thorough investigation could be carried out while the phenomenon was still going on. These phenomena usually tend to diminish or disappear when an investigator with serious intentions appears on the scene. Spiritualists coined the expression *Poltergeist* (German: rattling, blustering, bullying spirit) for such "ghostly disturbances," in which a destructive spirit was thought to be responsible. Now a purely descriptive term is preferred: RSPK, or *recurrent spontaneous psychokinesis*. The German word "poltergeist" now appears mainly in literature in English, while the Germans themselves talk of "Spuk," which means "ghostly disturbances."

As a rule these events appear to be connected with a young person at the age of puberty or in psychic situation of crisis. It appears as if psychic conflicts which cannot be resolved in contact with other people are released through "psychokinetic discharging" in inanimate objects. It has been observed that the closer objects are to the agent, the more they tend to move; PK, as opposed to ESP, appears to depend on distance, at least in spontaneous cases.

PK—Spontaneous or Controlled?

Another German case illustrates conceivable psychological workings of the phenomenon [5].

> Toward the end of 1965, newspapers discussed the curious events in a porcelain factory in Bremen. Glasses, cups, and vases were said to literally hop from the shelves. A detailed investigation by the police and various experts could reveal no explanation. The disturbances ceased for the first time when Heiner, a fifteen-year-old apprentice, was sent home. A person interested in parapsychology suspected RSPK and advised getting rid of the boy. Professor Bender began his investigations of the case two days later. The whole porcelain factory was full of shattered porcelain; the damage amounted to about 5,000 German marks (dollar value then about $1,250).
>
> Heiner had grown up in his maternal grandmother's home. He was not accepted by his mother, who was married to a man other than his own father. He was intensely unhappy with his work in the factory. "His destructive aggression seems to have turned into a psychokinetic discharge after the shock he received from seven hours' testing in a psychological laboratory." He was sent to a psychiatric clinic where the same occurrences continued, to the astonishment of the doctors and the psychologists. He came to his foster parents in Freiburg and began working as an apprentice to an electrician.
>
> In March 1966, new cables were to be installed in a new school: two hundred hooks had to be fastened to the cement walls. Two holes were bored for each hook and the hook attached by two screws and two plastic plugs. Heiner's foreman noticed that almost immediately after the hooks had been fixed, the screws worked loose, so that the hooks (which had been attached so securely that you could climb up them) could easily be unscrewed from the walls. He had heard of the occurrences in Bremen and suspected Heiner, who protested his innocence. But first in the presence of the foreman and later before a group of researchers from Freiburg, and various other people, the phenomenon could be observed and photographed under well-controlled circumstances. Hooks which had just been fastened

securely and checked and thus were firm as a rock, worked loose in less than two minutes in front of the witnesses' very eyes.

More recently, Heiner was again associated with new phenomena and lost his job. Contact with him was broken when his foster parents refused to allow further investigation. After July 1967, no further phenomena were reported.

It is typical of these cases that the disturbances gradually cease when the psychodynamic situation surrounding the agent changes. In Annemarie's case the relationship between her and her employer stirred up a psychic atmosphere conducive to RSPK, and this was moreover intensified when he became very interested in the phenomenon. On one occasion, in her presence, Adams, the lawyer, said, "The next thing you know the pictures on the walls will start swinging around too!"—and in a short while the new variation began. The phenomenon seemed to be related to him: on one occasion when he entered the office, a person from the electrical company who was there to investigate happened to be standing a meter in front of a picture and noticed how it quickly rotated about 320 degrees when Adams passed by it.

Several young RSPK agents have been the subject of exhaustive psychological appraisal in Freiburg. The following personality characteristics are considered typical [5]:

The intellectual endowment was normal, but her emotional development late. Her tolerance for frustration was very low. She reacted quickly to stimuli with a tendency to hysterical reactions: she was very easily irritated. One found indications of losing control and losing integration [ego weakness]. Projection was a dominant defense mechanism. She had a tendency to dissimulate and fabricate when conflicts occurred and for reasons of tension. Conflicts between her high ambitions and her limited resources, between her emotional need for contact and feelings of being a social outcast due to retarded psychosexual development, could be thought to explain the "psychokinetic discharging" of aggressive tension into substitute objects as a way of unconsciously resolving the conflicts.

Thus, several researchers consider that the ability to produce PK-phenomena is not a mystical quality possessed by a certain number of people called mediums, but rather a skill which could be acquired by almost anyone. The determining factor is the mental disposition: doubt and suspicion hinder the phenomenon; belief and expectation facilitate it. By practicing trying to relax tension while simultaneously maintaining an expectant attitude one can soon succeed in demonstrating PK. The Englishman Batcheldor, in particular, has set forth these theories. An interested group of three men and one woman who wanted to prove his theories became able to bring about remarkable phenomena [6]. They came together to see if some phenomena could be produced; the first objective was to try to make a table weighing 18 kilos rise from the floor while keeping their hands *above* the table. During the very first attempt, knockings were heard in the table, and after a few seances these movements occasionally became so violent that it was feared someone might be injured; the table swung in the air and no one had complete control over the powerful movements it made. In later experiments, people tried to make a lamp light by willing it. If a metal ring which hung down loosely could be made to swing upward through PK, then an electrical current should be able to be turned off and a lamp on a table lit. They were soon able to get the lamp to light and go out on order. It could also answer questions by lighting a certain number of times; occasionally it even gave them the answer before the questioner himself was conscious of the correct answer. They were able to repeat the phenomenon in several successive seances.

Those interested who would really like to contribute to parapsychological research have an opportunity to test their ability in this area. With the example of the British group's experiences, other groups would perhaps be able to demonstrate that long-sought-for PK conditions.

PK in the Laboratory

Experimental incidences of PK under laboratory conditions are not as strong or significant as those for ESP. The emotional storms and the special psychological situations which seem to be a necessary ingredient for RSPK also prove to be difficult to reproduce in laboratory conditions. Nor do RSPK agents always succeed in getting results during laboratory experiments. In Freiburg, Annemarie got significant results in ESP tests but not in those involving PK.

Numerous instruments have been constructed to investigate PK in the laboratory. The first basic approach was to cast dice with the purpose of calling a certain face more often than the randomly expected one sixth of the number cast. By deciding randomly which face you wanted, you could guard against the possible tendency of the dice to favor one face. Later, machines were constructed which cast the dice automatically. A variant machine throws down little polished cubes in the center of a horizontal slab. The idea is to try, using PK, to make the cubes reach one side or the other of a median line, depending on what has been randomly decided before the beginning of the experiment. The distance of the cubes from the median line is then measured, so that you can also obtain a quantitative measure of how you succeed. Using a device of this sort the Swede Håkon Forwald has, among others, made extensive experimental work and published significant results [7].

PK can also be investigated now with electronic devices which register automatically. Schmidt [7] has modified his machine for precognition testing (described in Chapter 5) to use in both clairvoyance and PK experiments, and obtained significant results.

Can PK also be thought to operate on living organisms? Barry [8] describes how one may impede the growth in a culture of the mushroom *Rhizoctonia solani* with "thought power." Various subjects each had nine seances of fifteen minutes each in which they tried by thought alone to impede the growth of the mushrooms in five plates placed 1.5 meters away from them. During the entire experiment, five control dishes were treated similarly except for the attempt at PK. Significantly slower growth was found in the experimental dishes (p less that 0.001).

Healing and PK

Might PK therefore be somehow connected with faith healing? Grad [9] let a person who considered that he had the power of healing attempt "the laying on of hands" on a group of mice which had been inflicted with sores of a certain size. A perceptibly quicker healing of the wounds was noted in the group of treated mice than in the control group, which was handled in the same way except that no "laying on of hands" had taken place, or at least none carried out by anyone who considered himself to have healing powers. In another experiment, jars containing grain were watered in otherwise absolutely identical conditions, some by a person considered psychiatrically healthy as far as anyone could ascertain, others by two people who were cared for in a psychiatric ward. Before the watering, the subjects held the bottle with the solution between their hands for thirty minutes. Quicker growth was found for the grain that was watered by the healthy subjects, but the differences were small. Others have reported that PK can significantly arrest the growth of tumors in mice [10].

J. Smith reported that the same "healer" who had handled Grad's mice could increase the activity of the production of the enzyme trypsin [11]. The resulting measurements of the differences of activity was, however, very slight. Swedish attempts to reproduce this experiment with a healer who said that he could heal from a distance gave no appreciable difference in the level of the enzyme before or after the treatment [12].

Healing presents difficult problems for the investigator. Some people maintain that they have this power or have experienced it from certain other people. But it is often impossible, after the fact, to reconstruct all the factors we must recognize in order to be able to determine if healing really has taken place. Was the diagnosis accurate? Had the person's condition already begun to improve before the treatment? Was the cure after the treatment checked and tested by adequate investigation? Did the cure last, or could it have been an impression of a temporary change in the activity of the illness? How great is the tendency of that illness to cure itself spontaneously? These are the questions we must face every time we wish to investigate the effect of a healing method, whether it is penicillin or the laying on of hands. Grad's experiments appear to have been well controlled and the results are noteworthy, but they will be of greater interest if other researchers can repeat them with similar results.

Nevertheless, several well-investigated cases exist in which an instantaneous and apparently inexplicable healing seems to have occurred. Bender [13], who has examined several such cases, considers that suggestion alone is not an adequate explanation. Hypnotic suggestion has a chance to work only if an "effective field," that is to say, a strong emotional bond, is built up mutually by a patient and a therapist. The therapist would contribute among other things an intense wish to help the patient and deep sympathy for him. Already under the influence of this emotional field, the unconscious mechanisms in the patient could accept the suggestion and produce the adjustments necessary for healing. Therefore, healing might also be seen to occur on the psychodynamic plane and therefore need not have anything to do with PK. It seems as if a similar emotional field is also necessary for RSPK, though in that case the nature of the emotions are quite different.

Psychic Surgery and Magic

"Psychic surgeons" might be mentioned in this context. In the Philippines it is said that Tony Agpaoa and his colleagues can perform abdominal operations with their bare hands without pain, without any sort of instrument, making large incisions which heal instantaneously and leave no scar. The operations as a rule involve a "tumor" being removed and exhibited in a big pool of blood, after which the blood is mopped up and the patient rises healthy and cured. These operations have been much disputed, and even Western doctors who have witnessed them have not been completely unanimous in their judgment. Obvious fraud has occurred: the "tumors" from human patients proved, under microscopic investigation, to have been animal tissue. From the films and color pictures I have seen myself, two things are often conspicuous: most of the patients are corpulent, and the patient is partially covered with cloth which is always laid out near the "wound." It is difficult to avoid the suspicion that the man performing the operation has a sponge or bladder of blood hidden under the edge of the cloth, from which he squeezes the blood while he presses down with his fingers into the abdominal fat, thus producing the illusion of an incision. The whole thing happens very fast. It is conceivable that the surgeon's main intention is to impress the viewers and facilitate the suggestion, which will have a beneficial influence in such cases. Whether or not any genuine paranormal phenomena occur would be difficult to determine from a distance. A definite investigation would not be impossible to undertake. Accordingly, American observers judged that deception was involved as early as 1967, but the phenomenon continues to draw distant voyagers to the Philippines [14]. German parapsychologists investigated the phenomenon during the summer of 1971, and perhaps their reports will definitely show once and for all if the operations are paranormal.

José Arigo in Brazil operated, on the other hand, with instruments—using ordinary scissors and knives, unsterilized, without anesthetics, without antibiotics, but at an unbelievable speed. And yet his patients felt no pain, had no significant bleeding, no infections, and the wounds healed quickly and without complications, according to the reports of several doctors, among them an American who himself had a small tumor removed by Arigo. No deception has so far been proved [15].

If the reports on Arigo describe the events accurately, then there are indications of undeniable psychosomatic mechanisms of a sort completely unknown to us. Indeed, the fact that healers in the Philippines on certain occasions have been guilty of fraud does not rule out the possibility that paranormal phenomena may have truly occurred in other instances. Arigo died in an automobile accident in February 1971. Detailed, extensive reports of his work have so far (June, 1971) not been published, but would, of course, be of the greatest interest.

The psychic surgeons' work seems to be related to the phenomenon of *magic*. Reference books define the word as, for example, "actions and processes of primitive man's belief in the possibility of influencing supernatural powers; witchcraft, sorcery. . . . [16]" But people who really have had a chance to study magical conduct from close at hand have sometimes doubted that superstition and superstitious faith are a sufficient explanation for what appear to be paranormal phenomena which have been observed [17–19]. Magic may be either "white," which is to say, aimed at protection against harmful powers, or else "black," that is, directed to produce harm or death in others.

A variant of black magic is called "voodoo." There are various and sundry reports of so-called psychic deaths or voodoo deaths in which a person has died after another, a magician or someone else, has predicted his death at a certain time. In some cases, it has been possible to follow the process in the hospital, for example, when a member of a so-called primitive people has become ill after being subjected to the incantations or curses of a medicine man. The individual has wasted away and died without any demonstrable sign of illness, and people have tried to explain the process as the result of strong autosuggestion. The more specifically related psychodynamic mechanisms remain, nevertheless, unknown [20] and the phenomenon's existence is doubted by many [26].

A variation of white magic are the rituals which appear to allow people to walk barefoot on glowing coals without danger of burning themselves [21]. These phenomena are poorly investigated, partly because magical practices are kept absolutely secret from outsiders. Parapsychologists have seldom had the financial resources to make such studies, and ethnographers as a rule are not familiar with parapsychological areas of questioning. Still, reports which do exist from many different cultures indicate the possibility that those people we may consider primitive can make use of psychic and psychosomatic mechanisms and powers which are completely unknown to us. (See also the section on ecstasy in Chapter 15.)

Psychic Photography and the Spirit Photograph

Finally, a phenomenon should be mentioned which may possibly be related to PK but which for the present appears completely mysterious and puzzling. This is the "psychic photograph" which has been produced by the American, Ted Serios. With a Polaroid camera held either by him or some other person near him during the exposure, a number of pictures have been produced which do not resemble the surroundings in front of the camera at all but instead show completely different subjects. Hundreds of such photographs have been produced, some under carefully controlled conditions. TV cameras have also produced abnormal pictures in the presence of Serios. No one has been able to prove fraud, and abnormal pictures have been produced even when independent investigators have held the camera [22].

Through the spring of 1969 some of the Swedish press printed a sensational "spirit photo" obtained during a seance in Eskilstuna [23]. Naturally, a photographic trick is a simple explanation for such pictures, in which case the photographer ought to have noticed it before he showed the picture to the public. But even if the picture is genuine, that is to say, not produced by some manipulation or trickery during the taking or in the darkroom, it does not necessarily mean that it is a "spirit photo." The fact that Ted Serios seems to have produced paranormal photographs without the help of "spirits" must raise a certain suspicion about other collections of alleged spirit photos which have been published [24]. So long as such pictures cannot be produced under controlled experimental conditions they will remain a curiosity in the outlying areas of parapsychology [25].

Thus we have discussed the phenomena considered to be ESP and PK. In the following chapter, parapsychology will be discussed as a science before we investigate totally different phenomena and experiences in Part Three.

7

Parapsychology — Fraud or Science?

A new scientific truth does not triumph by convincing its adversaries but rather by the fact that these adversaries finally die, and a new generation grows up familiar with the new truth.   MAX PLANCK

Criticism of Parapsychology

The first reports from Durham of Rhine's experiments stirred up conflicting emotions among American scientists. Between 1935 and 1936, five articles were published, and between 1937 and 1938, forty-two articles followed which were all critically opposed to parapsychology. The attacks followed several lines. One was mathematical: the statistical analysis of the experiments was rejected. As early as 1937 at a congress of American statisticians, a statement was made that "if Rhine's investigations are to be attacked fairly, then it must be on other than mathematical grounds."

The criticism also pertained to the experiments themselves, and the usual points of attack were: (1) faulty precautions against sensory cues, (2) poor shuffling of cards so that their order was not completely random, (3) unconscious faults in the keeping of procedural reports, (4) incomplete reporting so that only successful parts of experimental series were published. In several cases, the attack was clearly justified [1], but gradually the techniques were sharpened in all respects.

During the following ten to fifteen years, fewer works opposing parapsychology appeared. Parapsychology seemed to have won an easy victory. But in 1955 a Dr. Price wrote a long article in the distinguished periodical *Science* [2], the main points of which were: (1) If ESP really exists, it would be of enormous importance and it ought to be possible to apply it practically, for example, as a warning system before catastrophes. (2) But the occurrence of ESP is incompatible with modern scientific knowledge. Therefore ESP cannot exist. Parapsychology is superficially masked with some of the accessories, trappings of science, but it "bears the marks of magic." (3) "My opinion concerning the findings of the parapsychologists is that many of them are dependent on clerical and statistical errors and unintentional use of sensory clues, and that all extrachance results not so explicable are dependent on deliberate fraud or mildly abnormal mental conditions." (4) But part of Rhine's and most of Soal's work demonstrate that ESP seems to occur even under controlled experimental conditions, and their results cannot be explained or dismissed as faults in method or statistics. (5) Therefore Soal must have cheated, that is to say, the results he published depend on conscious fraud. Price then described different complicated methods he would have used had he been Soal and wanted to cheat.

Price was rebutted by a phalanx of parapsychologists and others. He had no proof at all to support his accusations against Soal, who very naturally felt that he had been wronged: "It is, I think, safe to say that no English scientific journal would have published such a diatribe of unsupported conjecture." Price had proposed a "definitive experiment," which, under absolutely "watertight" conditions and with a large jury, would determine whether or not ESP occurred during just that particular experiment. Soal thought instead that several researchers each should search for outstanding subjects and make similar experiments. A "definitive" experiment, however large the jury and strong the evidence, would in the end only disappear into the shadows of history, and then surely some new critics would arise and accuse the jury of fraud. The 1955 debate had an epilogue seventeen years later. In the January 28, 1972, issue of *Science,* the following letter from Dr. G. R. Price was published: "During the past year I have had some correspondence with J. B. Rhine which has convinced me that I was highly unfair to him in what I said in an article entitled 'Science and the supernatural,' published in *Science* in 1955. The article discussed possible fraud in extrasensory perception experiments. I suspect that I was similarly unfair in what I said about S. G. Soal in that paper."

After the debate in *Science,* the next broadsides against parapsychology appeared ten years later. Then, in 1966, Hansel published his *ESP: A Scientific Evaluation.* This book is obviously directed at the layman and thus for safety's sake is armed with the respectable word "scientific" in its title [3]. It is essentially a criticism of certain experiments which Hansel considered so important that the whole of parapsychology would stand or fall depending on their assessment. Many of the critical points taken in the book had already been published and replied to in parapsychological periodicals. The book was read with horror by parapsychologists and pleasure by their critics— finally someone had once and for all given parapsychology a death blow. Hansel was applauded with enthusiastic reviews in several scientific periodicals [4, 5]. In more well-balanced evaluations [6, 7], Hansel's strategies were revealed: he searched through reports primarily for the possibility of fraud on the part of the subjects and the researchers, however far-fetched and preposterous it might seem, and then he drew conclusions that since (in his opinion) fraud could not be ruled out, then fraud is also the most probable explanation for the results of all these experiments. But the book teems with faulty facts, which cause one to doubt that Hansel even read several of the works he flattens with his criticism.

And yet even this attack had its useful aspect: it caused parapsychologists to sharpen and refine their experimental procedures even more. A more unfortunate result is that interested laymen may have got a completely inaccurate idea of what parapsychology really is from Hansel's exceptionally biased and sometimes completely inaccurate exposition.

Do Parapsychologists Cheat?

And how has parapsychology tackled this purgatory? Has any evidence of ESP withstood the attack?

One of the main accusations both Price and Hansel made concerned cheating. But various research projects since Hansel's book was published have in fact been very well protected against the possibilities of cheating. Schmidt's precognition experiments gave highly significant results using a completely automatic method of registering them, something Hansel considered had been lacking. Experiments for clairvoyance can also be made in similarly safeguarded conditions [8]. Self-correcting procedures were used during the experiments with Stepanek—if a mistake was made, it was discovered immediately, since the sums would not match, and the final appraisal was first done by a computer. Nor did the subjects know how they would have to alter their reports to get results in the desired direction. I have personally taken part in several experiments in which significant results were obtained by Stepanek and I know that in each case there was no cheating in the experiment.

Cheating also seems to have been ruled out in for example Moss's experiments and at the Maimonides Dream Laboratory, where the result is first received, and then the reports are scored by, outside observers, and in which moreover the percipient is often situated far from the target object. In the event of fraud, these judges would also have to be implicated. But why would all these people cheat? What motivation would be strong enough to get a dozen researchers to take part in a conspiracy which runs great risks of being discovered —and to keep unswervingly, strictly silent about it? Furthermore, such a situation would present a marvelous opportunity for an opponent to join in such an appraisal group and disclose the cheating afterward.

Of course, not everyone is a saint simply because he is involved with parapsychology, and certainly it is conceivable that a researcher might fall for the temptation to improve his results, just as that possibility might occur in other branches of science—perhaps to increase his chances of receiving financial subsidy or promotion. Hansel maintained, for example, that Soal received his doctorate degree because of the significant results he obtained with Shackleton. He thought Soal would not have received the degree for a series with negative results, with the implied insinuation that this would have been a strong motivation for Soal to cheat. But the contention was groundless: Soal's work was judged on other grounds [10].

Even if some form of cheating could be proved in a parapsychologist's experiment, still hundreds of other such experiments remain to be explained away. An increasing number of people nowadays are completely unmoved by the accusations of fraud brought by Hansel and others, namely, researchers who have themselves obtained significant results in parapsychological experiments and who, unlike Hansel, *know* that they have not cheated.

The fraud debate is really, in fact, uninteresting. Scientists in any field can cheat if the motivation is strong enough. But only parapsychology has been set apart for this particular accusation of fraud, actually because certain critics experience the results of these experiments as a threat to their world view and therefore must explain them away. A small number of them are brave enough to acknowledge this candidly [11].

ESP and Personality

Another frequent point of attack made by opponents is that the psi-phenomenon, even if it does exist, is "lawless"; it obeys no natural laws but wanders independently and cannot be correlated with any other known facts, and, therefore, the study is of no scientific value. What is considered to be ESP is no more interesting than any number of pure coincidences which must occasionally be reckoned with in the laboratory and sometimes in everyday life.

But reality proves to be quite different. Various studies indicate that success or failure in ESP experiments (as in other kinds of performances) depend on the motivation to take part in the experiment. Gertrude Schmeidler [12] found in group experiments that subjects who believed in ESP ("sheep") got better results than those who did not believe in ESP ("goats") and considered the experiments meaningless. The results of later experiments varied somewhat but as a whole indicated the same pattern. Numerous studies have been made to illustrate the connection between the subjects' opinions and attitudes about the experimental methods and the person conducting the experiment and their ESP results. ESP is thought to function like other psychological processes related to performance. Too reserved and defensive an attitude blocks ESP, while an open, trusting attitude or a particularly strong psychological need tends to facilitate ESP in laboratory experiments. But researchers examining mediums have sometimes reported contradictory results: mediums have shown poor adaptation to reality and in psychological examinations have indicated very weak defense mechanisms, that is, unconscious psychological contents show themselves all too easily. Perhaps the individual's access to his unconscious is decisive: a person who allows his unconscious impulses to surface as conscious impressions and actions (whether this happens in the case of a spontaneous and balanced individual who may "relax" his defense mechanisms, or in the case of an individual whose defense mechanisms are too weak) appears to achieve ESP more readily than someone who maintains stronger defense mechanisms. The relationship between ESP and personality has also been studied, for example by H. J. Eysenck, who believes that extroverted people achieve better ESP results than introverts [13].

It is interesting to note that certain people tend to get significantly *lower* scores than those expected according to the laws of probability (psi-missing). This indicates that they actually receive ESP signals but, as a consequence of unconscious processes, prevent them from reaching consciousness and as a result choose wrong symbols more times than according to chance.

These studies show that ESP does not "hang free," unconnected with any other factor, but that the ability is actually related to other personality factors, even if the connection is very far from being clearly mapped out.

Psychosomatic Reactions to ESP

One of the important personality factors for ESP would thus seem to be the ability to allow unconscious signals, for example, a tele- pathic impulse, to become conscious. Perhaps everyone receives such signals but only a very few have the ability to let them surface as impressions in the conscious mind? Shouldn't we then be able to demonstrate and identify unconscious signals through a psychoso- matic sequence?

Dean is an American pioneer in this area. He has made studies with the help of a plethysmograph, an instrument which measures the current of blood in a hand or a finger [14]. The changes in the volume of blood are dependent upon impulses from the sympathetic nervous system and are generally not controlled by the will [15].

In his experiments, the percipient tried to relax in one room, while an agent in another room or in another building concentrated on a series of cards. On some cards were written the names of people who meant something to the percipient, the control cards were blank or contained names taken randomly from a telephone directory. The percipient showed significantly greater variations in his blood volume when meaningful names were "sent" by the agent. Here ESP was registered through a physiological course not directed by will power [14, 16].

ESP can also manifest itself in spontaneous cases through bodily symptoms. Barker describes how seven people who experienced a kind of "premonition" about the Aberfan disaster noticed psychic or bodily discomfort which seemed to be eased by the catastrophe itself or by what they heard about it [17]. One woman described her "disaster-vision-dream":

> A London woman, aged fifty-two, wrote, "At approximately 4 A.M. on the morning of the disaster I awoke choking and gasping with the sensation that the walls of my room were caving in. I have had this same experience prior to two other disasters, but on the morning of the Aberfan tragedy it was particularly terrifying."

A similar process appears to lie behind a "pain projection" which has been described during spontaneous cases of telepathy:

> A woman suddenly had severe pains in her right hip. The condition lasted several hours. She consulted doctors who ordered x-ray examinations. Then she learned that her mother, who lived far from there, had fallen and broken her hip [actually broken the neck of the thigh bone, but that was not clearly indicated] at precisely the moment her own pain began. It quickly passed, but her mother was operated on three times and became an invalid.

In this case, the ESP signals clearly never reached the conscious mind and the percipient perhaps didn't realize at all that the symptoms were caused by something outside herself.

A statistical detail which indicates that successful results of psi experiments are something more than random coincidence is that the results often tend to be better (more hits) in the beginning of each experimental series of, for example, five attempts. This is particularly striking in PK experiments. An obvious explanation would be that this is simply due to fatigue and boredom. Experiments with PK do involve a certain strain and expenditure of energy. The energy level is highest after a break and a rest; when the subjects are tired, their motivation decreases. Such a distribution of hits would not be expected in the case of cheating or random coincidence [19].

One form of physiological ESP is what is called "the removal of the tactile sense," which has been described by Fahler [20]. A person is placed under deep hypnosis and made to hold a glass of water in his hand. The hypnotist gives him the suggestion that the tactile sense in his arm and hand will "flow out into the water" and he tests that the subject cannot feel by pricking his hand. Then the glass of water is removed from the subject, who may be blindfolded, and the glass is held several meters behind him. In successful cases, if the surface of the water is soundlessly disturbed with a needle, the hypnotized person states that he can feel a needle pricking him on the hand, and if the needle is plunged deeper into the water, he mentions pain, and so forth. What would result if someone happened to spill the water, no one has actually ever dared to investigate. Fahler's report has been much discussed. However, no one has published any successful summary of his results, and in fact he has been successful with only one of his subjects. Nevertheless, others say that they have carried out similar experiments [21], and the phenomenon was described back in the nineteenth century [22].

Can the Experiment Be Repeated?

A regular point of attack against parapsychology is the scarcity of experiments that can be repeated. Some critics [5] mean by this an experiment that can be undertaken by absolutely any formally competent researcher and which will demonstrate "on command" that ESP exists. But it is easy to forget that ESP is something different from, say, the force of gravity, which can be demonstrated very easily by simply dropping something heavy on one's tender toes.

The possibility of repeating an experiment and getting identical results is very important in sciences like physics and chemistry. But the more complicated the biological processes involved in the experiment, the more difficult it is to produce identical results every time. The difficulties are particularly great when some form of conscious human activity is being investigated. For example, in psychopharmacology, when you want to prove the effectiveness of a new medicine, it is not sufficient to consider only the chemical substances you are examining. The patient's and the doctor's perceptions must also be considered; the doctor's opinion of the new treatment, the patient's personality and frame of mind—all this must also be taken into account. Within psychopharmacology it is therefore well known and accepted that we must take into account all these factors. In repeated experiments, in which we try to make the conditions similar, we may not get identical results. But no one consequently comes out with the attack that psychopharmacology is not a respectable branch of science and that it cannot be accepted as a science until it can produce an exactly repeatable experiment [23].

Conditions in parapsychology are of a similar nature. Schmeidler [12] and others have indeed shown that the results to a great extent depend on the relationship between the researchers and the subject. A subject who is convinced that ESP does not exist has more chances of obtaining negative results and thus becoming increasingly set and convinced in his attitude than someone who is open to all possibilities. For example, S. G. Soal began as a critic of Rhine's experiments and also believed in the beginning that his own experiments confirmed his doubts, until he went through his own data again and found indications of precognition.

Has parapsychology no repeatable experiments to offer? Certain critics would say not. Even the most outstanding subjects are not active forever; their interest diminishes, they fall ill or die or other circumstances hinder further work with them. Certain subjects like Shackleton and, to an even greater degree, Stepanek have been available for several years; different researchers have been able to travel to Prague to work with Stepanek. The focusing effect has been demonstrated as a repeatable experiment [9], though, of course, one cannot guarantee that Stepanek will also be able to demonstrate this ability in the future.

Some experiments can certainly be repeated. The dream investigations can be carried on in different laboratories; Moss's experiments with emotionally charged situations can be made and varied, a series of experiments concerning the relationship between ESP and attitudes could be repeated. But ESP is obviously dependent upon many subtle factors which have yet to be completely understood, and until more is known of them, and until they can be tested and controlled to a great extent, it would appear that the attempt to demonstrate ESP on demand will be no more than a cherished dream. What we can do is vary the conditions systematically: in one experiment collect all known conditions which favor ESP, in another similar one collect all negative factors. On the basis of what is known, we could therefore predict that the results will clearly be better in the first instance.

The difficulty of repeating experiments with equally good results may depend on the fact that, with most subjects, ESP can be demonstrated in the laboratory only as a marginal process. This is comparable to listening to a remote and weak radio station when the signal is scarcely stronger than the static. Hence, unusually lengthy experiments are necessary, with many guesses, to obtain significant results. The exception to this are the few "stars" among subjects.

A doctor who wishes to study a particular illness does not simply go out into his waiting room and fetch a patient at random. He must actively search out patients or wait until someone consults him and proves to have that illness. It is the same with ESP: if you want to study it you must either vary the conditions in some experiments to be as favorable as possible for the subjects without great gifts, or wait until a Shackleton comes your way. The scarcity of exceptional subjects has increased the interest in methods of developing, learning, or training a person's ESP; we will return to this in Chapter 15.

The above chapter has given examples of how ESP and PK, if they do exist, can be studied in the laboratory and how they may appear spontaneously. It is my opinion that this work and these experiments, together with hundreds of others which have not been mentioned here, have clearly demonstrated that there is something worthy of the name of extrasensory perception, and something else which is equivalent to the term psychokinesis. In the following part, Chapters 8 through 14, we will look more closely at some phenomena and experiences which are difficult to examine in laboratory conditions but which are of crucial significance to the question of what happens at death.

Part Three

IMPROBABLE
EXPERIENCES

8

In the World of the Dream and Out-of-the-Body

What if you slept? And what if, in your sleep, you dreamed? And what if, in your dream, you went to heaven and there plucked a strange and beautiful flower? And what if, when you awoke, you had the flower in your hand? Ah, what then?   S. T. COLERIDGE

Hallucination and Reality

Our ability to live together in physical reality depends on the fact that we all perceive reality in somewhat the same way. We have, for example, agreed that the sky is blue on a clear day; if someone insisted it was red and green checked, we would not believe him any longer. He takes us out into the yard, eager to show us that it is just as he says. We see only the ordinary blue sky, but he insists it is red and green checked. The doctor consulted announces that he is the victim of a sensory illusion, in this case a visual illusion, more precisely a visual hallucination. A *hallucination* is the experience of a sensory impression which does not have a perceptible equivalent for "normal" people in outer reality, an experience which is produced "from within" without stimulus from the corresponding sensory organ. Hallucinations may be experienced as perceptions from any one of our sensory organs: sight, hearing, smell, taste, or touch. They occur especially often under certain conditions of illness but can also be experienced by people without any apparent illness at all.

Imagine that some city dwellers are strolling in the country on a

91

summer evening. They have never heard a cricket chirp and don't even know that such a creature exists. Everyone there, except a young boy, is advanced in age and can no longer hear the high-frequency singing of the cricket. The boy stops to listen and describes this piercing sound to the others. The others are unaware of their diminishing auditory acuity and can't understand at all what the boy is talking about—their conclusion must be that he is hallucinating!

This example shows that we cannot always immediately decide who is "right" in his description of the truth, the one who seems to be hallucinating or everyone else. It could be thought that the one who is hallucinating may be experiencing something which really exists outside himself which the rest of us can't perceive. In the case above, we could record the cricket's chirp with a technical instrument and thus convince those who doubted that there really was "something" there. But in most cases of hallucinations, there is no such possibility. If the contents of the hallucination diverge from what the rest of us consider plausible and possible we're quick to draw the conclusion that it is a symptom of some kind of illness. But it is possible that in some cases hallucinations are actually experiences caused by an unusual sensitivity to something in outward reality which the rest of us cannot perceive. (I do not mean to imply that this is the case on all or even most occasions.)

We have seen examples of hallucinations as expressions of spontaneous paranormal experience, for example, Cases 1 and 16. A hallucination can also be collective, that is, experienced simultaneously by several people:

> 20. My wife and I had just heard that my mother-in-law was on her deathbed. We had just gone to sleep ourselves, it was quiet in the apartment. So then I clearly heard the outer door open and close, and then my mother-in-law's characteristic shuffling walk in the hall on the way to the kitchen. Then it faded away and nothing more was heard. My wife doesn't remember now whether she heard the door open, but she heard the footsteps as clearly as I did—you couldn't mistake my mother-in-law's slippers. It happened a couple of days before she died.

A remarkable collective visual hallucination is described by C. G. Jung in his autobiography [1]:

> With a friend he visited a church in Ravenna and in the Baptistery there found four large mosaics of incredible beauty. He

puzzled over how he could have forgotten them, but he had not visited the place in twenty years. Both friends stood before the mosaics for more than twenty minutes, discussing the Biblical motifs represented there. Jung wanted to order photographs of the mosaics, but didn't have time to get them, so when he returned home he asked an acquaintance who was going to Ravenna to get the pictures for him. This man could only reply that no such mosaics existed similar to those Jung and his friend had seen.

Jung comments: This experience in the Ravenna Baptistery left a deep impression on me. Since then, I know with certainty that something interior can seem to be exterior and also that something exterior can appear to be interior. The actual walls of the Baptistery, though they must have been seen by my physical eyes, were covered over and altered by a vision which was as completely real as the unchanged baptismal font. Which was real in that moment?

My case is by no means the only one of its kind. But when that sort of thing happens to oneself, one cannot help taking it more seriously than something heard or read about. In general, with anecdotes of that kind, one is quick to think all sorts of explanations which dispose of the mystery.

An even more dramatic example of how this inner reality can completely cover the outer is the following:

21. When I visited Egypt and the pyramids, I experienced traveling backward in time to the time when the great pyramids were being built. I looked very carefully around at what surrounded me then: the experience lasted a long time.

In the evening I was relaxing on my bed in the hotel, hadn't yet fallen asleep. Suddenly I was again transported to ancient Egypt and found myself in a huge grotto. I lay there fascinated, looking at the people around me and what they were doing. But then I had to get up for a necessary little job. The light was out, but the grotto was in fact illuminated. There was no light switch by the bedside, it was on the opposite wall. But I had a hard time finding it. I knew it should be there somewhere, but the mountainside was in the way. Finally I put my hand right through the stone wall of the grotto and reached the light switch, and when I turned on the light, the cave disappeared and the hotel room was present again.

The Lucid Dream

In this context a *dream* could be defined as a hallucination which covers the entire field of experience, that is, the person's whole experience and all his sensory impressions. The ordinary nighttime dream is a typical example and need not be described further here. It should only be emphasized that dreams are not just limited to visual and auditory impressions, with more or less strong colors and sounds. Sensory perceptions of intense smells, tastes, and tactile feelings can also occur, though not as often. While the dream is going on, dream experiences are therefore just as "real" as those perceived in a conscious awake state.

A special group of dreams has caught the attention of numerous parapsychologists in recent years. These are known as *lucid dreams*. A dream is called lucid not because its visual impression is unusually clear (which the adjective might imply) but rather because, during the dream, *the dreamer is conscious of the fact that he is dreaming.* This awareness is closest to an intellectual kind. What is fascinating is that the dreamer of a lucid dream, when he has reached a full realization that he is dreaming, achieves a certain degree of *control* over the dream's further development and it appears possible to develop this control through practice. Lucid dreams are usually also characterized by the fact that they are noticeably easier to recall than ordinary dreams [5, 11].

An example of incipient lucidity and control in a dream:

22. Walking to the train to travel far away, in a hurry and it's a long way to the station, but my legs can scarcely move. My joints have stiffened and my muscles are completely without strength, or the wind blowing against me is so strong that I can't manage to push myself forward—or I fall down from very high up. Fall at great speed and while falling I have a disagreeable feeling in my stomach and wonder whether I'll be able to feel the pain of crashing before I die. Or someone chases me through an endless forest. I don't know what he wants, only that it's something evil, bad.

Just when the fear begins, something says within me, "Why are you afraid? It's only a dream." I smile, relieved, and my legs move normally again, the wind dies down, and I reach the train. Or I fall much more slowly and land softly. Or I speed up very fast and escape my pursuer easily. As a rule, these dreams don't wake me up, but the memory of them is unusually clear in the morning. Or the dream fades away only very gradually.

Another variant: I receive a longed-for letter, open it, notice that it's very long and I've just started to read it, when I hear, "It's not really a good idea to read it here, it's only a dream." I put it aside, disappointed and angry, thinking I could have read it first anyway, but now I don't want to any longer.

The dreamer in the following example is interested in the idea of finding himself in the so-called spirit world (see further, Chapters 17–19) and there he examines his surroundings substantiated by a lucid dream:

23. I became conscious of a dream while it was happening. In it I was playing with some children in a sandbox. I was completely aware that the experience was not taking place on the physical plane and then I thought I would be able to test whether what M says is true, that on a spiritual plane you can influence your surroundings. It was very hot. I imagined a swimming pool instead of a sandbox and instantly I was sitting at the edge of a pool splashing my feet in pleasantly cool water. It was absolutely convincing. But then I wasn't able to keep my concentration on that experience but woke up completely.

The following example implies that the lucid dream can also be made use of therapeutically [5]:

When I was about nine years old, I suffered from nightmares occasionally, as many children of that age do. They were quite traditional nightmares, with a monster or dragon chasing me, always ending with my waking up in a state of extreme terror, soaked in cold sweat and totally paralyzed for a few seconds or a minute as I struggled to escape from the after effects of the experience. Somewhere during that period I came to the conclusion that I was very tired of being pushed around in my own dreams and that I had to do something about it. From then on, whenever I had a nightmare, I did the following: as soon as I became awake enough to realize that it had been a nightmare, I resolutely forced myself to go immediately back to sleep and into the nightmare. This usually resulted in the nightmare continuing where it had left off. However, at this point I took either of two courses of action. The first was to tell the pursuing monster or dragon: "Look, we don't have to do this sort of thing; this is all sort of silly, why don't we become friends?" The second course, likely to be taken if the first wasn't productive of results, was to play hero, whip out a sword, and lop off the monster's head! After doing this eight or ten times, I stopped having any nightmares. It was clear to me at that time that I had showed these various creatures of my dream world who the boss was. This simple therapy worked very well, and I have almost never been troubled with nightmares since.

As a child I had thus accidentally stumbled on the phenomena of the lucid dream and active dream control. These events and a very rich dream life in general have been among the sources behind my current professional interest in dreams. Dreams have always seemed incredibly rich, complex, and wonderful. I have never been very satisfied with the psychological literature on dreams, however, because it seems to take into account so little of this richness and complexity. Indeed, I am inclined to suspect that almost everyone who has written on the subject of dreams in the conventional psychological and psychiatric literature is himself a very poor dreamer; i.e., his dream life is rather impoverished compared to what dream life can be, and his own impoverishment is reflected in his dream theories.

False Awakening

In connection with both ordinary and lucid dreams, a *false awakening* may occur, in which a person dreams he is waking up, but actually continues to sleep and dream. Freud [20] would have called the following experience a "wishful-fillment" dream caused by the wish to go on sleeping:

> 24. The alarm clock shrilled, I shut it off, got up, went about my usual morning ritual, cycled off to work. After a while I woke again, felt completely bewildered to find that I was still (or again?) lying in bed—I should have already been at work, such a long time passed since I'd slipped off. Then gradually I got my thoughts together and understood that the first awakening must have been a dream. I rose up laboriously yet again . . . came to work two hours late. (The alarm clock had gone off.)

In the case of lucid dreams, several types of false awakening are described which are not as easily explained simply as self-indulgent dreams. In one variation, the dreamer is concerned with the preceding dream experience, ordinary or lucid. This condition can give rise to a new lucid dream. An example:

25. For several days I had been working on an article about, among other things, lucid dreams. One night during that time, I had my first clear, lucid dream. In it I was at some sort of holiday place, where I stood jumping on a long plank laid over two sawhorses. While I was jumping I suddenly realized that I was dreaming. I immediately decided to try to jump higher, and then I jumped dozens of meters up into the air but still landed gently on the plank. Then I wanted to see if I could fly, and immediately I swooped through the air as gracefully as a seagull. After that the clarity disappeared and my memory of the rest of the dream is uncertain.

When I woke up, I remembered the lucid dream with great pleasure, was almost childishly happy about it. The alarm clock said 6:45 and I saw clearly how the second hand was moving. I dictated the dream into a tape recorder I had by my bed for such occasions and then fell back asleep. Woke again at eight o'clock, remembered both the lucid dream and that I had woken up and recorded it, but then something happened that didn't make sense. I listened to the tape but no dream was recorded on it—it had been a false awakening.

Out-of-the-Body

Another variation of false awakening occurs when the dreamer, after having gotten up, happens to turn around and sees his own body still lying in the bed. This can, especially the first time, be so astonishing that the dreamer immediately "slips into" the body and awakens. Here we have a border-line case between the lucid dream and another experience, namely, the *out-of-the-body experience*. For the sake of simplicity, this experience will henceforth be referred to, following Whitman [19], as *separation*. The term suggests that the center of consciousness is split or separated from the body and exists somewhere else, for this impression is constantly referred to in descriptions of such experiences. The separation can begin in a sleeping state, in a lucid dream, or with a false awakening, but also in a completely awakened state. Three typical cases:

26. I had taken twenty-five of my nerve tablets and lay down, when I then awoke. I am certain that I wasn't dreaming. It was about eight or nine o'clock in the evening. So then I woke and wanted to get up but couldn't, I was so tired in my body, perhaps because of the pills, too. But I was determined to get up; I had

this feeling. But I couldn't, it was exactly as if I were paralyzed. And that was when it happened . . . I saw myself lying in bed, sleeping, while I myself or "my soul" floated in the air, in the same place where my body lay in bed, a meter up in the air, two or three meters to one side of the bed, I mean diagonally. There was another girl in the room who was lying there resting, and when I saw myself floating like that, I "walked" over to her, wanted to tell her about it so she'd look and see me floating. But in that same instant the eyes in the body opened and then I found myself back.

The whole thing lasted scarcely more than a minute, perhaps not even that long, difficult to figure out the time, perhaps only half a minute. When I had returned back I could get up, but I just lay there quietly thinking about it, and forgot what I'd wanted to do.

27. When I had my second baby I experienced the following in the maternity ward. I was lying relaxed in my bed. My body, so to say, remained lying there in the bed while another I (or soul) left the body. The soul (or I) got to sit up on the ceiling.

From there I could look down on the other mothers. Then I saw the doctors come into the room. Then a great rush down again. I jolted myself into my body. I got into it just as the doctors came up to my bed. They thought I was sleeping deeply.

28. It was an evening like so many others. I had put down my book, turned off the light, and was waiting to fall asleep. Suddenly I felt as if I was sort of swinging up from my body. My I—or the astral body, whatever people call it now—developed a clear light. I felt it as if it were not my body's dimensions but that I was instead very small. I felt very happy and not afraid as I slowly floated away toward the door. Just when I reached the doorway, I got to look back toward the bed and my body. "I mustn't disappear like this," I thought, "what would our daughter and my husband say." Slowly, sort of against my will, I floated back to my body. I turned on the light and suddenly had a whole lot to think about. I had never experienced anything like the joyful emotion I had when I came out of my body.

In psychiatric literature such symptoms are called *autoscopic,* defined as "a complex psychosensorial hallucinatory perception of one's own body projected into the external visual space [2]." The symptom occurs in certain states of illness. It involves seeing a "double" in the outer world viewed from the physical body. Separation instead involves more precisely the opposite of this: from a point in the outer world a person sees his own physical body. There are, however, connections between separation and reports of autoscopy, and a few cases in which the consciousness is thought to oscillate or shift between the physical body and the "double [3]." Psychologists and psychiatrists have shown very little interest in separation and lucid dreams, and parapsychologists are almost alone in investigating these experiences. I emphasize that the experience of separation or lucid dreams is not a symptom of illness but rather a common occurrence with the psychically healthy [4].

How It Feels to Be Out of the Body

Various firsthand descriptions of separation have been published. Some people believe that they can repeat the experience at will through some technique of "concentrated relaxation [6–8]." Several basic characteristics of this experience follow, collected from various sources, primarily from Green [9–11].

A separation can begin during sleep and also easily after a false awakening. But it occurs more commonly during a state of stress or illness when the body is awake, or when the body happens to be unconscious after an accident. There are, however, several published cases of the body continuing its activities in what appears to be a perfectly normal way, even though this may involve a complicated activity such as driving a car, examining a patient's teeth, or giving a sermon. The field of experience, that is, the surroundings which are experienced during the separation, may remain just as they are in the normal wakened state with the one difference that the point of view of the experience has shifted to slightly higher up, usually several meters over the body's physical position and slightly to one side (Case 26 is typical of this). But small differences in the surroundings can also be found which do not disappear until after the experience has ceased. The person often but not always sees his physical body. He may also feel that he has "another body" which is usually experienced as being the same size as the physical one (Case 26) but sometimes smaller (Case 28). The person can also perceive himself to be a completely "disembodied spectator." Sometimes a "silver cord" is described, a sort of "umbilical cord" linking the physical body to the separated self. But this is not experienced by everyone and has not been described by any of my personal case studies. Perhaps it can only be observed during separation under specific conditions. But it is described even by people who maintain that they have never heard of the concept [15].

The separated self experiences singular freedom of movement, and the testimony often emphasizes a feeling of joy, ease, and freedom. In a separated state, an individual is able to pass through doors and walls and float around unhindered. The experience may last only a few seconds or much longer, but the perception of time is uncertain (Case 26). The separation usually ceases spontaneously. Typically, the first experience of separation is very brief, only several seconds: the realization that one is experiencing a separation is so overwhelming that one instantaneously "travels back into" the body. Occurrences during separation are accompanied by a powerful emotional reaction and may also bring the experience to a swift conclusion, as for example, has often been reported in cases when someone happens to touch the physical body.

During initial separations, freedom of movement is usually restricted to the body's immediate surroundings, but with increased experience, a person has greater scope and can move further afield. In this state he may meet other people and find it difficult to know for certain whether or not they belong to the physical plane, that is, are in a physical body, or whether they belong to the "dream world." Objects and bodies in the physical world cannot be touched or influenced; or at least the contrary has not been demonstrated. In isolated individual cases, it has appeared possible to remove the self from the body's presence to regions which do not seem to belong to the physical plane, and in such cases it is difficult to ascertain whether the experience is separation or a lucid dream. Before and after separation, definite bodily symptoms may be experienced, not unusually a feeling of stiff numbness and a chill which starts in the legs and spreads upward throughout the body, sometimes intensifying into a feeling of total paralysis (Case 26) together with pressure in the head immediately before separation.

An example of increasing freedom of movement through several successive separations [12]:

> The first time that I consciously left my material body is as vivid to me now as the day it happened, though it was about twenty years ago. I awoke one night to find myself sitting up in bed. Puzzling over how this had happened, I had occasion to turn my head and then—I saw myself still lying there asleep

with my head on the pillow. I thought I was going mad, but then immediately the sitting-up part of my astral body sank back into the lying down body.

Several months later I awoke feeling a great wonderful rushing roar in my body, like a whirlpool. I was raised in a horizontal position over and above my physical body, the raising happened slowly and soon I sank back into the outer body. On this occasion the physical body felt stiff when I stepped out of it and was not able to speak. That was repeated and each time I rose still higher. Then gradually the astral body moved around the room but always stayed horizontal. But then one time the body happened to move to an upright position. The astral body faltered a couple of times before it got upright. The whole time a vibration was felt in it. I was conscious of what was happening throughout.

From then on it was much easier for me to leave the outer body. This was the start of a period when I wouldn't stay in the same room any more but wandered off on other excursions. I remember so well the first time I floated up against a wall. I thought, "I wonder if I'll feel the wall," but I didn't. Always felt so free and easy when I left the outer body.

Many times I've tried to take hold of something and lift it, but I still haven't succeeded. My hand just goes right through the object. On one occasion when I returned to the body I felt my pulse immediately. It was beating very slowly, almost not at all, but quite quickly it got back to normal again.

Two separations with visits to "other regions":

29. On two occasions I have experienced my soul separated from my body. The first time I was working in a restaurant, had just happened to injure one of my hands, and fainted. Then, while my body lay there on the floor, I felt I was traveling out into space, entered a white house, in an indescribably glowing atmosphere. A whole crowd of bright holy beings rushed toward me, among them my recently departed mother. "O come, here you'll be with us," I heard them saying. Then I heard a stern, decisive voice, "Not yet!" from the atmosphere or whatever it was and I was drawn away from that marvelous place and woke up in my body again. "Ugh," I said; it was like waking in hell after what I had experienced.

30. It was one morning early in April. . . . I awoke and watched the light filter in through the curtain. My husband was sleeping

soundly in the same room. I had a powerful feeling that something was about to happen. After a while a freezing cold began
to move from my legs up through my body. I couldn't move,
couldn't call out to my husband. Now I'm dying, I thought, but
without panic, I felt no fear. A strong pressure in my head and
then the soul or the spirit left my body. That spirit stood still
a while looking down at my lifeless body, felt infinitely free,
no sorrow over leaving husband and child. Immediately afterward I was standing under the linden tree beside my childhood
home . . . now I see it here before me just as I remember it,
the torrent rushing, the birds singing in the early spring morning,
the house, many hundreds of years old, stood silently in its proud
decay. As for myself, I was as light as down, incredibly liberated
from the body's weight and pains.

I walked several steps out into the grass, leaned down and
swept away the old leaves and rubbish and look! there I found
the stone I used to throw which had once disappeared and was
never found again despite all my eager searching. I laughed
happily, everything was so light and easy, now I knew eternally
much more. When I had lived before, my mind was closed tight
as a mussel shell, now it was open, gleaming clear. I walked
toward the house, that old house I had loved so deeply . . . went
up the worn steps and opened the heavy oak door and into the
room where my mother lay. But although she had already died
several years before, she was lying there smiling, looking younger,
she beckoned to me, "Come over here. I've been waiting for you."
I took a stool and sat down right beside her. We talked about
everyday things, about life on the estate, the neighbors, and we
were both very happy. After a while she said that now I had to
go. I protested but she insisted, "You must, you have people
waiting for you. Now you've been able to come here for a visit
and see how it is, but your time is not yet come." Good-bye,
Mother; good-bye, Maja. So then I walked out, closed the door,
stood outside in the bright spring morning; stretched my hands
out toward everything which had once existed and been mine.
A giddy dizzy moment and then I stood again in my bedroom
where my husband was still asleep and where my body lay lifeless
in the bed. I leaned down over myself and felt an aversion to
taking on the form of this strange being again.

Then my body felt a violent pressure in the head and a sensation of pain reaching every limb, the icy cold disappeared and
I was back in life again, my spirit was gone and my sorrow
was great. For a long while afterward I remained as if cleft
in two, but then very slowly I became my ordinary self.

The lucid dream, on the contrary, usually begins as an ordinary dream [5, 11]. The dreamer experiences himself in his ordinary body, and it is seldom that he sees his body in the bed, as he may in the case of separation. But some people also seem able to produce the lucid dream more or less at will [7, 11], and it is thought that a person may teach himself on successive occasions to increase his control over the dream. But still it is noteworthy that people who have described several lucid dreams remain cautious in their experiments. For though they are aware that they are perceiving a dream and, for example, decide to jump off a balcony to demonstrate to someone nearby who doubts their dream, some doubt still lingers: what if it were reality, then I would break my leg [5]! There are very few published reports of people walking through walls in lucid dreams, probably because it hasn't occurred to them to try. If they really made the attempt and didn't doubt the outcome, they would, presumably, succeed. The field of experience of the lucid dream differs more from the physical world than the field of that of separation, for it often contains more symbolic and fantastic elements. People who have experienced both lucid dreams and separations are inclined to value the latter more, for they involve much greater control over the situation, with greater possibilities of experimentation and of moving freely about, as well as deeper experiences of joy, freedom, and ease. But this does not imply that separation is always a positive experience:

31. During the evening I had been busy practising exercises in meditation and contemplation, and when I went to bed I was both tired and dull, weak in my body. After reading a little while, I turned off the light and calmly fell asleep. Abruptly—it was well into the night—I awoke, completely wide awake, and felt I was being lifted up toward the white-washed ceiling. I felt so incredibly, unbelievably light and featherlike and marveled as I noticed my own body which was lying there on the bed. But immediately afterward I was filled with feelings of terror. Fear of the unknown and of the weirdness of this kind of situation mounted within me, and before I was even aware of it, I had traveled back to the reclining body. I lay there in the dark and felt really very terrified. The occurrence was actually not completely inexplicable to me, for I had some familiarity with paranormal matters. But what happened next I find inexplicable. There I lay, terrified in the darkness, and in an attempt to ease my emotions, I thought I'd get up and go back to my writing table. But I couldn't! It didn't happen! A dark arm—I didn't

see the arm directly, but felt it—pressed me down on the bed. As hard as I could, I tried to force myself up from the bed, but I couldn't at all, the arm held me there and those seconds seemed to me like an eternity. But then the pressure ceased and after just a short while I fell asleep again. The room was dark, the arm was equally dark, it seemed to come from the window. I have no recollection that anything existed beyond the arm. I simply couldn't twist my head that far back.

Probably that "arm" was nothing more than a symbolic experience of the temporary feeling of paralysis which may occur after a separation.

It is striking how deep the impression of the first experience of separation often is on the percipient. Several describe it as if now, for the first time, they could really understand what it is like to live fully and completely. We cannot dismiss their experiences lightly as just the product of fantasy. But is it really conceivable to imagine a center of experience outside the body? Yes, and then is it conceivable that a person lying on an operating table, with every indication of being unconscious, who cannot react to impressions from the outside world, can nevertheless have these experiences? This is self-contradictory: an unconscious person who has conscious experiences, even if they are the result of a bodily state, cannot report them before the unconsciousness has ceased. An example:

32. I read a book in which a medium described how she could come out of her body during an operation. Having returned, she described to the doctor what had happened. He was moved and they became the best of friends [13]. This was not the case with me.

When I was five years old, I developed a throat ailment and was taken to the Karlskrona hospital. I was admitted and it was decided that I should be operated on.

. . . I was put in a chair and two girls fussed around me and put an apron on me. My mother had told me that Dr. Widén would operate, and we knew each other. . . . A pair of hands stuck a rubber sack from behind under my nose and held it there firmly. I tried to wriggle free but one of the girls took my hands and a man ordered me to breathe. I submitted, it prickled and was unpleasant and then everything was like night.

Suddenly I saw the room in a wonderful light without shadows. The first thing I saw was my hands, which were fastened down tightly to the chair arms with broad straps and a buckle contraption on them. My hands didn't obey my thoughts anymore; they were dead. Astonished, I slid down onto the floor and looked at myself. There sat a poor miserable little creature, pale, with some sort of contraption in her mouth. In front of me I had some sort of apron of something like waxed cloth with a pocket toward the bottom of it. My hands were lashed down and my feet tied tight under the seat. It was bloody and sloppy, a runnel streamed down the waxed cloth. A young, dark-haired doctor was in front of me. He had a chair, too. The two girls had suddenly put on surgical face masks. On my left side on a low table was a tray, and on it, instruments; their cold glint frightened me. I turned around. A big white box, its lid off, and on it stood a bottle which was brown with a white label, the contents of which I took. . . . I saw that the doctor changed something in my mouth—how little and miserable I was! I walked behind the doctor but the instruments scared me and I hid behind the protective white cover of the seat.

. . . I woke to find Mother sitting by my bed and I saw only her staring eyes. . . . I said to Mother that I hadn't seen Dr. Widén during the operation. How do you know, said Mother, after all, you were asleep. No, no, I said, I stood to one side and watched. Yes, but I especially asked for Dr. Widén, said Mother.

When the doctors came on their rounds, I complained that Dr. Widén had not operated on me. The big blond one wrinkled his eyebrows and said, what could you know about that? You were asleep! Well, no, I said, I stood to one side and looked on. Absurd, said the doctor. Then he walked off and over his shoulder threw out the words, "There's a lot between heaven and earth one does not understand." Afterward the nurses bawled me out, saying you don't talk to doctors that way. Doctors are gods.

[The records show that the patient was operated on by Dr. A-M, a Dr. Widén was also in the clinic. Operation: tonsillectomy plus *abrasio*, brief ether narcosis.]

Buddhist monks and nuns in Vietnam who have burned themselves to death protesting political conditions are a mystery in their way of dying: motionless, they sit in the flames and die apparently without pain [14]. Young people in Europe who have chosen the same desperate form of protest have burned to death while clearly suffering the most profound pain. A conceivable explanation is that the monks consciously "leave their body" just before they light the petroleum. The absolute mastery over the body which the monks strive for in their training over a period of many years may thus include the ability to will a state of separation.

Astral Projection

In books, the term *astral projection* is often used for the experience of separation. This term has its origins in the concept that, along with the physically perceived aspect of existence, the physical plane, there exist spiritual planes where "substance" is of another nature. One of these planes is called, in certain doctrines, the *astral plane.* Thus, similarly, it is considered that people can, outside and beyond their sensory physical bodies, also have normally invisible "spiritual bodies," among them the astral body, which resembles the physical one completely. This is called by some the *etheric double,* and several other terms exist.

During sleep and in certain other circumstances, according to this concept, the astral body can free itself from the physical body and move freely in the astral plane. There it is the bearer of the consciousness, the center of which has then moved out of the physical body. The separated being can then perceive the physical body's surroundings and certain aspects of the astral plane's surroundings equally well. With certain techniques, a person's observations can move "deeper into" the astral plane, which results in temporarily breaking contact with the physical plane. According to this concept, what happens at the moment of death is basically that separation between the spiritual bodies, among them the astral body, and the physical body, becomes total and permanent. Then the "silver cord" breaks, and the dead person is "born" into the spiritual plane [15].

We will return to this way of thinking later. Here it is sufficient to state that from the percipient's point of view, both the lucid dream and separation are played out in "another world," clearly distinguished from physical everyday life, with completely different "natural laws" from those of our everyday world. To what degree this "other world" may have any objective existence will be judged later (Chapters 17–19). But it is nevertheless noteworthy that descriptions of separation from different times and different cultures have so many common characteristics and are generally so alike that the experience of separation must be considered to be genuine and not entirely imaginary. Separations under different psychological conditions, for example, completely spontaneous occurrences compared with willfully produced ones, seem on the other hand to have some dissimilar characteristics [15, 16].

Work is also in progress to study separation and lucid dreams experimentally. An attempt is being made to correlate the EEG aspect with the subjects' reports of their experiences [17]. But it is difficult to produce these states on demand in the laboratory, and only a very small number of people say that they have the ability to induce separation at will. The majority of those who experience separation do it only one or a few times during their lifetime. Therefore, the focus has gradually shifted and concentrated on reproducing these experiences in conditions of altered consciousness, for example, during hypnosis [18]. We will return to this in Chapter 15.

The next chapter deals with two phenomena closely related to the experience of separation, namely, apparitions and ESP-projections.

9

Ghosts and Apparitions

Human beings are more versatile when compared with scientific instruments. Contrary to science's dissecting analysis, we experience all the various sense impressions simultaneously, and these combine instantaneously, spontaneously, into a synthesis of feelings, spiritual impulses, and thoughts, with qualitative values which natural science lacks. —CARL HØEGH

Apparitions and ESP-projections

A visual hallucination can sometimes be so detailed, vivid, and lifelike that the percipient experiences the hallucinated individual or thing as if physically present, nearby, while the rest of the surroundings otherwise appear quite normal. Such a hallucination is called an *apparition*. It may be accompanied by other sensory impressions, such as hearing, touch, or smell.

An experience of separation is called a (complete or total) *ESP-projection* if it fulfills the two following requirements: (1) the person who experiences the separation, the *projector* [1], experiences himself projected, that is, moved to another place from where his physical body is to be found, and he can describe how that other place looks, what the people are doing there, and so forth, and (2) a person who is in that place where the projector travels to, the *percipient,* can see an apparition of the projector, that is, he perceives a sensory impression of the projector and describes his appearance. An ESP-projection is called complete if it fulfills both these criteria, *incomplete* if it only fulfills one. If only criterion one is fulfilled, the phenomenon is called *traveling clairvoyance.* In such cases the projector does not always experience separation from the physical body but rather, "as if in a dream," experiences a shift to the place in question, for example, after hypnotic suggestion about it.

For a separation to be called an ESP-projection, the person separated must, basically, experience a move beyond the body's immediate surroundings, and he must be able to describe the place he travels to in such a way that it corresponds to the real situation there, which he could not normally know.

An example of an apparition:

> 33. On two occasions I have seen "things which do not exist." We were taking a coffee break at work, chatting and laughing as usual. Suddenly my dead mother-in-law appeared about three or four meters away from me, and she said to me, "You will be afraid of Elsa (my wife)." The vision lasted at the most fifteen seconds. She was completely lifelike, had on a dress with a blue flowered print. I can't say for sure whether I'd ever seen her wearing it. It was striking how bright the colors were, the blue was especially intense. When she talked she moved her mouth completely naturally. She appeared very distinct down to her waist, covered and blocked my vision of things behind her, and then disappeared sort of diffused down toward the floor. I took up my coffee cup and tried to act normally, I don't think any of the others noticed anything.
>
> I delayed a long while before I told my wife about the vision. Partly because I didn't want to frighten her, partly because we were in fact having some problems just at that time. The vision made a strong impression on me, and contributed to my not taking a step which I otherwise would have in my relationship with my wife. And thus it made me simmer down, which was good .

An apparition can also be experienced collectively by several people:

> 34. Mother, father, and I were invited to visit a Hungarian artist one day. When we got outside the house where he lived, we saw him sitting working at his drawing board by the window. But when we came up to his place, no one came to the door, which was strange since we'd seen him sitting there. All three of us saw him absolutely clearly. Finally Dad said that we should go down to the front door and wait outside. There was no

back door through which he could have run down to the street.
We walked down again and when we came outside through the
doorway, who but H was steaming along down the street. When
we told him that we had seen him sitting there he excused
himself by saying that he had thought so intensely about how he
would arrive late.

Animals seem able to experience apparitions, too:

35. Evening in the country. Father, mother, brother, and I
in the kitchen. Kille lay in his basket, he was the world's worst
watchdog: he loved people, good and bad alike, and never
barked.

"Someone's coming," said my brother, listening to sounds
from the gravel path. We all heard steps—they rounded the
corner of the house and approached the kitchen door. Kille
started growling deep down in his stomach. Someone knocked
on the door. In the country a person always knocks on the outer
door first, then opens and walks in and knocks on the inner
door, so no one bothered about opening. The knocking came
again. "Go open the door," said father. Kille raised a thick ruff
around his neck—the hair stood straight up. Mother walked
over to open the inner door; then Kille rose up cautiously, his
body stiff as a board and his hair on end. Just as she opened the
outer door, Kille flew like lightning out of his box, barking
loudly, and rushed into the wood-storage room and disappeared
under the stove there. Outside there was *nothing*. How well I
remember the open door and the darkness outside, and that
mysterious nothing which was there as if it were someone. Father
and my brother went outside with candles to see if a tramp was
there, but found nothing. The next day one of mother's relatives
came and told us that one of our close relatives had died. Later
when I reminded mother of what happened, she only answered
curtly, "Yes, that was the evening Måns Nilsson died."

ESP-projections can appear spontaneously or as the result of a conscious attempt on the part of the projector (and possibly the percipient). First an example of a spontaneous experience:

36. *Mrs. L:* We were building our summer cottage. Olle, one of
the neighbor's boys, went away on holiday just when the foundation was laid, and the house went up during his absence. One
evening at dusk my husband and I saw a neighbor striding
along the road wearing light-gray clothes. He disappeared in the

pine grove. I joked with my husband, saying, "Here's our ghost come to haunt us!"

Later that evening, it was still light, I saw another man, this time striding obliquely over the rise up toward the house, dressed in light blue pajamas and really just like Olle. The figure walked *right through the spruce trees* and up to the house, where he stopped, and with hands on hips, studied the house—and then disappeared into nothing.

After several weeks Olle strolled up just the way the figure in pajamas had, but now he avoided the spruces. He looked up at the house completely terrified and burst out, "But I've seen this before!"

Olle: The L family had just started leveling and grading for the foundation when I went away, so I had no way of knowing how the house was going to look when it was finished. One night I dreamed I was walking along the path that led up the O's site to the L's. In the dream, when I reached the cottage I saw it absolutely clearly. I wasn't at all surprised that it was finished, it just stood there. It had a verandah facing in my direction and I also saw Mrs. L standing on the steps as if welcoming me. I don't remember whether we talked or not.

Later, when I came back from the trip, I walked over to the L's to chat. I was terrified when I caught sight of the cottage; it looked exactly as I'd seen it in the dream, and Mrs. L sat on the steps. She asked me if I'd worn a pair of light blue pajamas the night I had the dream, and in fact I did. The time corresponded, too.

A deliberate ESP-projection which was incomplete:

37. *Tora:* It happened on Easter day, 1970. I was in the summer cottage, so overstressed that my heart began thumping and fluttering. I lay down flat to calm this distress. I was a little bitter toward Britta, as I can get sometimes. My last conscious thought before I fell asleep about eleven o'clock was to go out and play at ghosting her, just to scare her a little. Dreamed I was on my way out of the house, then everything got blurred and fuzzy and I half-dreamed that something happened.

Britta: At about eleven o'clock, when I was going to bed, I suddenly saw Tora sitting on a chair. She looked ill, more dead than alive. I'd seen her before when we'd tried experiments like this but then only hazily and half-transparently. Now she was absolutely physically vivid, she covered the chair from my sight just as an ordinary body would. She was dressed in some sort of nightgown with very short sleeves, a high neck with a little collar. I looked at her. It lasted a very short time and I didn't talk with her.

Tora confirmed: The nightgown looked just as she described it. It was kept at the summer cottage and she is sure Britta had never seen it.

Two projections with the same projector-percipient pair:

38. *Jakob:* Eva and I had agreed to note down the time, etc., of possible telepathic impressions of any sort.

The day after our decision I drove my daughter to her job, the time was 6 P.M. I was suddenly reminded of this agreement with Eva. Then I transported myself astrally to her home and found her sitting on the sofa, reading something. I made her notice my presence by calling her name and showing her that I was driving my car. She looked up and saw me. After that I left her and was back in the car which I had been driving all the while without any special awareness of the driving. The next day we corroborated the contact by telephone.

Eva: I was sitting alone in the room in an easy chair, waiting for the phone to ring, for some reason I can't remember now, thinking that Jakob would ring, or come. Suddenly I saw Jakob sitting in front of me in the car, saw about half the car as if I were in it with him. He sat at the wheel: I only saw the upper part of his body. I also saw the clock in the car, I think it was a couple of minutes before six. The car was not headed toward our house but in another direction. So then I thought: he has an errand somewhere, and that's why we haven't heard from him.

39. *Jakob:* I sat on the edge of the bed intending to read something. Then I heard someone call out, "Is there no one who can help me?" It wasn't loud, more like a whimper. I listened and recognized Eva's voice. I transported myself to where she was living and was standing in her downstairs hall when I saw her come hurrying down from the second floor, rushing past me in the hall, out into the kitchen. I followed her and placed myself by the window in the kitchen. Eva was in front of the sink. I repeated her name several times, and then Eva caught sight of me by the window. She stopped what she was doing and, standing still there, turned toward me, cried out, "Jakob!" Then I began talking, saying, among other things, "It isn't only Lasse and the children who need you, there are so many others, too."

I saw how she relaxed, and then I went away from there and did my reading. Who told me to speak to her as I did, I do not know. I hadn't the remotest idea of why I had to say just what I did.

Eva: I went down to the kitchen and was going to wash the dishes: I was alone in the house. Periodically around that time I had been extremely depressed and very tired. That day I'd felt very lonely and abandoned by people, and was totally fed up with life. Cried over my chores there at the sink. I didn't want to go on any longer. The thought of suicide was there. I felt completely worn out and a failure and everything was deplorable, I felt very sorrowful. Then suddenly from diagonally up on my right I remember hearing "light voices" and I saw a sort of luminous glow. Several voices said to me something like, "You do have friends anyway, we think of you and care for you; you are not without friends. We really are here." So then I tried to think through whom it could be and thought of some, among them of Jakob, but couldn't distinguish anyone definite. I couldn't identify the voices, rather felt that the thought behind it was sent out by a small group of people and that Jakob might be one of them. Then I felt very happy later when Jakob told me how he had felt my situation and tried to influence me. What he described about how I came down the stairs and what I did in the kitchen was perfectly accurate. The time corresponded exactly.

Case 33 clearly shows us right off the difficulties of interpreting an apparition. The percipient had earlier (Case 16) experienced a possible precognitive hallucination of a hospital bed which looked as real and lifelike as this apparition. That could indicate that the apparition was a creation of his own unconscious produced by the conflict in the house, which manifested itself in this way. On the other hand, this message could also imply that the apparition had some connection with his mother-in-law (provided that her personality continued to exist after death). Many apparitions behave like mechanical dolls, moving in a stereotyped way and unable to speak. But this one had a definite message to convey, which would have been characteristic for her had she been alive and aware of the situation in the home, quite apart from the natural motivation to help her daughter. As we will see later, it is just this sort of conceivable motivation from a supposedly surviving personality which is a strong element in the choice between different interpretations of phenomena.

(This same mother-in-law also appears in the collective auditory hallucination in Case 20. It is not impossible that the percipient would also have seen her apparition then, had he gone out into the hallway where the footsteps were heard.)

These cases pose certain questions. Is an apparition always only a hallucination created totally by the percipient (percipients) conforming to his (their) unconscious psychological needs, or can it have some independent existence? Could all cases of verified complete ESP-projection be explained simply as pure coincidence or, on the other hand, as telepathic contacts? Or can it be possible that the center of consciousness in the projector really has been transferred to another place and therefore finds itself in that something which the percipient perceives as an apparition?

Hornell Hart's Investigations

Apparitions were of primary interest to the researchers who founded SPR. Tyrrell summarized their findings in a book [2]. The man who studied apparitions and ESP-projections most thoroughly and deeply is Hornell Hart. Here only a very brief survey of his wide-ranging work on the subject can be given [3, 5, 6, 8].

Hart collected from parapsychological literature ninety-nine cases which fulfilled the criteria that the experience had to be reported by the projector or the percipient to some other person *before* confirmation came from the other party. In reference to the manner in which the appearance occurred, the cases were divided into five types —three experimental and two spontaneous:

1. Twenty cases in which the experience was induced under hypnosis.

2. Fifteen cases in which the projector caused the experience through "concentration."

3. Twelve cases in which the projection was caused by more complex methods than simple concentration.

4. Thirty incomplete cases.

5. Twenty-two incomplete spontaneous cases, which generally lack the second prerequisite.

Hart found eight characteristic qualities of a complete ESP-projection. The first two have already been named: (1) the projector's observations and (2) the percipient's observations. The projector moreover often reports that he (3) was conscious of being observed as an apparition, and that he tried to respond to the percipient's reactions; (4) he saw his physical body from a point outside it; (5) he was conscious of taking on a "projected" body (6) which could float freely through the air (7) and also pass unhindered through physical matter, for example, walls; and (8) it could "travel quickly through the air."

The projectors in Group 1 demonstrated principally the first of Hart's qualities, while the remaining were found to a varying degree or were lacking. On the other hand, the projectors in Group 2 mostly revealed the second quality and the others less often. Cases in Group 3 revealed several of the eight qualities most often.

An example of a successful projection from Group 2:

A man decided to attempt a projection to his mother, who lived in another place. After having concentrated his thoughts on her for five minutes starting at 11:15 P.M., he decided that the projection would occur at 12:30. Then, while his body lay on the bed, he experienced that he was seeing his mother in her bedroom. She sat on her bed, dressed in a light pink nightgown which was so low cut in the back that she was bare down to her waist. Later he broke off the experience and wrote it down. The next day, before she met him, his mother said that at 12:30 that night she had been awakened by a person leaning over her who brought his face close to hers. The apparition looked like a young man but did not specifically resemble her son. She confirmed the appearance of the nightgown, she had received it as a gift and it was too small. [Compare Case 37.]

Hart considered that neither chance, fraud nor telepathy could explain all these cases. Telepathic contact does not involve shifting the center of consciousness; the picture or impression comes while the receiver is fully conscious of his physical body and his normal surroundings. But it is characteristic of an ESP-projection that the experience occurs from a point in space outside the body, and the surroundings are experienced from a perspective which is completely consistent with and natural from that new viewpoint.

Basically, Hart recommends that hypnotic suggestion be used to try to produce ESP-projections experimentally. Similar experiments with "wandering clairvoyance" have been described by John Björkhem, among others. (See Chapter 10, Note 15.)

As for apparitions, Hart [3] studied 164 published cases, which fulfilled the following criteria: (1) they were based on evidence in so far as a description of the experience had been given to some outsider *before* the percipient received information of the projector's action at the actual time in question. (2) The apparitions were experienced with visual impressions (with one exception, see below). (3) The apparitions were seen by the percipient in a wakened state or in a trance; dreams were not included.

The apparitions were divided into five groups according to the projector's state during the occurrence:

A. Apparitions of people who had been dead at least twelve hours: thirty-eight cases.

B. Apparitions of people who had been dead less than twelve hours: twenty-two cases.

C. Apparitions experienced at the moment or close to the moment of the projector's death: forty-four cases.

D. Apparitions of living projectors who obviously did not recall their projection or possibly were not even aiming for one at all (ESP-projections incomplete from the point of view of criterion one): thirty-six cases.

E. Apparitions of living projectors who reported a moderately clear recollection of their actions and observations during the projection (complete ESP-projection): twenty-five cases.

The following characteristics of apparitions are discernible:

1. Distinctive indications that they are "material": apparitions are described as solid, palpable, vivid, lifelike; they cover objects behind them in a completely natural way. They can be perceived audibly and tactilely as well as visually, and the impressions from these three senses moreover correspond to ordinary natural ones. They appear therefore to be identical with material bodies. They adapt themselves to their physical surroundings in the same way that bodily-present people do. They are seen in normal perspective, both when they stand still and when they move about, and they can be reflected in mirrors and be covered by other objects. If they have belongings with them (clothes, walking sticks, house pets, horses, vehicles) these are perceived in the same realistic way. The details that are observed by the percipients would under normal circumstances be unknown to them but later prove to be correct compared with the projector's real experience at that specific moment. Apparitions may be seen by several people at once.

2. But the apparitions and their accouterments are only "semi-material" and therefore also have the following characteristics: they are glimpsed arbitrarily; they appear and disappear suddenly and

unexpectedly; they are not always seen by the people who would have seen them if they had been normal physical bodies. They can pass through walls and closed doors. They can glide or swoop instead of walk. They can relate ideas without words and gestures, that is, telepathically.

Hart compared the apparitions in these five groups with reference to these and some other (twenty-five altogether) clearly defined characteristics. His first findings were that the apparitions of the dead were essentially similar to those of the living. But some striking dissimilarities were found:

Group A included first of all those apparitions called "haunting ghosts," associated with a certain place rather than a certain person. The following experience belongs specifically to this group:

40a. One autumn day at about 2:30 in the afternoon I was on my way home after picking lingonberries in the woods. I had just cycled through Nyhyttan village and took the road heading toward Viksmanshyttan. The sun was shining, it was warm and beautiful. A little way ahead of me I saw a farmer bound in the same direction as myself. He had a four-wheel wagon with what's called a hayrack, and around that four boards were fastened. The horse was walking, the wheels rolling. I only saw the back of the farmer's head, sitting high up driving. I came nearer the wagon. Finally I was so close that I could almost touch it. I could clearly see the cracks that weather had caused in the boards and how the boards were fastened around the wagon. . . . The farmer wasn't going very fast, and I wanted to get ahead a little faster on my cycle. I looked down at the ground to see if there were any stones on the road. Then, when I lifted my eyes, the whole conveyance had vanished! I jumped off the cycle to hunt for traces of the wagon, but found nothing.

This really was something like the phenomenon which science defines as "impressions of eternity." Such people argue that all sounds and events which occur in this sphere last, and if one is lucky or whatever you want to call it, one can take part in past events. Had I suspected this was such a case, I wouldn't have looked down at the ground, but everything was so natural.

This particular percipient, now more than eighty years old, was himself very interested in paranormal phenomena and had reported several other experiences of a similar nature. Apparitions of this type do not seem to have been as unusual formerly in rural districts. Louisa Rhine [25] considers it is possible that apparitions have become in-

creasingly rare phenomena and that this is due to growing materialism. But still one can run across it unexpectedly, as in the following
case:

40b. At about ten o'clock in the evening in the beginning of
August 1967, I was driving on route 119 west from Ryd, about
a kilometer before the border of Skåne. The evening was star
bright, crystal clear, and completely calm. I was at ease, driving
about ninety, listening to the car radio, when a couple of hundred
meters in front of me something shadowed right in the headlights'
glare. First I thought it was an animal, but when I came nearer
I could clearly see that it was a person, walking along apparently
oblivious of the approaching car. I dipped the headlights without
result. Once, quite a while before, I'd driven past a drunken man
who had walked right into my path; with this in mind I braked
violently.

My astonishment grew as I neared the man. I had never seen
anyone now living with such old-fashioned clothes. Now I came
right up close by him and eased the car along slowly as far out
in the left lane as I could.

He was dressed in a loosely fitting, blouselike, collarless, gray
coat of coarse material gathered at the waist with a leather thong.
The coat hung down and swung loose below the thong. His
trousers were gray and of material similar to the coat, rather
sacklike and gathered up under the knees with thongs. These
had been wound criss-crossed down his shins and were tied
to a pair of mocassin-like soft leather shoes. On his head he wore
a dark, round, low-crowned hat. Hung from his left shoulder he
carried a hunting bag on his right hip, and on his left side a
powder horn. In his left hand he carried a long flintlock rifle
with a narrow butt and chin piece.

I could see that the man had long hair and wore a rather
massive beard. I hoped he'd turn around, so that I could see his
face. However, he took absolutely no notice of me but instead
just marched along with light, springy steps. Staring steadily at
his head, I rolled up alongside him. But at the very instant he
appeared through the side window, he vanished!

I braked hard, lit the back lights and hopped out, thinking
he'd fallen down, but the road was deserted and empty and the
forest stood dark and silent around me. Unfortunately I became
completely terrified and drove away from there at a terrific
speed.

At the end of November that same year I drove again on the
same road. At the same time in the evening and in the same place

I saw the man again. A difference was that this time the road was damp and wet and very dark. So I saw the man even more clearly in the headlights' beam. Besides, the law had changed and so I was driving then on the right-hand side of the road, so I should have been able to have a better chance of observing the man now that I would pass him on the right side. I also noticed that he was carrying the rifle in his left hand now.

It didn't look as if he'd harm me, I thought, and I felt brave enough to decide to get to the bottom of the mystery. So I put the car in neutral, opened the door a bit, lit the back light, and took out a pocket flashlight just before I slowly rolled up alongside the mysterious apparition. Just then I noticed that the man had a shadow! (I hadn't noticed it the first time.)

As I suspected, he disappeared in exactly the same way he had the first time. In a second, I was out of the car on the road, which stretched along just as silent as the time before. Not the slightest sound of footsteps or rustling in the woods. No one huddled down in the ditch by the roadside, no footprints anywhere.

I investigated the surroundings of this second occurrence: it was absolutely still and the sky was clear and bright, but there was no moon. The road had no lighting, no buildings in the neighborhood, no other travelers passing by could account for the light effects. No bushes, trees, or other vegetation, no milk-collecting platform, signboard, or anything similar was around, behind which someone out to trick me could have hidden. My windscreen was clean.

After the second experience I drove to a farm, knocked and asked to use the telephone. But this was just a pretext to ask if any eccentric was known in the neighborhood, someone who habitually went out walking with a flintlock. The people at the farm reacted visibly to my question but gave no definite answer. An old woman in the room who was hard of hearing didn't catch my question. When it was repeated for her she burst out, "Good heavens, he's seen the old man!" Then they said it was late and I had to go; I got the impression that they didn't want to talk about it but did want to get rid of me as quickly as possible. Since then I've driven on that road several times but never seen him again.

The percipient in this case is a folklore researcher, which accounts for his interest in the details of the clothing. Clothing of that sort might have been found in the district from the seventeenth century far into the nineteenth. The district is very "out of the way" and conservative: hunters with flintlocks were still known there even in the beginning of the twentieth century. There has been a road in the place where the man was seen for a very long time. (Apparitions of this type are also discussed in Chapter 19.)

Now we will return to Hart's material: Groups B and C together represent what are called "crisis-apparitions" which occur in connection with the projector's death. This category was first limited to experiences occurring up to twelve hours *after* death, but precise limits as to the time of death are difficult to establish. Apparitions in these two groups give the percipient information about the projector's death more often than others. Even if the projector's death itself does not occur in the apparition, the percipient often draws the conclusion that the projector is dead. An example [4]:

> A man in Dallas sat on his bed about midnight, pondering awhile before he went to bed. He looked up and to his astonishment saw his father before him, dressed in working clothes, with a slide rule in his pocket. He rose to greet his father, who then disappeared. Shortly after, a telegram came saying his father had died the same evening in California. He was wearing his working clothes and had a slide rule in his outer pocket.

Apparitions in Group D often occur in connection with the last illness of the projector, and Hart found it probable that the projector was often directing his attention toward the percipient. This applies to an even greater extent to Group E, where in almost every one of the cases, the attention was focused upon the percipient. As an example of this group, here is an old case which was first studied by the founders of SPR:

> A theological student dreamed that he visited his fiancée's family. He saw her up on the stairs on the way to her bedroom. In the dream he walked hurriedly after her and grabbed her around the waist from behind. He awoke, the clock struck ten, he wrote down the experience and posted the letter to his fiancée. Before his letter reached her, his fiancée's letter came to him, in which she described how that same night at ten she had been on her way upstairs and just reached the top, when she had heard his steps on the stairs and felt him place his arms around her waist; but she didn't experience any visual impression.

Hart investigated further how cases which were well verified (according to a scale which was developed for the purpose) compared with less well verified cases. He found no significant difference, that is, nothing which indicated that the latter cases had been embroidered or bettered. Nor were there any significant distinctions between older and more recent cases. In all these cases, it appeared that 56 percent of the observers who were so placed that they would have seen an apparition had it been corporeal, then actually did see it.

Hart summed up his investigations of the apparitions: Apparitions of the living, dying, and dead are seen so often and with such conformity in essential features that the phenomenon must be accepted as a part of our reality. Apparitions are typically perceived in ordinary clothing and accompanied by normal possessions or house pets. In many cases, they cannot be distinguished from normal bodies, but they also have their own qualities which distinguish them from these, for example, they can disappear spontaneously. If the apparitions communicate, they tend to limit their words or impressions to a simple idea or group of ideas. They can be seen by strangers who happen to be nearby and by people with whom they have no emotional connection, and they can be seen collectively in more than half the cases in which they could have been so perceived. They can be seen in a completely normal perspective, as if they had been physically present, and stand in the way of, or may be obscured by, other objects.

Apparitions of persons who have been dead a long while can be seen even by strangers in the place associated with tragic events of the deceased. These apparitions are more marionette-like, tend to move through certain rather simple ritual movements. The sight of an apparition often gives information about matters which the percipient could not normally know, for example, of the projector's death.

During ESP-projections, a person can see his own body from outside it, can be conscious of finding himself in a projected body, and can be perceived by others as an apparition. This projected body functions as a center for action and observation for the projector. But the apparition can also occur when the projector is completely unconscious of it, and may even be involved with other matters. A person can see his own apparition from a point of view outside his own body or (in autoscopy, but seldom) from it. During projection, the physical body can continue its normal activities.

The Etheric Double

After going through all these factors, Hart [3] arrived at a hypothesis scarcely a stone's throw from the conception of an astral world mentioned briefly in the preceding chapter. Rather than an astral world, he talks of an "ether," and his hypothesis may be summarized briefly:

Suppose that all physical bodies have an "etheric" counterpart resembling them in every detail. These must be considered to be primarily potential, that is, they exist as potentials which are manifested through psychic activity. Like physical objects, they have three spatial and one temporal dimensions, but these dimensions usually do not coincide with those of the physical world. The etheric bodies do not exist in physical space but rather in a "psychic" universe, although both these universes may coincide in space and therefore penetrate each other. The mutual bond and connection between etheric and physical objects is determined by the strength of common associations of ideas and feelings rather than by a purely physical connection. The clothing of an apparition is determined, for example, by the sort of clothing usually associated with the projector. An etheric object's intensity and accessibility is determined by the intensity and frequency with which it is bound to a consciousness. For this reason, a person's body has a pronounced characteristic and intense etheric counterpart, or "double," after it has actually been connected with a consciousness for a long while. An active and observant person (the I-consciousness, Hart calls this person "I-thinker") can use his physical body's etheric double as an instrument for observation and action. The etheric body's placement in the physical universe is usually connected with that of the physical body, but in certain circumstances (dreams, ESP-projections) it can occupy another position, and the I-consciousness can thus alternately use either the physical or the etheric body as an instrument for observation and action. The etheric body's tangibility can vary from, on the one hand, a completely subjective impression to, on the other, an almost complete materialization. The more materialized an etheric object is, the more easily it can be observed by the percipient in his physical body.

That which a percipient sees of a projector during an ESP-projection would therefore be his etheric body, which happened to have left his physical body temporarily. It is sometimes difficult to follow Hart's train of thought, but he obviously thinks that the etheric body definitely breaks its connection with the physical body at death and yet probably continues to exist in "the psychic universe" and functions there as the instrument for the I-consciousness' observation and action [3]. He also seems to believe that these hypothetical etheric bodies comprise the "material" of our "inner" world, that is, the world we experience both in dreams and when we are cut off from sensory impressions from the outer world [5]. Apparitions and also telepathy would then be explained according to this theory as the percipient in the "inner" world having made contact with and observed the projector's (that is, the agent's) etheric body. Clairvoyance, then, would indicate that the percipient had perceived the inner world's etheric counterpart for an object or a group of objects.

Time does not have the same meaning in the "inner world" as in the physical. The etheric image can even be perceived at a point in time when its physical counterpart, for example, a person's body, no longer exists in the physical universe (Cases 40a and b).

But what does this theory of apparitions have to say about the question of survival after death?

Hart's supposition [3] is that consciousness is absolutely dependent upon the function of an individual's brain—a very common viewpoint (which will be discussed in greater detail in Chapter 16). The phenomenon of ESP-projections indicates that at least a substantial number of apparitions of the living are instruments for consciousness, and their behavior is connected with such aspects of conscious behavior as memory, opinions, emotions. He argues further that we arrange all verified cases of apparition in chronological order, beginning with those long before the projector's death and ending with those long after his death. The supposition that consciousness is absolutely dependent on the function of the physical brain should therefore indicate an abrupt alteration in the character and behavior of the apparitions when the point of death is passed. But the observed facts do not indicate such a change—nothing other than what could be expected from the altering of viewpoint and motivation which death could be thought to produce in the projector. The conclusion is that "the burden of proof" now lies with those who argue that apparitions do *not* give any proof of survival after death.

ESP-projections may also appear in dreams, the so-called *shared dreams*. A hypothetical example: a young man far from his fiancée, dreams that they are eating together in a restaurant neither of them has actually visited. He sends her a letter with a description of the dream including the bizarre dishes they ordered and receives from her a letter with a description of a dream at the same time about a meeting with him in the same restaurant with the same courses. Some verified dreams of this sort have been published [6]. Here is a rich field for experimentation if one could find some method of producing these dreams more often. Hart proposed hypnotic suggestion with couples in love as subjects [5].

Different Opinions About Apparitions

Hart's interpretation of apparitions has not remained unchallenged. Louisa Rhine has studied the thousands of reports of paranormal experiences which have come to the laboratory in Durham, North Carolina, over the passage of years. Eight hundred and twenty-five cases of "psi-hallucinations" have been collected, which represents about 10 percent of all the material. Of these apparitions, 440 had living projectors (corresponding to Hart's Groups D and E), 88 projectors were dead (Groups A and B), and the remaining 297 were dying (Group C). But of the 440 living projectors, not a single one of them had intended the projection or was even conscious of it; the same applied therefore to Hart's Group D. Hart actually built a conspicuous part of his reasoning on the 25 cases in Group E (and on earlier studies of similar material) in which the projectors had intended the projection or were conscious of it in each case.

Louisa Rhine's interpretation of her material concludes that the experience of an apparition of a living projector is created entirely by the percipient himself according to his unconscious psychic needs and demonstrates his equally unconscious ability to "dramatize." The cases with dead projectors did not give her any lead clues either, and her conclusion was that hallucinatory ESP experiences, apparitions and others, have no particular significance for the problem of survival after death [7].

It must be noted that Rhine's cases, unlike Hart's, were not checked with the intention of verifying them, and several were secondhand accounts. Hart therefore protested. The crux of argument was that Hart and Rhine had completely different views of the value of spontaneous cases. Rhine considered that spontaneous cases could only provide suggestions for research in the laboratory but could never prove anything. Hart, on the contrary, believed that basic studies of well-verified spontaneous cases could also give information and even allow for certain conclusions [8].

Others have pointed out that complete ESP-projections can be seen as ordinary telepathic experiences. The fact that projector A and percipient B perceive each other simultaneously could be explained simply as telepathic "return transmission": B unexpectedly receives a hallucinatory experience of A, and that is such a shock for B that he sends a telepathic impulse to A, who then receives the information of B's actions and reactions to the apparition [9]. This interpretation may be supported by the fact that A's description of

B's behavior is often not completely clear—it is accurate in essentials but may be incorrect in details, for example, as to whether B is lying down or standing up (see page 115). On the other hand, this theory seems to me inadequate for those cases in which A and B have more lengthy contact (Case 39); ordinary telepathic contacts are usually of short duration.

In a famous case of this sort, Mrs. Garrett, the projector, sat in her home in San Diego, California, dictating to her secretary what she was experiencing simultaneously in a projected state in Reykjavik, Iceland. The percipient there had agreed to arrange a situation at a certain time which couldn't easily be foreseen and which Mrs. Garrett could then describe. And so she then described the objects on his writing table, his movements in the room, and a book which he took down from the bookshelf and read. He was himself conscious of her presence the whole time, and his description of the course of events agreed with hers. Mrs. Garrett clearly experienced telepathic contact with the percipient when he read the book, but emphasized that in her "double" she really had existed in his room [8]. If such an experience can be explained simply by telepathy, then it is a form of telepathic contact which, in intensity and quality, widely surpasses what has been known to date.

In a later discussion [25], Louisa Rhine develops her views on spontaneous cases and spontaneous apparitions in particular. Her main arguments are:

(1) In the earlier studies of spontaneous telepathic cases, researchers were interested in the role of the agent. The agent was considered the active partner, he "sent" something which the percipient apprehended. (2) Those researchers were also concerned with the question of survival after death. Therefore they tended to judge the cases in so far as they considered them relevant to this problem. (3) Apparitions provided such relevant cases, giving impressions that a dead projector had been the "active" partner. Apparitions might then indicate that he had survived. (4) Rhine studied her vast material of (unverified) spontaneous cases, giving special attention to the agent's role. She found many cases which implied telepathy, in which the situation was not such that some conscious thought could have been sent by the agent, and in which nevertheless the percipient had received a telepathic experience. Such cases resembled other telepathic ones in everything except in regard to the agent's role. This implies that the agent's "transmission" was not a necessary, es-

sential part of the process. Telepathic experiences can occur without any "transmission." Whatever causes the percipient's experience, it is not necessarily dependent upon any conscious activity of the agent. The percipient could be thought to be the active party, in clairvoyant and precognition cases as well, in which no agent exists. (5) Since apparitions are a form of telepathic experience, the conclusion is that the agent (= the projector) need not be in any way active in these experiences either. The experience is therefore probably caused by the percipient, and from this it follows that apparitions have no special relevance to the question of survival after death. If a case of apparition is in fact relevant to it, then this is due to aspects other than the fact that the experience has taken this specific form. (6) Rhine concedes that her conclusions are only drawn from studies of a large body of material of (unverified) spontaneous cases. Experiments which would relate directly to illustrating the agent's role in telepathy have yet to be made. But she emphasizes that the opposite interpretation, that the agent is the active party, according to her opinion, is not based on any studies at all but rather simply on wishful thinking.

Hart's studies of apparitions did not receive the great attention and credit which he considered they deserved in relation to the discussion of survival after death. But the cases of living and conscious projectors remain for us to consider and they suggest the possibility of something more than "ordinary" telepathic contact. However, these cases are rare, and if we are to go further and draw more definite conclusions from them, we must find methods to reproduce and study them experimentally. (We will return to Hart's etheric hypothesis later.)

Deathbed Visions

Apparitions appear to be seen relatively often around the time of the percipient's death. An example:

> 41. When my father died, my mother was sitting by his death-bed. At the moment before his death, he said, "Now Father is coming." A glow of ease spread over his face.

Karlis Osis sent out questionnaires to 5,000 nurses and an equal number of doctors to investigate their observations of the experiences of dying patients [10]. But it roused little interest, only 355 nurses and 285 doctors answered. The answers were followed up by telephone interviews if they were granted. The 640 people who answered said that they had seen at least 35,000 patients die, but only about 10 percent were conscious in their last hours. The reported phenomena therefore involved around 3,500 conscious, dying patients in almost similar cases.

Osis received particulars concerning 753 cases of exhilaration or exaltation of the dying. Anxiety and terror were not the dominant emotional expressions; both painful discomfort and a neutral sensory mood were reported more often.

Visions, that is to say, hallucinations of "not-human" content were described in 884 cases. The content of these was in accordance with traditional religious imagery (heaven, the eternal city) or scenes of beauty, bright colors, similar to scenes which can be experienced under the influence of certain drugs. Only two patients described experiences of something which could be called "hell." But any connection between the sort of vision and the patient's religion could not be specified, since too few cases could be followed up.

The most common deathbed experiences were hallucinations of people, 1,370 cases of which were described, and 135 could be followed up. The majority of these patients were not influenced in their hallucinatory course either by illness or medicines, instead the majority were fully conscious and in contact with their surroundings. The hallucinations had the characteristics of apparitions, that is, the dying person was conscious of his normal surroundings. This finding confirmed earlier observations that the dying primarily describe apparitions of departed relatives, who often announce their intention to help the dying enter into "the other world." Religiously involved patients seem to see apparitions more often, but otherwise age, sex, education, and type of illness did not seem to have any significant importance.

The low percentage of answers is partly indicative of feelings of duty to remain silent, since the questionnaire was not sent out by a medical doctor, and otherwise it is probably due to lack of time or simply lack of interest. Those who answered often seemed to have had their interest grow after observing a phenomenon for the first time, and that could have made them more observant of deathbed phenomena from then on. Despite the low percentage of answers, the investigation was not without interest, and it should be repeated in other countries.

Ghosts and Haunted Houses

Apparitions that are called "ghosts" sometimes appear in "haunted houses." Moss and Schmeidler have described an experiment for investigating them [11]:

In a "haunted house" in Los Angeles, four witnesses, independent of each other, maintained that they had seen a "ghost." They were thoroughly interviewed, and three lists were made of words they used to describe the ghost's activities and physical characteristics. The witnesses received these lists and were asked to mark the words which best fitted their experiences of the apparition. An experimental group of eight psychic individuals and a control group of eight non-psychics were then sent to visit the house and similarly marked their impressions on the lists. For various reasons, the reports from two psychics could not be used, but three of the six remaining ones marked the lists in ways which corresponded significantly with the witnesses' descriptions ($p = 0.03$, 0.0004 and 0.00008). Only one of the eight reports in the control group appeared somewhat similar to the witnesses' descriptions ($p = 0.05$). The remarks were also compared with reports from another haunted house which had been investigated earlier. In this case, no witnesses or psychics and only one from the control group had any significant correspondences in their descriptions.

The results were judged from three alternative hypotheses: (1) There was something in the house which had been perceived and described by the four witnesses and the three psychics. (2) There is a stereotype pattern for the appearances of such ghosts, which these people have described. (3) Three of the psychics reacted to the lists with ESP. The differences between the control group and the psychics' reactions were definitely taken to indicate hypothesis 1. The results also indicated that a "ghost" can have individual characteristics which make it possible to distinguish one from another. Continued investigations of "haunted houses" with this and other methods appears justified.

The Etheric Body and the Aura

A phenomenon like separation or an apparition can be taken to indicate that an "etheric body" really exists. But then couldn't this be registered objectively?

Clairvoyant mediums sometimes maintain that they can see and describe a person's *aura,* a glowing field which is perceived around the body. According to them, the aura can vary in different colors depending on the person's spiritual mood and physical state. Experienced mediums should be able to notice a presently latent illness by observing certain changes in the aura before the illness has revealed any symptoms [12]. The British physician Kilner described a method for increasing the eyes' sensitivity to the radiance of the aura by looking through colored glass [13], but his results are widely disputed. The method demands lengthy training and great patience, which may have contributed to the fact that no one seems to have definitely confirmed his results using this method. Another conceivable explanation is that Kilner's auras were something completely different from the physically glowing field others have said they are able to perceive. If Kilner actually perceived the aura clairvoyantly, or if, on the other hand, it was a purely subjective hallucination, then it is not remarkable that others have failed to see it through colored glass.

Nevertheless, Kilner has received certain confirmation from some later investigations. Since Burr and Northrop [14] demonstrated the existence of an electromagnetic field around living organisms, others have reported a glowing field around the living human body which disappears at death. This field consists of something other than ordinary heat waves and may possibly correspond to the aura [15, 16].

It has also been reported that an amputation does not affect this energy field—the voltage difference characteristic of the body is also registered in the space where the amputated part of the body would normally be. This might indicate the existence of an etheric body. There are also separate accounts that this voltage field, located where the amputated part of the body would be, has been made visible [17].

Now if the etheric body exists, could it not in some way be demonstrated at death, when it leaves the physical body?

A researcher at the beginning of this century, Duncan MacDougall, believed that this bearer of consciousness after death must also take up some place in space and have physical characteristics, for example, weight. He placed dying patients in a bed on a weighing platform. As was expected, a slow, gradual diminution of weight over the last hours was registered as an indication of the loss of moisture through perspiration, evaporation and expiration. This loss of weight was measured in one case as 28 grams an hour. But at the moment of death, a sudden inexplicable weight loss of 21 grams was registered. The measuring was repeated with several patients with similar results [18].

The American Watters constructed a variation of Wilson's room

[19] to study what happens when an animal dies in it. On several occasions he was able to photograph a substance over the animal's body which bore a striking resemblance to its physical body [20]. But in later experiments, when he had refined his apparatus much more thoroughly, he did not succeed in getting any similar pictures. Either the successful pictures depended in fact on the apparatus being incomplete and were therefore the result of "pure coincidence"—or else he was not able to repeat that combination of circumstances which had created these occasions and which had made it possible for him to actually photograph the etheric body [21].

The Frenchman Baraduc photographed first his son and then, six months later, his wife on their deathbeds. The pictures showed a cloud-like substance concentrated a little way above the dying body [22].

But such research has not been followed up. Watters did not succeed at all in repeating his first results. Evidently no one could repeat MacDougall's weight experiments with similar results, and so they were forgotten. Nor has Baraduc's photographic experiment been repeated, from any known reports. This may be due to the fact that no one has made a serious attempt. His results, on the other hand, agree with clairvoyants' observations of the dying. There are various descriptions of a mistlike texture condensing a little above a dying person, sometimes with a "silver cord" which breaks at death. This substance is perceived to be diffused or like an exact copy of the physical body, until it disappears sometime after death [23]. It is possible that this substance can be photographed only if it is more completely materialized and that this can occur only under certain specific conditions which are not yet known.

However noteworthy and remarkable these results may be, this whole area of research has been forgotten and is known only to historians of parapsychology [22]. A thorough perusal of these earlier reports and new experiments with the technical resources which now exist should actually be able to help us ascertain whether some sort of energy field around the human body other than heat waves does exist. By means of new measuring devices, especially on amputated persons compared with persons who lack a part of the body as a result of a birth defect, we could also perhaps register traces of the possible etheric body. If a person loses an arm in an accident in his maturity, it might be expected that the etheric body, if it could be made visible, would remain complete even after the accident. If, however, the arm were missing from birth, then he would not have the same conception of it as part of his body, and probably no trace of an arm would be found in the etheric body.

In 1970 a book was published in America which became a hotly debated bestseller: Sheila Ostrander and Lynn Schroeder's *Psychic Discoveries Behind the Iron Curtain* (New York: Prentice-Hall, Inc., also Bantam Books). It received very negative reviews in *JASPR* (vol. 65, pages 88 and 495, 1971). The book describes, with all the advantages and drawbacks of journalistic reporting, how two journalists traveled around Eastern Europe visiting parapsychologists and research centers, and it contains a good deal of sensational information. Among the information which roused the greatest interest (and which, unlike much of the rest appears to be correctly and objectively reported) was the so-called Kirlian effect, named after its discoverer S. Kirlian. If a leaf is placed in the dark on a piece of film and a high-frequency, high-voltage electrical field is turned on both the leaf and the film, remarkable pictures of light images are obtained. Similar pictures can be produced of people's fingertips and the light glow varies according to the subject's attitude and frame of mind. The connection of the phenomenon to parapsychology remains unclear to date. Work is being done now in several places in Europe, South America and the United States. Some researchers consider that the pictures are related to the aura or the etheric body. See for example, *Psychic,* June, 1971, or July, 1972.

Separations and ESP-projections can be seen as accidental visits to "another world" by people still living. In the next chapter we will look more closely at the information about this other world which spiritualism can provide us [24].

10

Spiritualism and Spirits

But even though the spirit world exists,
however it may act,
it cannot prove itself as fact.
And even though God shows himself
upon his throne of might,
the thought will out despite:
"hallucination!" some will insist.

V. RYDBERG

A statement from a TV discussion about death: "That you have to die, be reduced to nothing, not get to be part of anything more—I think it's a damn curse!" But the problem of death usually does not become acute and intrusive until someone close dies.

> 42a. My wife, whom I loved more than anything, died in 1966. Up until then I was a person like everyone else, living in the present, mostly interested in the world of the senses and pushing the problem of death aside, as everyone who is even vaguely happy will do.
> But when she passed away, my despair was so deep that I was close to taking my own life. I saw no way out of the darkness, because it was for her and her family that I had lived and struggled. The teachings of the church couldn't give me any comfort. The half-medieval articles of faith it offered and, above all, the self-satisfied complaisant attitude of its representatives caused me to steer completely clear of its ideas. I was as alone as a hermit in the desert, like most people who have lost the meaning in their lives. No one visited me, no one could answer the burning ques-

tion that preoccupied me: did she or did she not still exist? Doctors could only offer me sick leave and sleeping tablets. All the religions of the world talk about another world beyond material things, but I had no information about that world.

. . . So then I rang a medium, a charming lady in her seventies and asked for a seance. I was so doubting that I requested to remain anonymous. I went there with a tape recorder. The old lady fell into a trance, and in that state she told me about thirty facts she couldn't have known under any circumstances, since I was anonymous and she didn't know where I came from. Finally she mentioned my wife's name and told me that she said, "If you want to make me happy, you must go on living and making friends!" And then she told me about how she saw her standing leafing through loose sheets of paper. I knew immediately—they were my poems. Overwhelmed, I left. I realized I must continue to live, even if it would be difficult, because I wanted to make her happy. Where no religious concepts had helped, contact with a medium did help me.

This man was helped in his mourning by a medium in the spiritist movement. We will investigate what sort of information about the significance and meaning of death this movement gives.

The modern spiritist movement began around 1850 in a small village in America. In one family's house, people could hear in the walls mysterious knockings which were thought to be directed by an intelligence; answers to questions were given by a certain number of knockings and a "spirit" announced itself. (Personalities who were thought to have survived death were usually called spirits within the movement.) The phenomenon aroused great attention, and, "half as a parlor game, half as spontaneous sorcery, spirit knockings spread throughout the United States." A number of spiritist circles were founded which held seances to make contact with the dead, and new phenomena were produced. The interest reached its peak at the turn of the century and later continued rather diminished, but the First World War, with its many casualties, gave rise to a spiritist wave. The number of followers over the whole world can still be counted in the millions [1]. The word spiritist has a bad connotation for some reason, and so followers now call themselves *spiritualists*. We will use this term from now on.

To quote from the Swedish spiritualist movement's statement of purpose: "Spiritualism is a strongly idealistic, religious and politically neutral movement, the basic concept of which is that mankind sur vives bodily death. . . . It is involved partly in disseminating information via lectures, discussions, literature, etc., partly in seances and work in development and meditation circles [3]."

Phenomena at Seances

Seances are the part of spiritualism's activities best known to outsiders, but at the same time a great deal of misinformation about what occurs during a seance abounds. Many appear to believe that seances are something frightening and dangerous, but they need not be for people who have some degree of psychic stability.

In a *seance,* people gather around a medium; the number of participants or sitters, not counting the medium, may vary from one or two to hundreds. The seance is begun and concluded with meditation, music, prayers or psalm singing, depending on the group's religious affiliation. The medium may be completely awake but usually goes into a *trance,* which in principle seems to involve a self-hypnotic state. The seance itself often begins with a trance talk. This is a form of sermon which is thought to come from the medium's *guide,* a spirit on the "other side" whose specific task is to help and lead the medium in this process. The guide or another soul may also function as a sort of chairman presiding over a seance, in which case the spirit is termed a *control.* He may "release" other souls, who are often described as waiting in line, eager to contact the people who are alive.

> *Question:* If I go to a seance, can I be sure of contacting a relative?—*Answer:* No one can know in advance whom we will contact. It is our loved ones on the other side who seek the contact with us, not we with them [3].

The trance talk may be beautiful and inspiring, but sometimes extremely worldly sources can be traced in them. During one seance I listened wonderingly as a trance talk began to sound very familiar—in form and content it reminded me increasingly of a lecture given by an author I knew. It later appeared that the medium had also heard his lecture.

After the trance talk the medium remains seated or walks among the participants, describing visual and auditory impressions of the souls. These impressions are thought to be received through clairvoyance or clairaudience. Example: "An older woman, in a long red dress, white-haired, stands beside Erik. She is smiling sweetly and beautifully. I get the name Anna. She sends greetings, she is well." And Erik joyfully recognizes his old Aunt Anna.

Sometimes the information is more precise and could only be known by the deceased and a particular surviving relative. For example, through the medium, Aunt Anna might describe a little thing Erik once gave her, which he himself had almost completely forgotten about. Through the medium a conversation might also develop between Erik and Anna, and the surviving family member may receive advice and help.

Sometimes the medium's voice may become completely altered, in which case the medium is said to talk with the *direct voice,* which resembles the departed. Often, during the golden heyday of spiritualism, so-called *physical phenomena* also occurred, above all *materializations.* White forms which clearly resembled the deceased took shape before the eyes of the seance participants and could even be photographed. Unfortunately, these impressive phenomena seem to have completely disappeared now, just when we would be able to record and investigate them. In any case, no materialization medium seems available for investigation in Europe. Various individual mediums have been caught cheating, especially in connection with these materializations, but, on the other hand, there are certain individual mediums who have been investigated by critical researchers for decades without any attempt at cheating having been revealed. Whether some materializations were genuine paranormal phenomena or whether all were created through fraud would be difficult to ascertain in retrospect. Such a critical, objective observer as Ducasse was able to photograph a materialization himself. Poul Bjerre, himself highly skeptical of the belief in spirits, became convinced, after several personal experiences, that materializations could be true phenomena [4].

During *direct voice,* which is seldom reported now, little trumpets may be used, held by the medium or swaying apparently freely in the air. Ordinary seances can be held in daylight, but with seances in which physical phenomena appear, the room is in darkness or lit only by a weak red light; therefore the trumpets are painted with luminous colors. Voices, which are said to come from the spirits, are heard from the trumpets. In this case, the spirits are said to talk directly, without using the medium's organ of speech.

One of the most remarkable factories in the world can be found in the city of Columbus, Ohio. There spiritualist aids are manufactured on conveyor belts: swaying and talking trumpets, "life-like" spirit manifestations in natural size, "ectoplasm" by the case, and different models of astral bodies. In other words, here is everything a medium needs to perform a spiritualist seance, and false mediums from all over the world place orders through this firm. These false mediums, who operate in most countries, then appear to make contact with "the other side" and let in-genuous, faithful, mourning people believe that they are meeting dead relatives, while in fact the manifestations were bought by postal order from a firm in the USA!

. . . We have sent for material for an hour-long trick seance and can assure you that the effects are fantastic. People who were not let in on the secret believed that they were seeing a genuine miracle. A number were so terror-stricken that the hair literally rose up on their heads—and we had to quickly turn on the lights and turn off the spirits, which for the most part were made of luminous material. . . . [4]

The fact that one can buy "spirits by the case" proves nothing more than that fraud exists, which has been known since the beginning of spiritualism. It does not prove that all the alleged paranormal phe-nomena in the history of spiritualism have been hoaxes.

Even if materialization could be investigated all over again and proved to be genuine, even then it would not prove that they are al-ways what is maintained, namely, a manifestation of the deceased. Alexandra David-Neel, who spent decades with monks in Tibet study-ing their methods for spiritual development, describes how she could, by concentration, create a "phantom" in the form of a monk—a last-ing, complete materialization. His constant presence began to irritate her eventually, and she determined to send him away again. But he was marvelously tenacious; it took her six months to get rid of him completely. This experience can be explained simply as autosugges-tion. But if David-Neel tells the truth when she relates that others could also see her monk before she introduced him, then perhaps the explanation becomes somewhat more complex [5].

Other physical phenomena include *apports*—foreign objects which suddenly pop up in the seance room "from nowhere." Descriptions exist of the apparition of exotic plants with lumps of earth still at-tached to them and also of people who were in another place alto-gether when the seance began. The phenomenon of apports has also been described in investigations of RSPK. If they are authentic, they still need not necessarily be caused by spirits. The knockings and table rappings are plausible—to the extent that they are paranormal —psychokinetic phenomena released by living people [6].

Unfortunately, physical phenomena are seldom produced nowadays. The most common content of seances (at least in Sweden) are greetings to the living. Such greetings, especially if they are detailed and personal, can certainly be a positive experience for a person in sorrow and can assure the mourner that the departed still exists and that contact can be made with him or her. There is no objective way of judging these experiences; their value for the individual can only be judged by himself. But what the survivor experiences as proof need not necessarily prove anything to an outside, objective observer, however many details may have been produced which are accurate and could not normally have been known by the medium. Even people who otherwise do not acknowledge the presence of ESP hasten to explain the medium's knowledge of the personal behavior of others as telepathy in these situations, and with good reason (provided that the seance participants really are anonymous to the medium). An alternative explanation is object association:

A medium is given a watch which belonged to a deceased male relative. The medium then gives such intimate information about the deceased that it can only be confirmed by questioning another relative who never had the watch and didn't even know about the seance [7].

The medium could indeed be thought to experience those present as psychometric objects and could describe associations received from them in the same way that the medium in this description received associations from the watch. The departed relatives would thus be included in the histories of those taking part in the seance.

The situation in the seance room often seems conducive to telepathic and other paranormal phenomena: the participants are full of expectation and establish an emotionally charged atmosphere around the medium. But in circles in which the medium is well acquainted with the participants, often no paranormal explanations have to be resorted to at all. One may marvel over the eagerness and ingenuousness with which even the vaguest and most diffused messages of the seance are sometimes accepted as "proof" of the survival after death.

Parapsychology is often confused with spiritualism. The difference can be best and most simply expressed thus: parapsychologists seek knowledge and pose questions, while spiritualists have faith and give answers. Certainly much that is of great interest to parapsychology may occur during seances, but no proof of eternal life will come from the commonest types of greetings from the deceased.

Automatic Practices

There are other ways of seeking contact with the spirit world than attending seances. Signals given by knocking sounds have been mentioned. *Table rappings* were popular for a long while: the participants sat around a three-legged table and laid their hands on the surface. Questions were asked which could be answered by one leg lifting for yes, another for no, and a third for don't know. Another instrument is the so-called *psychograph,* of which there are many variations. In its simplest form, the psychograph consists of an alphabet written on a big piece of cardboard and an overturned empty drinking glass placed on the surface. The participants sit around the board, each placing a finger on the glass. Questions are asked which are answered by the glass moving and indicating the letters. The "writing" may happen with incredible speed; sometimes it is impossible to decipher the message until it can be read as a whole. This can give a very strong impression of an outside intelligence influencing the glass's movements, a being who also seems well informed:

> 43a. My boyfriend Nils had been in Göteborg a couple of days. A few of us sat around with the glass, and someone asked what Nils had been doing in Göteborg. The glass wrote that he had been "out with a nurse." He blushed beautifully, and when the others had gone he admitted it was true. None of the rest of us could have known about it.

In this case the explanation appears simple enough: Nils himself had directed the glass's movements, consciously or unconsciously.

If a person wants to seek contact with the spirit world alone, he can resort to automatic writing: all you have to do is sit relaxed with pen in hand and a lot of paper. After some ridiculous attempts your hand may begin to move "by itself." First it will produce only illegible scribbles, but then words and ideas can be formed while the writer may remain unconscious of what is written and has his attention focused on something completely different. Later, when the writing is interpreted—a time-consuming chore, since the words are usually

written all joined together or without spaces between the lines—
meaningful messages from deceased relatives and known or unknown
spirits can appear. They may give advice and comfort, joking, comic
allusions, or even severe scoldings. The expressions and style are
often completely distinct from those of the writer's normal communication, and words from languages which are foreign to him can also
appear. The personality in the writing may demonstrate literary or
artistic ability widely surpassing that of the writer.

In the following case, an inspiration of unusual power, not completely due to automatic writing, was experienced as coming from the
spirit world:

> 42b. Since my wife passed away, something had begun to work
> within me alongside the sorrow, with incredible force. I received
> an inspiration which was not of this world. In ten months I wrote
> about eight hundred poems . . . It usually happened this way: I
> would come home to my empty house after the work day was
> over, sit down at my writing table and burst into tears, and then
> the spirit of inspiration would descend upon me. I wrote and
> wrote with a swiftness I could not comprehend. I was not in a
> trance but I didn't know what I was writing until I set about
> making a clean copy, and the speed was sometimes so great that
> I could scarcely read what I had written. None of the poems
> took longer than three or four minutes, or about as much time as
> was needed to write them down. With some exceptions, the ma-
> jority of the poems in "Conversations with the Invisible" came
> this way. I almost never altered a line.
>
> What astonished me in particular, besides the speed of writing,
> was that each poem was different from the others. In one poem
> there'd be one theme, in another, another theme would surface.
> So it couldn't be a question of some sort of automatism. But I
> conceived these poems as if they were not written by myself [8].

In the following case the inspiration was heightened to complete
automatism:

> An American woman with a very elementary education, Mrs.
> Curran, automatically dictated a group of novels, plays, and
> poems that were considered by critics to be of high literary
> merit. But the most remarkable feature was that they were
> written in several kinds of English, from old to modern, and in
> each case perfectly consistent. According to philologists, one
> story in verse, containing at least sixty thousand words, with a

medieval theme, did not include a single word which had come into the language later than the seventeenth century! The personality that appeared in the writing called herself "Patience Worth" and was clearly very superior to Mrs. Curran intellectually [9].

Of course, the spiritualist explanation of these phenomena is that spirits manifest themselves and communicate in these various ways— by the table rappings, the glass moving or the automatic writing. We may call this the *spirit hypothesis*. It appears to be corroborated by the fact that other paranormal phenomena are not unusual in association with it, sometimes in a frightening way:

43b. I was keeping company with Rolf, a pilot studying in Stockholm. He had said six months earlier that perhaps he would fly down to Ängelholm, in which case he would come see me, but nothing came of this trip. Now I hadn't heard from him in a while and had no idea whether or not he was planning any flying trips.

When we sat down with the glass, we always asked first off, "Who is there?" but we didn't get any answer this time. Then Lisa asked, "When will Kerstin marry Rolf?" and the glass answered, "No." She asked, "Why do you answer no? Won't they marry?"—Then no real ideas came, just words, but then the glass answered, "Dead" and then, without any further questions, "crashed," "Stockholm," and "Ängelholm." We thought it was terrible and stopped immediately, asking neither who was there nor when and why.

The next day, in the afternoon, I was sitting alone at work when I suddenly fell asleep and slept a while in my chair. It had never happened to me before or since. In the evening I heard about the accident: Rolf had flown from Stockholm to Ängelholm and turned and crashed on the way back in a forest. The accident happened at the very time I'd fallen asleep at work.

Then a long time passed before we tried the glass again, but then gradually we did anyway. When we asked who it was, we received "the Devil." Then we said, "We don't want to talk with you because you only bring misfortune" and the glass answered, "Dead on the highway." We felt this was unpleasant and stopped. I was scared and the following day I waited, wondering who would die now. The following day, a man I knew died in an automobile accident. His wife had formerly lived with my brother, but that could have been simply a coincidence. One time later, the glass said that Nils, a boy I was with then, would also die in a traffic accident and described the day and how it would happen. He came to see me that day, and I was so afraid that I got him to spend the night because I didn't dare let him cycle home, but I really couldn't tell him why.

Paranormal messages also appear meaningful and motivated from the viewpoint of a presumably deceased person, surviving beyond death, as in these two cases cited by Bender [10]:

A medium writes automatically in the deceased's handwriting, giving a comforting message which soothes guilt feelings of a survivor. She didn't know the deceased and didn't know the guilt feelings.

Writing with the glass, a woman received a clear message from her brother who had died several years before. One day he asked her to help "Uncle Florian," who he said was in need. She didn't know any Uncle Florian, and then, right off, the glass said this was a nickname and gave the correct initials. With these, after great difficulty, she figured out who the uncle was, and in fact he turned out to be indeed in very dire straits.

But is the spirit hypothesis the only conceivable explanation?

The Unconscious

It is well known nowadays that at any given moment a person is not conscious of the entire content of his personality. On the contrary, his normal waking consciousness at any given moment contains only a small part of his total psychic content. He has, for example, a vast memory outside of his immediate awareness that he cannot even summon into his consciousness without making an active effort. Such material is usually called *preconscious*. But for different reasons, certain memories cannot be recalled so easily. These, which may be memories of painful events in childhood, cannot be recalled without the help of special techniques, for example, some form of psychoanalysis or hypnosis. These memories represent the psychic material that is called the *subconscious*. This includes not only memories but also impulses, instincts, longings, needs, wishes, and tendencies which have been suppressed by the consciousness. The reason for this suppression may be that the drives and personality characteristics war with the person's conscious moral attitudes and thus create anguish, which is eased by their becoming subconscious. But the fact that these aspects of the personality have been "banished" from consciousness does not mean that they have been permanently silenced or that they remain passive. They may now appear in dreams in a symbolic form or through so-called neurotic symptoms. Here we will not discuss theories of the subconscious in greater detail. For those interested in the subject, there is a rich and varied literature from psychoanalytically oriented authors, and Schjelderup [1] has also described the relationship of the unconscious to the paranormal phenomenon. But it should be said here that subconscious material can also surface in personified form, that is, as a definite personality. C. G. Jung, in particular, has described aspects of the subconscious which appear as a person in dreams [11].

The book and the film *The Three Faces of Eve* became famous as an example of so-called multiple personality. Eve acted alternately different parts of her ordinary, everyday personality—sometimes becoming a very contradictory character—which represented subconscious tendencies and impulses. Through her progress in psychotherapy, a third personality appeared which could be thought of as a synthesis of the other two, and, when a critical event in childhood had been recalled to her conscious mind, this third personality became the "survivor" and the other two disappeared [12].

This is mentioned to illustrate what can happen if one devotes oneself too diligently to practices which give access to subconscious material, for example, table rapping, glass writing, or automatic writing. The spirits who are thought to manifest themselves need be nothing other than personified aspects of subconscious psychic material within the participants. Hypnotic trances also give occasions for subconscious material to surface. Hypnosis primarily involves displacing attention from the outer world through instructions which are given by the hypnotist and which produce a relaxation and possible plunging into an "inner" world. This condition can also be reached by a person on his own and, similarly, the medium's trance is possibly a self-hypnotic state.

Figure 2A roughly and simply suggests the connection. Circle A represents the total personality, including both the conscious and the subconscious. B is a complex of instincts, wishes, and characteristics which exist in A but are subconscious in relation to its "I," perhaps because they are "not worthy of being wished." This may be because of tendencies which war with A's moral or religious outlook, and

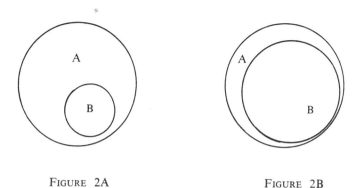

FIGURE 2A   FIGURE 2B

which he consequently cannot consciously recognize or accept as characteristics within himself. They may also be fantasies and cherished dreams which have been forgotten. Under hypnosis "a doubling of personality" or multiple personality may appear. This involves A's now behaving in a way which conforms with the characteristics of B, that is, with a totally different personality. B has access to A's memory, but the reverse is not the case—when A awakens from hypnosis he usually remembers nothing of B's behavior. But during the next hypnosis, B may return and remember everything that happened during the previous hypnosis.

Person and Persona

A person involved with automatic writing and similar activities puts himself in a state of concentration, expectation of what will happen, and diminished attention to other aspects of the outer world. This is also a state which is conducive to utterances from the subconscious, and it can be heightened to a nearly hypnotic trance. The characteristics of B easily make an impression and, just as under hypnosis, they may become personified. This would imply that writer A receives something written from someone who is *not-I*—from spirit B, but, in fact, it may come from characteristics of B in his own personality.

Hart has proposed the term *persona* to indicate everything one can observe of a person [13]. One could say that A experiences B as a persona, that is, as a picture of all the aspects and characteristics of a person which may be observed by another. A *persona* is, therefore, everything that can be observed or perceived of a *person*. In the material world, a persona includes a person's physical body, clothing, habits and manners, social position, and so forth. When an actor assumes a role, he changes into a literary or historical persona. A mimic tries to present the persona of the person he imitates. When a person dreams, remembers, or fantasizes, he temporarily shifts to a dreamed, recollected, or imagined persona. An apparition may be described as a persona which has become directly, distinctly visible. (The term persona is used in quite another way with another meaning in C. G. Jung's psychology.)

Risks Involved in Automatic Practices

It is *not* an indication of some psychic illness to be psychic or to have paranormal experiences, even if these consist of alleged contacts with the deceased. But the crucial determining factor is how the individual reacts to these experiences, how they affect his ability to live with others and manage his everyday tasks. For to force abilities which are not natural or ordinary is to run great risks, and it is dangerous to be habitually involved in activities which contribute to the doors of the subconscious swinging wide open, especially if a person does this alone without insight and awareness of what might happen. As the complex part of a person or persona B, in Figure 2A, is strengthened by repeated exercise, there is the risk that it will take over a greater and greater part of person A's consciousness and means of expression and finally intrude into that part of himself which acts. Eventually it might dominate it completely—the situation represented schematically in Figure 2B. This is a condition of split personality or *dissociation*. Person A has become "possessed" by a "spirit" B which thus need not be anything other than an aspect of his own personality. This state of conflict is not therefore to be taken lightly. The presenting symptoms of the alteration can resemble schizophrenia, and the condition may require psychiatric treatment, as in a case cited by Bender [10]:

> A sixty-nine-year-old woman lost her husband after a late and short marriage. She sought solace in spiritualist literature and found a description in a periodical of how, by holding a pendulum over an alphabet, one could make contact with the departed. Immediately before that, she had read Yogananda's *A Yogi's Autobiography* [14], which had made a deep impression

on her. Right off, in her first pendulum experiment, Yogananda's guru Yukteswar introduced himself. [He is described in the book as a great spiritual leader, and the author mentions miracles of his, such as contact with him after his death.] The woman became so seized by this contact that she burst into tears and she swung the pendulum throughout whole nights for several months. It soon became an obsession which she tried in vain to resist. She began to become aware of spirits "within" herself, telepathically. She received advice and instructions and she carried out meaningless compulsory tasks. She began to hear the spirit as a voice, several voices, finally a whole chorus. She suffered more and more from this condition and sought help. Because of her strong will to become healthy, all she needed was information through conversation and literature to realize that the "spirit theater" was completely directed and produced from within herself, and she soon recovered and was freed from all her troubles.

This should not be taken to imply that the spiritualist movement as such is dangerous from the viewpoint of mental hygiene. "Whatever else they may be, the spiritualists are spiritually oriented people. As such, they cannot be a negative movement in our present-day culture, and this is more than one can say of the majority," wrote John Björkhem [15]. Case 42a is a not uncommon testimony of how personal experience of the survival of a relative after death has had profound, pervasive meaning for a sorrowing person and restored his will to live. What can be dangerous is the excessive and habitual preoccupation with practices which facilitate dissociation, together with a completely uncritical faith in practically everything as a sign and miracle from the spirit world.

The guide or control of a medium may, of course, also be a persona of the sort produced from her own subconscious. But this possibility does not preclude the fact that this persona may have paranormal import.

A person P, in Figure 3, comes to a seance in the hope of contacting his departed wife C. Naturally, he is thinking of her and building an impression of her, person C1. His performance is perceived through telepathy or object-association by medium A, who unconsciously personifies it and thus describes person C2, that is, the outer characteristics of C which are picked up from her husband. The way this operates is illustrated by the presumptuous but effective investigation of British mediums made by a group of journalists. Using fabricated life stories and completely nonexistent relatives, they

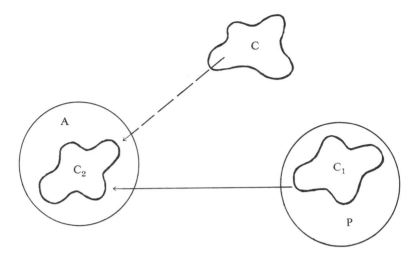

FIGURE 3

attended seances in which medium after medium described the desired "spirits" with supporting details from the invented life stories. The investigation caused a great uproar, and one medium could not understand why her guide had not warned her [16]. On other occasions, mediums have described a person as a spirit whom both the medium and the participant in the seance believed dead, until later, after the seance, it was revealed that the person presumed dead was still very much alive [17, 18]. This does not suggest that the medium is a fraud. She may be working in absolute good faith—but she could not herself discriminate among the pictures and impressions which she was receiving and out of which she subconsciously constructed a person.

Finally, as Figure 3 illustrates, it is also possible that the surviving wife C herself gave the material to the medium's persona C2—if, in fact, she did survive death. But we know now what a great talent A has for creating a persona C2 by dramatizing and personifying from her own subconscious material, or material from the participants in a seance, normally or paranormally received. It is very difficult to determine whether persona C2 comes from C or from another's performance of C. Telepathy between the living is still more probable than between the living and the dead.

Many experiences in spiritualism are truly consistent with the spirit hypothesis. But for the hypothesis to conform with facts it is not enough for it to be proved or confirmed. It must explain the facts *better* than other hypotheses. To find confirmation for the spirit hypothesis we must insist that information which is said to come from the departed shall be such that neither the medium nor those taking part in the seance could possibly have known of it telepathically, clairvoyantly, or through object-association. Precognition must be ruled out as well. Moreover, the person surviving death should be thought to have a strong motivation to communicate, in any case stronger than the participant's wish to receive information.

> 44. My uncle was run over by a truck in 1928 when it drove up on a sidewalk and slammed him against a wall. He was unconscious for three days and nights and then died, as we all thought he would finally, of a concussion in the back of his head.
>
> During a seance in England in 1934, my father was put in contact with someone said to be his dead brother. He told of his death, and stated that he did not die of his skull injury but that "it came from the bones." This was considered strange by his relatives, for they all believed he had died of the skull injury; they had accepted that as a fact and had never discussed any other cause for his death.
>
> It struck me first in 1956 that I could check the facts through the hospital records. They indicated that he had received a concussion at the back of his head at the time of the accident and he was then operated on. But his unconscious state did not alter and so then he died three days later. During the post-mortem the cause of death was found to be not the skull fracture but a brain embolism caused by a lower bone thrombosis (a clot from the bone which causes a blood stoppage in the brain). So verification of the 1934 communication came about twenty-two years later.

Here the information was completely unknown to the medium and obviously to the brother as well. To explain such cases one must invent a hypothesis of "telepathic links [19]." Perhaps the brother had had contact with someone in the hospital who had contact with the pathologist who carried out the post-mortem and wrote down the findings, and through this chain of "links" the medium received the information telepathically or psychometrically. This hypothesis does not receive much support from experimental results and seems to have been conceived primarily so that people might avoid the spirit hypothesis. In case 44 it is also not possible to rule out the contingency that the brother, in spite of everything, might have picked up a word of something about the cause of death through contact with the hospital and then later completely forgotten it, that is, he might have experienced what is called *cryptomnesia*.

Sincere mediums also recognize the difficulties in distinguishing what comes from "the other side" and what they contribute themselves [20]:

> Is the message which comes through the medium always unmixed? Are the teachings always genuine? How much of a medium's own world of thought is added?—Actually relatively few messages are completely genuine . . . it is a question of collaboration. I experience it as if *they* bring the contents and then I, to some degree, help formulate it.

Another medium, in his book *Private Dowding,* comments [21]:

> I must treat the whole experience as real. Otherwise it would not have been worthwhile setting it down. To me, my communications with Thomas Dowding were so real that he seemed to be in the room sitting at my elbow, prompting my pen. I know there have been many books written containing messages said to have been passed down from another plane of existence. One cannot doubt the possibility of "spirit communion," as it is often called. It seems to me that there can be no final proof concerning these matters. One must be guided by the interior worth of the messages themselves. I tell you, for instance, that I am satisfied I have been speaking with a soldier who was killed in battle seven months ago. I have set down the experience in writing exactly as it came to me. I cannot, however, prove the genuineness of the experience to anyone else. I cannot even prove it finally to myself.

"One must be guided by the interior worth of the messages themselves." But this is purely subjective: however intense and powerful a person's experience of the inner worth of a communication may be, he cannot prove it to anyone else, nor, for that matter, could anyone disprove or contradict his experience. This should result in an obvious openness to different experiences and many different perceptions resulting from them. It should also lead to a concerted effort to strengthen one's frames of reference and widen one's horizon in order to be able to experience more.

Other mediums still consider that they can distinguish between impressions from the spirit world and impressions received through, for example, psychometry. A medium describes:

> When one makes contact with those who have passed over, they come and talk to one directly. The words are lightning fast, the

message quickly gone through and irresistible. One can carry on a conversation with them.

That's not the case with psychometry: one hears a story, one sees an event, but one cannot talk with them—they mind their own business.

Cross-Correspondences

A medium who practices some sort of automatic activity, usually automatic writing, will be called here simply an *automatist*. The word *communicator* defines a personality (or, more precisely, a persona) which *communicates,* that is, appears in mediumistic messages, regardless of whether this happens verbally during seances, through automatic writing, or other activities. The communicator usually identifies himself with the deceased's name and also states that his home is in the spirit world. Naturally, this does not prove that the messages really come from that deceased person. The communicator could also be a subconscious personification from within the medium. The question of the communicator's true identity is what really should be investigated. The opinion that the communicator *cannot* be identical with some aspect of the deceased's personality is, on the other hand, only an expression of preconceived notions and unwillingness to study the facts.

Myers and Sidgwick, pioneers in the British SPR, died around 1900. Automatic writing was a common form of expression with British mediums, and a Mrs. Verrall, who had been fired by Myer's enthusiasm for "psychical research," began as an automatist immediately after Myer's death in 1901 with the clear intention of giving him an opportunity to communicate, if he could. After three months, a communicator did appear who said he was Myers. Then something completely unexpected happened. Other automatists in England, India, and the United States began to produce references to the themes which appeared in Mrs. Verrall's automatic writing. Fragmentary allusions to themes in classical Greek and Latin poetry appeared in a way that was often incomprehensible to the individual automatists, among whom only Mrs. Verrall had a classical education. Only when material from several automatists was gathered together could it be studied and coped with more comprehensively by outsiders. It seemed as if someone wanted to prove his identity by making a "classical puzzle" in a manner one might have expected from

Myers and his colleagues. Other allusions to events in their lives also appeared. These cross-correspondences continued for a decade and became increasingly complicated.

One of the automatists involved was a woman well known in public life in England, who in this context hid herself behind the pseudonym of Mrs. Willett. Her communication was to some extent of a different character than the first cross-correspondences. In those, the same communicator had expressed himself through several automatists. But two different communicators appeared through Mrs. Willett, in what could be seen to be intimate collaboration. One of them was Mrs. Verrall's husband, who died in 1912, and the other a good friend of his. The writing indicated both men's common interest and close relationship and gave correct allusions to events in their lives. Mrs. Willett was also remarkable as an automatist in that she did not lose conscious control over her personality during the seances. She seemed able to shift "talks" with the experiment leader to the communicators. Moreover, the communicators presented complicated theories about the nature and difficulties of the communication itself, and these theoretical reasonings were completely foreign to Mrs. Willett's conscious personality. The communicators emphasized that they did not possess Mrs. Willett completely but that it was a question of telepathy.

It is impossible for an outsider, without classical education, without access to the thousands of original documents and time to go through them, to get a clear conception of this voluminous material. The complete history of the cross-correspondence literature is yet to be written. Much of the material is of such a personal nature that, out of consideration for the people involved who might be hurt by it, it has not been possible to publish it to date. But critical researchers, some of whom knew Myers, Verrall, and their colleagues personally, and some who have studied the cross-correspondences very thoroughly, have been convinced that this really does represent the expression of an intelligent, coordinated activity, and comprised of material that could not simply be explained as telepathy among automatists' subconsciousnesses [22].

Mrs. Willett died in 1956. Several months after her death, another automatist, Miss Cummins, began to write messages of which the communicator was said to be . . . Mrs. Willett. This writing continued for several years and was published in 1965. It alluded to personal situations in Mrs. Willett's life, unknown to the medium, who was not aware of Mrs. Willett's real identity until the writing had already been

going on for a while [23]. It is remarkable and noteworthy how many memories "belonging to" Mrs. Willett are communicated in this writing. But, as Stevenson [24] points out, it is no less noteworthy how few memories there were in this writing which could *not* be Mrs. Willett's. It is difficult to avoid the thought that some organized activity had taken place which selected the memories that belonged to Mrs. Willett and discarded the rest. But the only person who would be able to cause such activity is Mrs. Willett herself, and this therefore, might also indicate that she had survived beyond death.

The cross-correspondences seemed to develop into a "serial story" which in different variations and with long gaps has continued for sixty years. Several researchers have thought it provides strong indications for survival beyond death. In later experiments with mediums, cross-correspondences have also appeared, following similar patterns, but with completely different communicators [19].

"Drop-in Communicators"

One phenomenon experienced during seances might be seen to support the spirit hypothesis. This could be called "unknown spirits" or, rather, "drop-in communicators [7]." During a seance held by a small group of people, a completely unknown and unexpected spirit may make himself known. He states his name and details from his life. None of those present know anything about him. Research later reveals that the information fits with facts of a certain deceased person. Such cases are naturally easy to fake completely. Cryptomnesia, another possible explanation, would have to be ruled out. But if, after a thorough investigation, it appears that the case is genuine, and that no one present could have read or heard of the deceased, then the case would constitute a certain support for the spirit hypothesis. It is strengthened to some degree if the information given during the seance is neither printed nor written in one single place but must be gathered from several sources so that it would be in itself improbable that the medium or the seance participants would have had access to it. In the best cases, the information is only known to a narrower family circle of the deceased, who are themselves completely unknown to those taking part in the seance. Moreover, the communicator can sometimes reveal strong motivation on the part of the deceased to deliver the message, something which must also be explained along with the information itself. In this case, to avoid the spirit hypothesis, one must adhere to the theory of "super-ESP." The medium's ESP could, like light from a lighthouse, actively search into the darkness until the medium made contact with just this particular piece of information. But there are hardly any other experiences which support this hypothesis [25]. Nor does it explain why the medium should make contact with information about a particular person who, in many cases, would have a strong reason to wish to communicate, had he survived death [26].

In the following case, a "drop-in communicator" appeared:

45a. *Mrs. L:* The first and third Thursday of every month we held a seance in Erik and Barbro's circle. It was a help circle—spirits came who didn't know that they were dead. Erik went into a trance; Barbro was psychic too and gave the straying spirits help through him.

It was Thursday, February 1, 1968. Toward the end of Erik's trance talk, I felt something strange where I was sitting in the half darkness. I felt as if something strange had come from somewhere, like a force field. Foreign words reached my mind, sort of like this, "I am lying in the south. I am dead. I do not want to lie here—I'll be discovered. In Hägersten. I am lying under pillows."

The feeling became suddenly macabre. I felt it was strange and thought, "I can't help you. Go to Erik—Barbro helps the dead through him—we have a help circle here." The feeling of a magnetic field left me, but after a short while, Erik grabbed his throat and cried out like this, "He's strangling me, the devil! I'll get him, I'll be revenged, do you hear! I'll be revenged! So he took the car, damn him, he took my car. He strangled me and I'll get revenge. . . ."

I was scared because Erik had a bad heart and high blood pressure and I thought now it would get worse. Barbro, who heard most of it, took it calmly and asked him not to be so roused to revenge. "Pray to God that He will help you, for you are dead now, and. . . ."—"Pray to God, I know all that backward, but He can't help me. I'll get my revenge!"

Erik was restless and disturbed and was given heart-calming tablets. He didn't remember anything about it afterward, he never recalled what had happened during that trance.

When I got home in the evening I was at a loss, asked Lennart [husband] if he'd listened to the news. He had, but no murder or anything like that had been mentioned. I discussed the seance briefly, "but it must have all been imagination."

The following day, Friday, I searched through all the newspapers I could find. Nothing. On Saturday we were in the country and I didn't see a paper. When I did get hold of a paper, I read: *Dagens Nyheter,* Saturday, February 3, 1968: "A twenty-year-old flower-seller and Salvation Army soldier, NN, Y-street in Hägersten, was discovered murdered in his apartment. N lay half dressed in his bed and had been strangled with an electric cord. The body and the face were covered with a bedcover and two pillows . . . The murderer . . . stole the victim's gray Volvo, which is now being searched for throughout the country. The murder is supposed to have taken place on Monday night."

"That's the man!" I shouted. "He came to the seance!" But that's really impossible, since when the seance took place [Thursday evening] no one had the slightest idea that he was dead—except the murderer, who was far away.

This account poses several questions:

1. Did the seance really take place before the murder was known about? Mrs. L is sure that it was the first Thursday in the month, for several reasons. She "read the papers like a vacuum cleaner" and would have immediately recognized the murder if it had been described before the seance.

2. Is her account of what happened during the seance accurate? No tape or notes were made. Erik was in a trance and doesn't remember. Barbro doesn't recall anything either, now two and a half years later. When the seance took place no one knew anything about the background of the event. The next time they met two weeks had already passed and no one thought to document the matter. Remarkable things do happen at every seance. . . .

3. Did she really tell her husband what had happened *before* the murder was known? He now only remembers vaguely that she came home from a seance and asked whether a murder or something like that had happened, and then she searched through all the recent days' papers. It is also relevant that she had been collecting clippings from *Dagens Nyheter* for a long while. A year later she wanted to hand all these over, with other material, to someone interested in parapsychology for possible investigation. When that person did not appear to take her experiences seriously, she got angry and threw everything away. Therefore, when she told me about the occurrence for the first time in March 1970, she had no clippings left. After searching lengthily through newspaper archives and in the library, she and her husband found the paper in August. Then he too recalled the story immediately.

Unfortunately, this case does not fulfill the criteria one must impose to ascertain the verification satisfactorily. It would be a great help if mediums like Mrs. L would write down or tape their experiences while they are fresh in the mind and get them witnessed by someone else immediately, someone who will testify to the date and the time. But this is a good deal to demand of a woman who also has a stressful job and a household to look after and who periodically experiences similar occurrences in her daily life. A later experience can illustrate the difficulties:

45b. Wednesday, September 16, 1970, in the morning. I was standing in the subway, wasn't thinking about anything, when a thought suddenly struck me:

In my thought I saw a burning car. I remembered Lennart talking about how people lock their car doors from inside and then when the car crashes and burns they can't open the doors and so they burn up. I thought intensely that I was participating in that fire. I saw how several people came running toward the burning car, I thought I screamed (that is, in my imagination), "Break the windshield, and pull them out." The first person to arrive quickly tried the door, then the side window, then he shouted to them to crouch down and he smashed the front window so that the chips flew, and then he knocked out the sharp edges and began to pull and shove, then he crawled in and went on gently pushing and shoving . . . I felt the fuel was really going to explode then . . . the heat was like a grill . . .

I was completely out of the world around me until I woke again . . . Arrived in the old city—yes, my job . . . then the whole picture disappeared. It was just a thought. I would ask Lennart when I got home if you could break a windshield with a stone or something hard, or have a hammer handy in the car in case an accident might happen . . .

Then work started and I forgot all about it. On the way home I was tired and bored. I bought an *Expressen,* which I didn't feel like reading. Prepared dinner, a friend of Lennart's came. We talked about this and that and I began to ask about burning cars, but was interrupted by Lennart who said that a car had burned—didn't you read the paper? But I hadn't.

Expressen, September 16, 1970: "Three cars were involved in a violent traffic accident in Stockholm at eight o'clock this morning. . . . Both the severely injured men were trapped inside their burning cars. No one in the rush-hour traffic on Sockenvägen dared approach the fire until Harry Karlsson and Karl Wennerström came. . . . Karlsson tells us: 'I heard a terrible crash. I saw two people struggling in the burning car. The others didn't

dare get involved. Then Wennerström and I smashed the windshield of the car. We tried to crawl into the car and managed to
pull the two people out.' "

Both these cases illustrate the difficulty of judging psychic experiences. If we surmise that Mrs. L reported essentially what she had
experienced, then four possibilities are suggested:

1. She remembered the time incorrectly. She first saw or heard
about the events in the papers or on the radio and imagined the rest
from that, and then later transferred the experiences in her memory
to the incorrect time.

This interpretation cannot be absolutely ruled out because she did
not write down her experiences and did not have them certified by
another person with the date and the time of day. The conditions
surrounding the first case still argue against that alternative. In the
other case, it would indicate that she had lied directly by emphasizing
that the experience came before she began her day's work, that is,
several hours before the evening papers had come out and about the
same time as the accident occurred. Then it would not have been
reported yet on the radio news.

2. The similarities between her experience and the real events
depend on pure coincidence. How often has she imagined something
which has not happened in reality? This alternative cannot be demonstrated either. At least in the first case, with all its details, it still appears to be less likely.

3. The experiences were precognitive. She experienced ahead of
time what would be in the paper, in one case two days and in the
other several hours later. This possibility cannot be totally ruled out.
Still, it is argued that Mrs. L had seldom had any precognitive experiences. She has reported hundreds of possible paranormal experiences
(of which only a fraction could be verified by others) and most of
them are telepathic in nature or of a type which will be discussed in
Chapter 13.

4. The experiences were telepathic. In the second case the agent
was living, in the first dead (as long as one does not maintain that the
murderer was the agent). This hypothesis is consistent with all aspects
of the two cases, but because it implies that the murdered man could
communicate after his death, it is rejected by most people.

The cases illustrate the mediumistic situation. Mrs. L comments:

> To be a medium involves being two people who do not always
> work together. What one experiences, the other rejects with his

physical, thinking, logical mind as "idiotic." I move in two separate worlds. I don't talk onto a tape—that's just as difficult as
writing.

I have "two minds." It's impossible to dismiss the impulses of
one mind and at the same time with the other mind crassly think
about what should be done to get the testimony properly correct. If you succeed with this correctness, then science says it is
too correct to be true.

A psychic person experiences the ordinary, everyday world as we
all do, ordered by commonly known physical laws, the world we are
aware of through our sensory organs. The psychic also experiences,
as we all do, a *psychic world* of dreams, images, and impressions;
moods, thoughts, and feelings. But that psychic world has a special
quality for the psychic and a connection with the material world
which it lacks for the rest of us. Sometimes the medium can connect
with, can contact, the psychic world, for example, by going into a
trance or some other special state. More often the contact and the
experience, too, come about completely spontaneously and unantici-
pated. A medium does not know why it occurs just then; she experiences something but doesn't know what it means. She sees before her
a burning car but doesn't know if it is only a fantasy image, created
by her self, or if the vision is related to some event in the material
world. She hears a murdered man who wants to be discovered and
revenged, but doesn't know if this is imagination or a communication
from someone. Time in the psychic world is not divided into past,
present, and future—everything happens in the present. The medium
does not know, in the moment of her experience, if the car has already burned in the material world, if it is burning right now, if it is
in Stockholm or New York. In the psychic world, time and space
present no obstacles; its laws are different from those of the material
world.

With experience, a medium can gradually learn to distinguish with
some degree of certainty between impressions and images that come
from the self and those that come from "without," from other living
beings who can be observed in the psychic world. But she cannot
prove her experiences to anyone who has not experienced similar
impressions. Her only chance to be believed is to show that through
her experiences in the psychic world she can receive knowledge of
situations in the physical world, situations which she could not know
about normally. She experiences contact with people in the psychic
world who have definitely left the material world, who are therefore

dead—but how could she ever prove this to anyone who has not had the same experience? (We will return to these questions in Chapter 17.)

To summarize the appraisal of spiritualism: the most ordinary types of greetings from the deceased provide no proof of survival beyond death. The seance phenomenon can often be explained as the personification of subconscious material. Information which indicates ESP is often supplied by mediums, but the same mediums may give poor results in formal ESP experiments. (Therefore methods have been developed to study spontaneous information in seances statistically as well [27, 28].) An extensive amount of seance material throughout the spiritualist movement is actually consistent with the spirit hypothesis, but the facts which, on the other hand, would support it are relatively scarce, above all cases of "drop-in communicators" who could be verified. It is regrettable that spiritualists themselves do not pay more attention to such cases and report them to interested researchers instead of, as so often happens, accepting their vague and scanty utterances as proof of survival beyond death. By such a simple procedure as taping the seances consistently and keeping the tapes a certain length of time, worthwhile material could be preserved.

In so-called spiritualist help circles, it is believed that contact is made with spirits who do not know that they are dead yet. This often includes spirits who are presumed to have "passed over" recently through an accident or murder, as in Case 45a. The medium then considers it his mission to help these straying spirits find their way on "the other side" by telling them that they are in fact dead. It would be of great help to the parapsychologist if, for a moment, the medium would play detective and ask the communicator for facts about his life and death, details which perhaps would make it possible to identify him. The communicator can seldom say his whole name (we will return to this in Chapter 18), but most of the time he can say his first name and perhaps the name of some close relative. With a little questioning from the medium, perhaps he could recount some of the circumstances surrounding his death. By watching for such cases, which possibly could be verified later, spiritualists would aid in making the spirit hypothesis stronger than it is now.

In the following four chapters we will touch on other types of spontaneous experiences which appear within, as well as outside of, the spiritualist movement.

11

Possession?

The previous chapter has shown how in certain circumstances a person can be "possessed" by forces from within his own unconscious. But in some cases of possession this explanation does not appear sufficient.

The Case of Latimer

The American minister and psychologist Walter Franklin Prince, who had become well known for his investigation of a case of multiple personality, was consulted one day in the beginning of May 1922 by a Mrs. Latimer, a "highly cultivated" lady. She begged for help; she was convinced that she was possessed by a spirit [1].

A male cousin, Marvin, who had died two years previously, had known her well. A day or two after his death she began to hear a voice that sounded like his and insisted it was his. The voice spoke to her hatefully, explaining that it wanted to make her suffer and that it had reasons for this. At first the voice sounded completely "outside," as if an invisible person were in the room, but soon it became an "inner" voice, though no less realistic or distressing. It continued to plague her for two years and made her life nearly unbearable. She was often told, "You made me suffer and I will make you suffer." She could not understand the reason for this and asked for an explanation, which finally came. The voice sought to revenge a certain occasion when, without her knowledge, Marvin had seen her writing a letter. The letter contained a remark about him that had hurt his feelings profoundly. That was just before his death. She recalled the occasion and the letter and realized that he could have been upset by it, but she doubted that he could have seen it.

The voice threatened that actions or attitudes of living people would torment her, sometimes describing them very thoroughly, and the predictions were later fulfilled. The voice scolded her for not having sent flowers to his funeral. She had sent roses for the coffin and thought that they had been arranged upon it, but on checking she discovered that they had not been placed visibly.

Her nights were almost never peaceful. Sometimes she awoke screaming so loudly that the whole house was wakened, once even the police had been called. Scarcely a day passed without these persecutions. The "spirit" explained that he wouldn't stop tormenting her until she had made a certain "mental apology" which she considered she couldn't do conscientiously.

Prince diagnosed her condition as a serious case of paranoia or persecution mania. He had been able to help patients with various forms of psychic troubles through psychotherapy, but "in no instance where there was what is known as the delusion of persecution accompanied by auditory hallucinations was instruction, persuasion, analysis, or suggestion of any avail whatever." He determined to attempt a completely different treatment. He explained that he was not convinced that there was such a thing as a possessing spirit, but, on the other hand, facts suggested that it might really exist. Other parapsychologists said they had helped suffering patients by communicating directly with the "guilty" party, the spirit, through a medium, thus causing him to leave his victim. "According to the standard teaching of our time, your trouble is solely one of your own mentality or your own brain. But I am willing to try an experiment on the basis of your own belief that you are really possessed." Mrs. Latimer willingly agreed.

"The address which I then delivered to nothing visible, but ostensibly to the spirit obsessing Mrs. Latimer, will, in bold print, look so absurd and superstitious to many readers that I might well hesitate to set down its outline. But I do not hesitate, for more than one reason. The experiment may be regarded as merely a clinical one, a psychological device which luckily succeeded in speedily removing the worst symptom of the case and in laying, apparently, the foundations for the eventual cure. Regarded in this way, it is of importance to know just what was done. If the process of improvement was one following verbal suggestion, one would like to know just what were the suggestions which led to so happy a result."

Prince stayed in the patient's presence talking for about fifteen minutes, friendly but seriously, speaking directly to the alleged spirit. His most weighty arguments were:

"I wish to speak with the gentleman who has been troubling Mrs. Latimer and whose voice she has been hearing for two years. If he is not here, I hope someone will report what I say to him. But I assume that he is here.

"I wish to talk with you as one gentleman talks to another. Partly on this lady's account, but partly in your own interest. I do not propose to scold you, but to reason with you and, if possible, to be of some assistance.

"You probably think that you are justified in your treatment of the lady, and I shall not deny that you may have had provocation. I do not deny that you are getting a degree and kind of pleasure, but feel sure that you are depriving yourself of greater and a superior species of happiness, and that such pleasure as you get is mingled with bitterness. . . . You are also preventing your own development and progress. . . .

"Should you forgive this woman for any injury which you think she has done you, or which she may in fact have done you, should your hatred turn to pity and friendliness, you would begin to experience a higher and far greater pleasure. . . . Your habit of ill will against this woman results in what is called her possession. In fact, you yourself are obsessed by the habit. . . .

"I understand that you had an emotional shock as the result of something your cousin did shortly before your death. You probably brooded over it in your last hours. That may be the reason that the matter seems so important to you since your death. I don't know, but am only suggesting that the accident of your dying while this matter was troubling you may give it a seeming importance far exceeding its real value.

"I do not expect you to accept what I say as the truth, on the moment. But I think you will admit the truth of what I now confidently assert. You are not happy. Even if tormenting this woman gives you pleasure, the pleasure is poisoned, and is brief. It is followed by deeper bitterness and pain. That means something is radically wrong. . . .

"I suggest that you make an experiment. Even if not convinced, as an intelligent person, knowing that something is wrong with you, you should try the experiment. . . . But you must try the experiment sincerely.

"The experiment is this: Review the whole matter with the desire to do this woman justice. . . . Try to look at it from her viewpoint. . . . Consider her sufferings. . . . And see how efforts to help her, to be good to her, affect you. You may begin to experience glimpses of a happiness you have not known since you left this earth. If so, you will surely go on, and the time will come when your life will become so transformed that you will be very thankful for the suggestions I make today.

"If you begin the experiment, you should use all possible means of making it successful. There is a Power in the universe which is at the call of all who make such experiments, and you should invoke it. There are wise and kindly intelligences about you who will gladly be of assistance to you. . . ."

Prince then instructed Mrs. Latimer not to answer the voice should she hear it and to refuse to converse with it if it should continue to show ill will. But if it showed signs of improvement, she could give it some attention.

That night Mrs. Latimer dreamed that she fought free from spider webs she was snared in. The next night she had a completely different dream: "My mother came to me and said, 'We heard what the man said. I will take care of Marvin. Go to sleep.'—'But I am asleep.'—'No, you are not. You haven't been asleep for a long, long time. You are very tired—listen . . . '" Then the mother sang a couple of lullabys and Mrs. Latimer slept (in the dream) and awoke at nine o'clock, more rested than she had been in years.

On May 9, Mrs. Latimer returned for a consultation. She had not heard the voice at all, but had had the feeling that someone was trying to communicate with her. Prince gave new instructions to the purported spirit, congratulated him on the success he had had so far with his experiment and encouraging him to continue. "I talked to him about as I should have talked to a living person after his few days in trying out a mode of thought and action which had been recommended."

That night Mrs. Latimer dreamed that her mother came again and said, "Go to the man; he will help you. Tell him not to let the facts hinder faith." Then two nights in succession, "Marvin came while I slept and just stood silently and sorrowfully."

After another visit on May 16, Mrs. Latimer failed to appear for some weeks because of illness in her family, which scarcely even gave her time to change her clothes for several days. But this severe strain did not result in the return of the paranoidal symptoms, which one might have expected.

She didn't hear the voice at all until one day she got a quiet moment and began the conversation herself. "I am now willing to listen to you, though we must not talk long." "I shall not ask you to listen long, nor shall I ask you to hear me often hereafter. I am going away. But before I go I want you to understand better what happened to you." The voice described how he had died with embittered thoughts toward her, and how he could not free himself from them after death. "And after that, it was not I alone who molested you. Others grouped themselves around me, joined their efforts to mine, and urged me on. But I took the advice given me, sought the aid of those who were wise and good, and became free. And now I shall soon be gone away."

After a return visit to Prince in June, Mrs. Latimer heard the voice briefly a few more times, and then it ceased altogether. The feeling of being subjected to a person's enmity and direct attack had disappeared from the first conversation in May and had not returned. During the autumn and winter, Mrs. Latimer often felt tired and had a vague feeling of being "the bone of contention." But on January 14 of the following year this feeling suddenly disappeared completely and something told her, "You are now free." During that spring, Prince's treatment of relaxation and suggestion restored her vitality completely, and subsequently she was free from any symptoms of psychic illness for as long as Prince heard news of her.

The Case of Tyrrell

Prince had an opportunity to repeat the experiment. A man, to whom Prince gave the name of Leonard Tyrrell, whom he had treated earlier for alcoholic problems with some success, consulted him one day in 1919. He described with terror how he had been just "sitting thinking" and found himself with pen in hand. Then he looked down and saw that his hand had written something without his having been aware of doing it. The writing contained some warm, friendly thoughts directed to him and was signed Diana. This was the name of his favorite niece, a young woman who had died several months before. The next evening the writing was repeated, and he was now requested by Diana to contact Prince. He did so, full of fear that he was becoming mentally ill. Prince emphasizes that Tyrrell was not in the least interested in spiritualism, nor did he know any more about it than one could pick up skimming through articles in the daily papers. He definitely couldn't recall ever having read anything about it.

During the following year, Tyrrell had nine consultations with Prince and wrote automatically. "Diana" wrote about a man, "Murray," who hated Tyrrell and tried to kill him. Prince suspected Murray was alive and asked where, but got the answer, "Murray is dead and he is trying to kill him." He was called a spirit who tried to tempt Tyrrell to drink and tried to harm him in other ways. Prince discovered that Murray was a man Tyrrell had known well, but who shortly before his death had become hostile toward him. During one seance Tyrrell seemed to see something horrible for an instant, and the related automatic writing read, "Murray." But Prince did not allow Tyrrell to read what he had written automatically, and he himself had no memory of the contents of what he had written. He never revealed any conscious knowledge of his own claim that he was possessed. He didn't like writing automatically. He was afraid of going insane and stopped coming to Prince.

Nevertheless, in March 1922, he did return and described that on several occasions, while at work, when he was supposed to be supervising other people, he had fallen into a state of such confusing thoughts that he could scarcely speak. It might last only a few minutes but seemed to him like an eternity. Prince gave him a couple of calming treatments and didn't hear from him again for several weeks. But in the early summer of 1922 he returned in a condition of complete terror and recounted how after a terrible dream the night before, he had found himself lying on the floor with the sensation of hands gripping his throat trying to strangle him. His condition had thus steadily deteriorated: first merely an illusion of being possessed which was only revealed unconsciously, on one occasion a visual hallucination which frightened him, then several confusing, bewildering states, and now also an experience of terror with a tactile hallucination.

Now for the first time Prince asked Tyrrell if he knew about the idea of spirit possession, which he denied emphatically. Prince described Mrs. Latimer's successful treatment, and Tyrrell was willing to take part in a similar experiment. He sat down, ready for automatic writing.

First "Diana" wrote complaining that Murray's rage had reached its culmination the previous night. Then several words appeared which were said to come from Tyrrell's mother, and later the writing shifted character suddenly and became much stronger. With forceful pressure, it wrote violently, "Here I am, damn you, what do you want?" Prince answered, "I am glad you are here. I want to talk to you as one gentleman with another." The answer was, "Well, I am waiting." The pencil was laid down. Tyrrell crossed his arms; his expression was forbidding.

"Thereupon I made a speech very much on the model of that in

Mrs. Latimer's case, adapted to this one. The figure remained with arms folded until I was through, but it seemed to me that the face gradually softened. It should be remembered that the core of the address was that the tormentor was cheating and injuring himself, that much more happiness was obtainable by the contrary course of getting rid of malice and helping rather than plaguing others, and that, at any rate, it would be wise to try the experiment for a few days and see how it worked.

"When I was through, the pencil was taken and substantially this sentence was written, 'Well, there may be something in what you say; I had never thought of it in that light before.' After a few thoughts came, 'Well, I'll think about it. You may tell him that I won't trouble him this week.'

"A week later Tyrrell came again, in good spirits, declaring that his mind had been clear and that he had had no unpleasant experiences. . . . 'Murray' announced that he had accepted the suggestion to try the experiment of letting Tyrrell alone, of trying to think kindly thoughts, and of seeking the aid of others on 'his side.' "

In a subsequent seance, the conversation continued with "Murray." He was grateful, said he had made progress on his side, and could begin to enjoy his existence. He never disturbed Tyrrell again, as long as Prince had contact with him.

Spirits or the Subconscious?

Prince presents these cases primarily as a report for a new method of treatment, successful in both cases. The diagnosis was "paranoia"; now one would more precisely diagnose a paranoid form of schizophrenia. The stubborn, recurrent, and long lasting symptoms of possession together with hallucinations, which both patients did indeed reveal (but Tyrrell's belief that he was possessed appeared only unconsciously, through automatic writing), caused Prince to judge the outlook for cure as slight; in other words, the prognosis was bad. But in both cases the conversation was carried out—an argumentative appeal in ordinary, serious conversational tones directed to the alleged possessing spirits—and it brought about a dramatic and permanent improvement.

These cases reveal conspicuous differences when compared with the case of "possession" discussed in the previous chapter. There the patient had devoted herself to automatic practices regularly, the symptoms developed gradually, and the treatment involved getting the patient to see that "the spirits" came from her own subconscious. But neither Mrs. Latimer nor Mr. Tyrrell were involved in such activities, and Mr. Tyrrell was completely ignorant of spiritualism. Their symptoms appeared suddenly after the "possessing" person's death. The treatment consisted of Prince accepting the recurrent "delusion" as possibly true, and as a result directing his words not to the patient beside him but rather to the invisible, possibly present spirit. In two later cases of persecuting voices, Prince tried the same method, but in these cases the patients said that they could not recognize the voices as belonging to any definite deceased person; it was rather a matter of different voices thought to come from undetermined spirits. In both cases the treatment failed.

Two alternative hypotheses are conceivable for these remarkable results. The first is that both these cases of persecution mania, lasting several years, consisting of recurrent symptoms of delusion together with hallucinations, were cured by "suggestion," by a dialogue in which the therapist entered into the delusion itself.

According to a common point of view, these patients experienced anxiety faced with certain tendencies and characteristics in themselves which they could not tolerate. These tendencies therefore had to be made subconscious, had to be suppressed. By later personifying them and describing them as belonging to a completely outside "spirit," the patient could facilitate his handling of them. Prince, accordingly, talked directly to this personified complex in the patient's subconscious, and it was to this that he directed his words. By accepting the recurrent performance of these "spirits" as credible fact, the patient's need to be taken seriously was satisfied, a prerequisite to any cure. Although the patients did not seem to have any guilt feelings or other complicated, emotionally laden reactions toward their "possessing" spirits, the "persecutions" had begun completely unexpectedly following their deaths; in Mrs. Latimer's case, anyway, completely abruptly. The hypothesis must then be enlarged to include the assumption that the patients experienced guilt or other complexes in relation to some other person, and that these complexes, for some reason, were shifted over to the dead people in connection with their deaths. In addition, the hypothesis does not appear to explain all the aspects of the cases as Prince has described them.

The second hypothesis is that the cases are what they appear to be, that is, possession. The patients were helped by persuading the invisible but actual personalities, or "spirits," who had influenced the patients, to change their attitudes and behavior. This hypothesis also explains why the same treatment failed in both the later cases: those did not involve an actual possessing spirit but only illusions and hallucinations.

Four cases are too meager a basis for a definite choice between these hypotheses, especially since the cases cannot be studied further. If current therapy could test a similar treatment in similar cases, a great deal more could be learned. Until then, each and every case must be judged from both hypotheses. A believing spiritualist would surely consider that these cases prove the spirit hypothesis; perhaps a psychologist would argue with equal conviction that the hypothesis of subconscious mechanisms was proved. I can only state that these cases are completely consistent with the spirit hypothesis.

Spiritualistically oriented doctors have treated various cases of psychic disturbances in similar ways but with the help of mediums [2, 3]. Alleged possession can also express itself as a sudden, abrupt, profound and lasting alteration in the personality of the possessed. Such cases will be studied in greater detail in Chapter 13 [4, 5].

In the next chapter another phenomenon will be discussed which can be explained either as utterances from the subconscious or contact with "spirits," namely, what is called "voices from space."

12

The Voices from Space

Jürgenson's and Raudive's Experiments

One summer day in 1959 the artist Friedrich Jürgenson wanted to tape the song of a chaffinch. He used his tape recorder in the usual way. But when the tape was played back, a strange, indistinct sound was heard which Jürgenson first thought came from a nocturnal bird. He recorded further tapes, and thus he stumbled upon the traces of a completely unexpected and hitherto unknown phenomenon. When he played the tapes over, actual, inexplicable, strange voices were heard which seemed to speak to him personally. Gradually he became convinced that the voices were not of earthly or human origin. He worked with the tapes for several years and in 1964 published the results in his book *The Voices from Space,* which attracted considerable attention [1]. Experts from various technical firms investigated the recordings and were present when new ones were taped, but opinions about the origins of the phenomenon remained divided. Jürgenson's results caused several people, in Sweden and elsewhere, to instigate similar experiments with tape recorders. One of them, like Jürgenson an immigrant from a Baltic country to Sweden, became the first to publish a systematic and in-depth study of this strange phenomenon. This was Konstantin Raudive, now living in Germany, who in 1968 published the voluminous book *Unhörbares wird hörbar* (*The Inaudible Becomes Audible*), published in English with the title *Breakthrough.* This discusses three years' work with seventy-two thousand identified voice phenomena [2].

A successful taping can, in principle, be made in three different ways. (1) Several people sit around a table talking together; on the table rests a microphone connected to the tape recorder. A calm conversational rhythm is maintained, with many short pauses; questions may be directed to the alleged spirits. Strange voices can be heard later in the pauses on the tapes, voices commenting on the conversation and answering the questions. (2) The tape recorder is connected to a radio in the usual way, and the wave length is changed until a place is located with continual static. During the replay of the tape, voices may be heard through the static. (3) The tape recorder's microphone is used instead, to amplify the radio. The microphone is placed near the radio speaker. Conversation can then be carried out with the radio voices in the same way as with the voices from the tape recorder's microphone.

Results cannot be expected immediately. This work demands a great deal of patience, and a person's ear must become accustomed to unusual noises. Raudive perceived the first voices after three months of fruitless attempts. Five minutes taping may require an hour of listening and transcribing.

A skeptic immediately asks: Isn't it simply self-deception? Natural sounds, mumbles which may be misinterpreted as words by those who want to hear words? Variations in the radio static, single words from distant stations? Objections are obvious and natural but can be easily refuted. Here we are actually concerned with a phenomenon that can be controlled and checked very easily, and judged by outsiders. The voices remain on the tapes; they can be played over innumerable times and copied onto other tapes. They exhibit great variations in clarity and distinctness, from scarcely audible to the unaccustomed listener to voices which anyone can hear the first time without any doubt or hesitation. But it is an objective phenomenon: the tape contains voices which have been produced by paranormal means.

The question then is, how have the voices appeared on the tape? Three conceivable explanations can be found. (1) Through fraud. (2) Through normal microphone pickup and radio transmission. (3) By paranormal means. The fraud hypothesis is easy to check. All people present can be searched for mouth microphones, and the whole seance can be filmed. Sound waves which reach the microphones can then be registered with oscilloscopes. The observer can provide his own tape recorder and a sealed tape from the factory. Strict controls have been made: still the tape contains voices which cannot be explained in a normal way. Raudive describes tapings made in the presence of a great number of people and under different conditions. In Jürgenson's experiments, too, the recordings were controlled experimentally in such a way that one can state that paranormal voices did actually result [3].

During a demonstration in London on December 12, 1969, a tape recorder fresh from the factory was used with new, unused, sealed tapes. The experiment was organized by electronic experts. Two requirements were set for the results to be considered successful: (1) the voices should specify someone present by name, and (2) they should answer a question. A voice came, "Raudive is there." A Catholic bishop "called out" a deceased Russian friend by the name of Stefan and asked him to speak Russian. A voice was heard, first speaking German, then Russian: *"Hier ist Stefan. Koste glaubt uns nicht.—Ocin trudno. My po-ucim Petrum."* (Here is Stefan. Koste [nickname] does not believe us. It is very difficult. We will teach Peter [4].)

To favor hypothesis 2 we must look more closely at what the voices say. They are clearly different from ordinary human voices: they have their own unique language, unlike any known earthly language. Very often sentences consist of words from several different languages. The words are grammatically altered, compressed, shortened, or have suffixes from another language: the results become a personally constructed telegram style with a marked rhythm. No language like this exists on any known radio transmitting station. Moreover, radio voices have even personally contributed to the experimenter's work and taken part in conversations with him in a way that would be inconceivable in an ordinary radio broadcast.

In certain conditions a tape recorder can function as a radio receiver. Besides the three methods of recording mentioned, Raudive's technicians therefore devised four additional ways, which, according to their specifications, definitely ruled out the involvement of radio transmissions. Voices were picked up with these methods equally clearly [5].

Some examples of the characteristic mixed tape language:

A microphone voice: *"Jundal kan gå själv. Oh veca pott, bindu han an de (n) Mortbed."* The words are from five languages: Swedish, Lettish, German, Latin, and English. They mean: "Jundal can walk by himself, the old pot. Tie him to the deathbed." According to Raudive, the meaning should be interpreted: Jundal's soul can walk itself, but his old vessel [body] remains bound by the deathbed.

A microphone voice: *Guten Abend med dej, I wishy your bebi Wein.* German, Swedish, English, Spanish. "Good evening to you, I wish to drink your wine." The German and the Swedish words are changed, the English "wish" and the Spanish "beber" have had extra endings added, which result in a marked rhythm. The recording was made one evening while Raudive sat with a glass of wine.

A radio voice: *"Pà Kostes central."* Raudive's studio was known as "central," and his first name, Konstantin, often has the nickname Koste.

The voices identified themselves by name, often as the deceased relatives and friends of the experimenters, but sometimes only as distant acquaintances or completely unknown people. Famous persons' names also appeared: Hitler, Churchill, and those long dead like Goethe and Descartes. But the communications from actual historical people are too short for these voices to be compared with accessible authentic recordings, something which would obviously be desirable.

The contents allude sometimes to the situation in the studio and to the experimenter's personal condition, sometimes to situations in the voices' world. Allusions to war often appear, usually references to events in the Second World War, but Vietnam has also been mentioned by name. References to life in the world are mixed in with rather contradictory, sketchy indications of the situation in "the other world." Most often, evasive answers are given to questions about what it is like "on the other side." Different voices argue and disagree, sometimes scream. Whatever the origin of the voices, and whether they do have their own existence, it is difficult to determine conclusively whether their communications are memories of earthly life, which still occupy their thoughts, or whether they refer to their present existence. They seem to be aware of Raudive's intention to make contact. They complain about interrupted contact, they notice when he leaves the room; he is urged to talk. He is invited to use the radio more; the voices seem to prefer the radio to the microphone. They are noticeably pleased with the contact; they line up to use the microphone. Conditions on "the other side" seem far from permanently blissful. Instead, many voices give the impression of finding themselves in something resembling the popular concept of purgatory.

It is noteworthy that the voices use the languages of those present. Raudive is unusually multilingual. But others, for example Swedes, have received ordinary Swedish [6].

The recording does not succeed every time, but sufficiently often for the phenomenon to be called repeatable. But how can it be explained?

Psychokinesis or Spirits?

If we reject the hypotheses of normal explanations for the voices, including fraud (and there seems to be good reasons for this), then paranormal explanations remain. Two hypotheses are conceivable: (1) the voices are caused by a hitherto unknown form of psychokinesis which in some way influences the magnetizing of the tape. According to this theory, the voices would be caused by those present in the room, perhaps in a way analogous to Ted Serios' psychic photography. (2) The voices are what they say they are: "voices from space," from the psychic space where "the spirits" exist.

It is too soon to choose once and for all from between these hypotheses. Supporting the argument for psychokinesis, the voices talk the languages of the experimenters or someone else present at the taping, and they have some connection with what they are doing. The contents of the tapes could be considered, as in the case of mediumistic phenomena, to be entirely or partially produced by the unconscious of those present, and the voices would thus be considered a form of "persona."

The experimenters are actually very involved emotionally with the experiment, which furthers the appearance of psychokinesis. Personally, during group recording sessions, I have experienced something strange several times: I have heard my own voice very clearly on the tape, talking words and using expressions which as far as I know I never said during the conversation several minutes earlier. Naturally, it is easy to say that my memory is faulty. But the utterances did not fit at all in the context of the conversation as we remembered it or as it appears on the tape. These statements are so out of context that otherwise the group would surely have reacted and asked what I meant by them. But they had not heard me say anything out of the ordinary, and were equally astonished by what was heard on the tape. Others in these particular groups have produced the same phenomenon, and there have been other reports of similar happenings. If this phenomenon is paranormal, then it is obviously a form of psychokinesis.

But support for the spirit hypothesis can also be found. Thus the languages could be explained naturally: the energy supply is obviously limited, and therefore it is necessary to express as much as possible with the least effort and expense of energy, hence the telegram style and the marked rhythm. The words are used symbolically, one word can carry a great quantity of information for those who recognize what the contents allude to. The origin of the voices acts as an independent personality, with individual characteristics. They give information which the seance participants do not recognize but which can be verified. They are pleased by the contact, which for some reason has great meaning for them. These conditions are recognized in other psychic contexts, for example, within spiritualism.

How the process functions is completely unknown. But since the voices can come through two such diverse channels as the radio and microphone, the simplest explanation is that what affects the tape happens completely electromagnetically. Some form of "psychic energy" can cause electromagnetic wave movements which are registered on the tape. That psychic energy could be thought to come from those present or from "spirits." But for the present this is all only guesswork.

There would be stronger support for the spirit hypothesis if the voices could identify themselves as deceased persons completely unknown to either the experimenters or others present, and if they could give sufficient, verifiable information to prove their identities. We would in that case have a phenomenon analogous to that of the "drop-in communicators" of spiritualistic seances. Hopefully they might also speak in a language completely unknown to everyone present, which could later be identified. But perhaps the communication is telepathic and in some way dependent on words which exist in the consciousness of those present.

Raudive emphasizes one circumstance which favors the spirit hypothesis: no voices have identified themselves as living persons. Once a voice identified himself as the Latvian artist Strunke. Raudive knew nothing about him other than that he was alive, and took that as an indication that "living" voices could also be received. But it turned out that Strunke had died several days before the seance. If the voices could be explained as psychokinesis caused by unconscious powers of those present, then it must also be explained how these unconscious forces can sort out communicators who, as far as the participants know, are alive but who then later prove to be dead. According to Raudive, this also occurred with voices who identified themselves as unknown to those present.

The investigation of the voice phenomenon continues, and as several people in different language areas take up the work, comparative material will be produced. Several individuals and groups are working on recordings, more or less systematically, in Sweden. For the present, we can state that the voice recordings can so far be considered a repeatable paranormal phenomenon. If further investigations can strengthen this hypothesis, that in itself would be of epoch-making importance.

13

Reincarnation?

Many, many must come to grief, fall
Victims here: this is no small
Attempt. Folk slain and kingdoms dashed.
Towns and palaces lost in smoke.
Like jugs and crocks whole armies smashed.
Blood of the young on the earth has run.
The Lord God shall experiment
Thus, till He creates the human.

HJALMAR GULLBERG

A Review

We perceive ourselves all too easily as separate, distinct entities, each with an identity discrete from every other person's, defined and cut off from each other and from the outside world by the determining limits of our skin. We readily believe that we are, basically, each a sort of biological machine, although slightly more complicated than other machines. Numerous facts suggest this is the case. But not everything fits into this picture. There are "impossible facts"; what should be impossible does, nevertheless, occur. We have considered a small selection of experiences which suggest that people can communicate with the surrounding world and with their fellow creatures without using their five known senses. These unsettling facts do not agree with the ordinary picture of human beings. Many people flee from this difficulty simply by totally refusing to concern themselves with these facts, and thus they ignore the problem completely.

The occurrence of paranormal phenomena implies that human beings are something more than just complicated machines. The human can communicate with the surrounding world and his fellow creatures beyond his sensory limitations; he is not completely isolated, cut off from contact and involvement. Humans are connected with their surrounding world in an even more profound, potent, and mysterious way. This need not mean something "supernatural," only that our knowledge of nature is not complete.

But what have we found out so far about the question of survival after death? We have studied several different phenomena and experiences: separation, apparitions, ESP-projection, deathbed visions, medium's experiences, voices from space. None of these phenomena alone gives any proof of the survival of life after death. It would be completely absurd to expect that such a complicated problem could be resolved by studying any single group of phenomena. But by attacking the problem on a broad front, from all conceivable angles, we can hope to come a little closer to the truth. Possibly the only way to prove survival is to experience it—to wake up after the death of one's body and find oneself conscious, possibly in another sort of body. But then perhaps it is too late to communicate this to anyone else: perhaps contact with people living on the earth is impossible. The different phenomena and experiences which have been mentioned so far are all in themselves completely consistent with the hypothesis of survival after death. Some of them seem to be more in accord with it than with any other hypothesis. Superstition and superstitious beliefs are not essential for one to accept survival as a working hypothesis. The material which supports the survival hypothesis is today so voluminous that one can accept it with a calm "scientific conscience," even if definite proof is still lacking.

Experimental Research Attempts

But are there no possible ways of solving the problem experimentally? Think of a person who has certain information or knowledge which only he and no one else knows. It exists only in his consciousness, not written down anywhere, but at the same time it is such that it can be verified only if someone else states that he knows it too. During that person's lifetime, mediums and others so disposed attempt to get that information, through ESP or any other means. No one succeeds. Then the person dies; afterward a communicator appears through a medium, announcing that he is that person and giving the correct information, which can be verified. That would be a strong support for the survival hypothesis, but not definite proof. For it might also be possible that the medium perceived the verification of the communication through precognition. But the likelihood of such an explanation is diminished if the medium and others have tried to solve the puzzle during the person's lifetime, perhaps stimulated by the promise of a financial reward for the person who first succeeds.

Several such attempts are being made now. The British parapsychologist Thouless [1] (and after him, Wood [2]) published ciphers, the key to which is a word or phrase known only to the one who thought it up and which is not written down anywhere. After his death, each intends, if he does survive and the possibility exists, to communicate that key word through a medium. The ciphers published between 1948 and 1950 have yet to be solved. However, this system is rather laborious. Stevenson has suggested a simpler method [3]: a combination lock of a certain type which permits the possessor himself to choose a combination of six numbers to open the lock. A key word or phrase can be translated into numbers, using a code. This code is written down and deposited together with the lock, but the key word exists only in the consciousness of the possessor and is never written down. After his death, he will try, if he possibly can, to communicate the key word through a medium. Here too mediums and other interested people must try to specify the combination during the owner's lifetime, with prizes offered to increase their motivation. Three possible means exist to guess the correct combination before the agent's death: a systematic test of all 125,000 conceivable combinations managing to guess correctly by chance, and guessing with ESP. After the owner's death, a fourth possibility exists, that of receiving a message from him. If a greater number of people got themselves such locks and key words to be communicated following their deaths, then the survival hypothesis might be strongly confirmed.

Conceivable Forms of Survival

The various phenomena we have studied so far all point to the same form of survival: that person A, who lived recently, shows signs of having communicated after his death and is perceived as communicator A1. This might be illustrated schematically thus:

But another form of survival is also conceivable. Person A1, now alive, may behave in a manner indicating that person A, who was formerly alive, is making himself known through him. A1 may demonstrate paranormal knowledge of A's life and may, moreover, feel he is identical with A. He may describe memories which could be A's very own. This can be illustrated:

The interval, the time from A's death to A1's birth, may vary. Three possibilities exist:

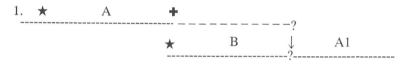

Here a person B is born, who at the time of A's death or thereafter, undergoes a sudden and profound personality change, begins to identify himself with A, and demonstrates paranormal knowledge of his situation, that is, behaves like A1. These cases, of which only a few are known, can be taken to indicate possession, but a more profound, comprehensive possession than the cases we have described earlier [4].

Here A dies before A1's birth, but the interval is shorter than the nine months which A1's body needs to develop from conception to birth. This is a relatively unusual form of passing over. The next type is the most common:

Here the interval is of varying length, but clearly longer than nine months, usually several years. These cases may be seen to indicate reincarnation.

The Concept of Reincarnation

The conception of *reincarnation* (from the Latin, *"re-in-carno,"* "again in flesh") is very old. It can be found in various forms in many cultures and religions. In the West it is, for the most part, completely unknown or ridiculed as a superstitious belief in "soul wandering." But for millions of people, especially in Asia, the concept of reincarnation is a fundamental part of life, and prominent Western thinkers have also been drawn to it [5]. It appears to offer a solution to many of the injustices and the grimness of which life seems so full. Thus, those who are unhappily situated in one life are pictured as able to receive compensation in the next, and in the long run, an adjustment and compensation will be effected. But the consequences of reincarnation could be otherwise. It is no proof of the concept that it offers a reasonable explanation for the injustice of life. Existence could indeed be considered just as grim and ill-disposed toward justice if one holds this view as it could be when looked at any other way.

A constant objection to reincarnation is that, since, after all, we do not remember a former life, we cannot have had one. But though it is most unusual for people ever to be able to remember anything about their very first days, weeks, or months of life, still they do not deny that they lived them. Memory can even desert us much closer to the present moment.

Moreover, recollections pertaining to a previous life are, in fact, considerably more common than we might imagine, even in Europe and America. Perhaps such memories are talked about so seldom because people who have them have been hushed up, laughed at, or scorned when they have tried to discuss them, and so they have taught themselves to keep quiet. Here are some examples of such experiences, collected from northern Europe:

46. A spring day, before I had learned to talk properly, I found cracks in the drying earth in front of my parents' home. A memory surfaced that I had seen things like that before—and that the cracks had widened—and I knew that they were the first indications of an earthquake. I couldn't say "earthquake" so I screamed "the trembling, the trembling," but no one understood me.

47. This I remember: a burning house, my home, my husband standing on the verandah roof surrounded by flames. Is he sing-

ing, drunk? or crazy? I run away from there, turn and look back to see it all.

The house is on the edge of a wood and I stumble and fall by a stump. There are several centimeters of snow, a pretty little spruce tree grows by the stump. There I die: my clothing is nineteenth century or the beginning of the twentieth in style. My age is around thirty-five. I don't remember any names, not even my own.

My memory of something diffused and vague from the past has been there as long as I can remember, but this experience came when I was just over fifty years old. Then it came to me in a fully awake state; there it was, all at once, like when you pull the curtain up at the theater. I knew all the time it was myself I saw, and felt the pain and the anguish the woman experienced, and the tranquility which came when she (I) sank down by the stump and everything was over.

48. When I was a child I could experience myself as a middle-aged, very strong, sharp-tempered woman, big and powerful, a country woman with masses of sons. I had a rather violent temper. I can remember how I was dressed, but no name. I felt it all painfully—I was, after all, a little child, but at the same time adult. I couldn't talk with grown-up people or give them the advice I wanted to. I wanted to say, "Do this, because I did it," as I used to say to my children. But then I'd be laughed at scornfully, and the adults said, "That girl, she talks so wisely, like an old woman, but she'll die soon enough." So you really do have to keep quiet and hold yourself in. This happened in primary school, then the memories gradually disappeared. The most powerful still stick with me: I'm walking to a well for water, it's an old-fashioned well the likes of which I've never seen anywhere nowadays, nor have I seen the village. I carry a yoke on my shoulders and I'm deeply disturbed about one of my sons.

The memories started coming as soon as I began to talk, but disappeared when I went to school, they faded away and became less painful. They also disappeared when I had to pull myself back inside my own skull and just be an obedient silent little child.

49. I was born in 1915, and what first dominated my mind was the feeling of homelessness. I experienced this consciously, the images didn't come until later. . . . I wept within myself, and it took several years before I taught myself to laugh and be happy. It was during that first lonely helplessness that the loss of my son first surfaced. He was a bit of myself torn away—I can't explain any better than that how it felt.

I was a very good child, though I'd have considered my docility to be really apathy. . . . In my third year I began to let on that I had my son with me. I used to smooth my pillow and lie down and caress the pillow as if it were my boy's cheek. In my memory pictures he was four years old, never older. Then someone took charge of me because I was "precocious." I used to hold myself very carefully upright, with my neck straight, and I felt I was grown up. So strong was my anchoring in the past that I felt exactly how the clothes covered my ankles and that my sandals were soft. I had a hard time learning to sit on chairs, would have preferred to sit with crossed legs most of all.

It's impossible to say when the pictures from the past first appeared, they came and went with haziness in between. Only my love for that little boy remained there all the time, first as a pain in my soul, later as a kind of knowledge about that one particular little person. The pictures have been the same since early childhood. But I can't retain them for long except for the one that remained burned into my mind as late as 1962.

The place we live in, in that memory picture, must be a very big house. The windows are high, like ordinary doors, with deep niches but no glass panes. I can't actually see that they have no glass, but I know it, definitely. The floor is made of thick polished tiles, about 40 x 90 centimeters. They look like marble, the colors are red-brown and gray-green. If I were to stretch out my hand as I lie on my divan, I could touch a tile which has an unusually big red-brown design. It feels as if my divan is placed almost in the center of my room. To the left, diagonally behind my head on the same side as the two windows, a couple of steps lead to a roof garden with a dazzling white balustrade. There's no door, but half of the wall is missing, and there, in front of the opening, my son is playing. Sometimes he comes over and playfully traces his fingers over my face. That's the memory which gives such pain, why I don't know. The boy is dressed in white, not Western style; he has bare feet. My clothes are thin, I'm resting on my left hip, and on my left foot I see the soft, lion-colored sandal. I lie there looking down at my brown wrist with the thin soft fabric around it. Though I can't really see it, I know I have white pearls in my black hair. Even in this present life, I "know" that my hair is black though it never has been black, really. As a child I was always so disappointed when I saw my mirror image—I didn't recognize myself at all. . . . I also have a memory of dancing in some dark room with light veils around me. It's often happened to me in this life that when I step inside a church I want to lift my arms and dance forward. For me dance means devotion as well as joy.

Although in my childhood I never heard about reincarnation, I believed the memories I had arose from the time I was with God before my birth, and that perception made me never doubt the existence of the spiritual world. I really have experienced that it is good and full of light.

As late as 1963 I began to suspect that it might have been India where I lived in a former life. A friend suggested that I read about that country because she found so much which could be connected with India in my images and personal characteristics. Then, with the joy of recognition, I found the lotus flower I had started to draw even before I went to school. But also OM, the holy sign, the symbol of God, was something I recognized and I had mulled over in vain since the age of five, when I saw a beautifully stylized number 5 on my father's cigar box and was absolutely convinced that it had to be something other than a number, which my father told me it was. The numbers 5 and 3 hid a secret for me which I never could puzzle out of them. I've never forgotten how I used to trace the number 5 on the wood of the box while deep inside I struggled to remember something very important.

50. As a child I often had such memories [of earlier experiences] and sometimes tried to talk about them with Mother, who hushed me up and threatened me with a beating if I dared go on with such raving. When I was eight or nine, war broke out in Finland (we lived near the border). I didn't understand very much about it, but all the anxiety and thundering and crashing, that no one could miss. It was hard to get food, a real shortage then in our district. I remember it once came to me with incredible clarity that I was adult and had four children, a newborn I carried in my arms and three clinging to my skirts, screaming and sobbing. I found myself in church and round about me were people in strange, mostly gray clothes. All the women had very long full skirts, down to the ground, I had a very full one, too, a white blouse with wide sleeves and a bodice which was done up in the front, and on my head a white hat with a wide brim turned up in front. I've seen a style somewhat similar in pictures from Holland. It was a little church on a hill and all these people had gone there in flight because of a battle, and we were being shot at with big black balls from cannons, and then the people screamed that now the tower was going to collapse. My children screamed and clung to me, then there was a terrible crash and everything was over. . . . I remember how I trembled and held my head and thought of running to Mommy and asking her, but then I remembered the whipping I'd get. I didn't dare

go home for a long while, then was declared ill and put to bed. There I lay remembering everything so clearly and wondering and not being able to understand.

Of course, I grew older. . . . I never dared utter a word to anyone (and also had many other experiences), but I knew that I had lived before and kept it to myself. I didn't want to hear that I was talking crazy nonsense and didn't want to get a beating. Then in later years I've been aware of such things . . . but I suppressed it all in childhood and it's now so fuzzy and incomplete.

I'm not pretending, I'm not inventing, it just was that way. I know, for example, when someone dies, a dear friend or relative, long before I'm told about it. All I know is it's *now,* and who it is I'll soon enough find out. I look at the clock and note down the time. Weird when it corresponds.

Experiences of this sort can give the percipient an absolute certainty that he has lived before, but, of course, they have no value as proof for anyone else. As long as they cannot be verified, the simplest explanation is that they are only fantasy images or forgotten memories of pictures a person has once seen. Children do imagine a very great deal. But it is remarkable that some people imagine with detailed pictures and situations which they do not recognize but later identify in pictures from other countries and other areas. Nor did these children have access to TV. Sometimes such experiences may have been an expression of wish fulfillment. But they are often far from pleasant, on the contrary, they are usually associated with unpleasantness and violent events which quite often lead up to death. It is completely natural that they cannot be verified, since the children are not even able to tell them to anyone who would listen seriously. But sometimes the experience strikes with full force in adult years and sometimes it can be verified:

51. As a child I used eagerly to tell my brother, who was some years younger than I, what it was like "when I was big before in the world." I had a lot to tell, especially about America, among other things about when I was along when living people were thrown into a well (something which as far as I know I had never heard about). Later I read about the Aztecs and recognized my story exactly. The name Arras also existed for me even when I was very little; I kept repeating it to myself but didn't know what it meant. Later it disappeared, but the awareness that

it was something special returned in the Forties, when I heard the name for the first time.

What I'm about to tell you is one experience from several I've had during the last ten years. They come sporadically, and I'm always amazed and startled by them. In my family many of us have paranormal gifts. I did not have any paranormal experiences myself before the first in this series. I've never sought out anything like this, it has always come spontaneously. Pervading the experiences has been a deep anxiety and unsettledness, great psychic fatigue, or sometimes a feeling of anguish. The state in which these events are experienced could perhaps be called a sort of trance, in some individual cases a deeper trance (if this means that one's awareness of what is taking place in one's normal surroundings is strongly blunted or completely cut off). After the experience is over, as a rule I slowly return to normal but still often continue to "remember" the continuation of what I have experienced.

*

Out of the night and fog, great roarings and alarm, the picture appears of an enormous railroad station with roofed-over tracks and a great number of trains in the station. A troup transport train, just ready for the soldiers to board. The platforms are overflowing with people: soldiers, functionaries, crowds of relatives, all strained, pushing and shoving and shouting.

The noise of the locomotive, the uproar from the moving, banging, slamming wagons, and the crying shouting people is all deafening. Through the vast doors and the partly open gigantic windows I see rows of horse-drawn carriages outside on the street. Lanterns on the vehicles and gaslights on the street look diffused and unreal in the fog.

Gradually it dawns on me to my astonishment that I—like thousands of other young men—am being shoved into one of the trains. I'm already on the train, half hanging out a window. Our uniforms indicate the time of the First World War. . . . Now I feel it is late autumn in 1914. There I stand in the window, feeling wild with desperation and despair. I know the train is leaving for Flanders, to the front. . . .

Now I know why I'm hanging out the window, because, in fact, I'm clasping a woman's hands. She's standing out there on the platform, young like myself, perhaps twenty or twenty-five, and very pretty. . . . Her eyes have the same desperate expression as my own must surely have. She's squeezing my hands hard in hers. Inaudibly we whisper each other's names as if this could save us.

I hear someone shout "St. Étienne!" several times—but that

doesn't affect me. I just focus on the terror which will happen
. . . that we who love each other so rashly will now be separated
from each other, forever. Inaudibly she whispers my name,
"Marcel, oh mon Marcel . . ."

Loud, harsh orders sound through the disturbance. O God,
now my train begins to move. Slowly, creeping like an evil person, it moves alongside the platform. Functionaries, police, offi-
cers, railroad workers try in vain to push away all the sorrowful
people. People cling to the train in the end, try in vain to prolong
the inevitable departure, still a few seconds more. . . .

. . . in vain, we can no longer touch each other. My comrades
call to me, I don't hear what they're saying. They hold onto me,
drag me into the carriage while I wildly cry out her name,
"Catherine, ma Cathy . . ." and far off I hear her increasingly
wavering, despairing voice, "mon Marcel. . . ." Then her face is
swallowed up by the darkness. . . . The last I see is her deathly
pale face shining for an instant like a single candle in the
night. . . .

My comrades pull me in and lay me down on a bench. They
talk to me, I don't hear them. I feel an icy coldness grip my
heart. It doesn't matter what happens now because I'm already
dead, I died the instant my beloved's hand slipped out of
mine. . . .

Slowly I wake up again, lying there on the bench. My comrades
talk to me, but I don't answer. The wheels clatter and clatter
against the tracks, clatter and clatter ceaselessly . . . until at long
last our train stops. It is dark outside and raining, but nevertheless we're pushed out of the carriages. Someone straps a knap-
sack on each of us and hands me a rifle, and we start walking
across a field where the clayey ground immediately sticks to our
shoes so they become shapeless and heavy. We stumble forward
in the darkness, now and then lit up by rockets. On the horizon
we see something like waves of fire sweeping the dark sky—these
are the flames from the cannon muzzles and the burning towns
and villages—after an eternity of endless, heavy, wandering footsteps down along the hollow of the valley, we arrive at a place
where there are hordes of other soldiers, where shelters are being
dug in the slope, and where the wounded and the dead lie. We're
told that now we're not far from Arras.

I live as if deafened by this misfortune which has overwhelmed me—I don't know if it's day or night, if days or weeks
have passed—but one day it is our turn to try to storm the rise in
front of us where the enemy holds the village. We worm our
way forward along the trough of a deep ravine where a stream
usually trickles, now swollen with the rain into a muddy river,

obstructing our progress. But that is the only protected angle of
approach we have and the only stream nearby. It winds its way
in narrow loops down the hillside and has dug out that ravine
with slopes toward the enemy side, slopes that are difficult to
storm.

The last stretch we slither our way up to the village, near the
edge of the ravine. The clay is all pervasive, slippery as soap; I
slither and slide in it. Then comes the signal to attack. With
superhuman effort we cast ourselves up over the edge of the
ravine, but at the very moment I see the village lying there before us, the bite of bullets from the enemy's machine guns strikes
our front. I feel a powerful blow in my chest and a burning pain.
My last thought is, "Here's where I die, I am, as a mattter of
fact, already dead."

*

This experience came the evening of June 21, 1966, between
eight and nine o'clock. That whole day I'd felt incredibly exhausted, uncomfortable and dull, and sometimes anguished, as if
something terrible were about to happen. When I got home I
threw myself down on the bed, lay there feeling low. Then I felt
the mist come over me again. I heard all the noises around me,
but more muted, and at the same time I felt my legs go completely numb and heavy. This dead feeling slowly spread upward over me, without my being able to stop it or do anything
about it. It was frightening and unpleasant, I wanted to scream
but I couldn't, and slowly I felt myself glide out of my body.
When I had actually come out, everything got much easier, but
I still could do nothing about taking the initiative. Instead, I was
moved even further away from my body and slid out into a
milky-white, dense mist where everything was deathly silent.
When I had glided a while through a silent universe, I felt A [a
woman colleague at work who appeared in an earlier experience
in this series] glide up beside me, and together we continued
this remarkable journey. I couldn't talk, I was very surprised that
she had come this way, but it was really as if I'd been paralyzed,
as if I'd got an injection of curare. It seemed as if we traveled a
very long distance that way, but finally the silence began to be
disturbed by a sound which grew stronger and stronger and
finally mounted into the tremendous tumult which led into the
experience at the station.

When I slowly returned to consciousness again, I didn't know
where I was. It was as if I could return to my own body only
with incredible effort. It continued to feel stiff and cold for a
long time, and I couldn't move, but at the same time I felt an
unbearable burning pain shooting across my chest especially in

the area of my heart, as if there was a huge gaping wound there. Finally I could open my eyes, but I didn't recognize myself, everything was so strange . . . it was as if the room where I lay echoed ceaselessly with Catherine's desperate call and the rumble of train wheels against the tracks. Everything which had happened was so lifelike and frightening, and it concerned me.

After a while I could move. Taking up the writing pad beside the bed, I wrote it all down, because I had it all still fresh within me. Then I tottered down to my family who stared, frightened by my distressed appearance, and I told them, but only the rough outlines, that I'd had a vision of an awful event in the First World War.

The next day I went to the library and borrowed books about the First World War. I'd never read anything about it before except what you find in history school books, whatever they put there. I was really terrified to read anything about that war, somehow I had a bad feeling about it, but I didn't know why. So then I found out that a big battle had taken place near Arras at the time I had thought. I felt that the French soldiers' uniforms were so familiar.

When I got to my work, I faced an even more remarkable experience. My colleague A, who had, indirectly, taken part in the evening's events, phoned and said in a very distressed voice, "I have to tell you something very strange that happened to me last evening between eight and nine o'clock. I was sitting listening to the radio when I saw you walk into the room, and then it was as if I lost consciousness and traveled far away, and when I woke up later, after a long while, I wept uncontrollably and it felt as if I'd taken part in something very terrible and mysterious." I tried to belittle the whole thing but felt even more shaken. Shortly thereafter she traveled to America, to be away for a long while, possibly to stay there. Some weeks after she left, I had two further experiences in which she appeared, but these were light and harmonious. Obviously everything was in some way connected with her, or perhaps she was even the "catalyst" who gave the impulse for this "memory."

I cannot free myself from the intense and vivid connection between these events and my own personality. It is not something which I merely observed or witnessed: for it involves me totally. I have experienced all this and remember it as something vivid and real, like every event which concerns me in my conscious everyday world.

*

In August of 1966 my family had been in England, and I decided we would travel home by way of Arras. I had a vague hope of recognizing the place if the vision did have a foundation in reality. In the beginning nothing happened, everything was unfamiliar, unknown, but when we neared Arras I had a weird feeling of seeing everything "from behind." (Later I came to think that if the experience was real, then in 1914 we had approached the town from the direction we drove up from now.) Several miles away from the town I began to say I wanted to catch sight of a stream which went into a deep ravine, winding through the landscape, but none could be found. When we entered the town it seemed completely unfamiliar . . . exhausted, I decided we should have taken the road to Charleroi in Belgium. As we criss-crossed around looking for a possible way out, my heart suddenly rose in my throat. We had come to where four roads met, and on a signpost stood the name Bapaume. Without thinking, I turned onto that road, although it led us in the wrong direction, toward Paris rather than toward Belgium. . . . After four or five kilometers we came to a little village I began to recognize. I turned off through the village onto a narrow road, crossed a railroad track, and now my recall became crystal clear. I turned around completely, drove back over the little road, crossed the big road down through the village to the other side, headed on between the houses, down the narrow wandering village streets, drove through like a sleepwalker, and finally came out of the village into a field. There I stopped, jumped out of the car, pointed for the others, saying, "There it was!" There was the ravine with the wandering stream and the village behind, where I had died in the vision. We had to drive back to the main road to get to the other village (Henin St. Cojeul), and I looked for the church but was seized again by doubt and disappointment, for I recognized neither the village nor the church. It hadn't looked like this even supposing it had been badly damaged during the war. This church looked undamaged. Meanwhile my son struck up a conversation with a very old man who was walking down the village street, and they disappeared, chatting away. After a while he came back with the information that the church and the houses which stood there now had been built during the Thirties, the church in 1934. The village had been completely destroyed during the violent fighting in Arras in November 1914. The Germans had occupied the rise just behind the church.

I don't know what the name St. Étienne stood for. Neither the Parisian station by that name nor the city seemed known to me when I saw them the following year. Possibly it could have been my own name which was called out. The Gard du Nord in Paris, however, had a ground plan and style which corresponded to my vision.

*

I really can't rid myself of my skeptical disposition and often puzzle over how much my subconscious could have deceived me. On the other hand, when such an experience happens, I have so little to say about it. But when it is over, as a rule I begin to doubt it altogether, and when I go back over my notes, I am almost astonished that I really did experience what I've written down. I would like to be tested some time about these experiences under deep hypnosis. Then mightn't I learn whether it was reality I had experienced or some "false play" of the subconscious?

[His son confirmed the conversation with the old man, and also that the vision had been told before the journey.]

One obvious interpretation would be that the woman, A, appeared in these experiences because the man was somehow involved with her, for example, in love, and could not consciously accept it, and therefore she took a symbolic role in the performance his unconscious created. But still this does not explain the paranormal aspects of the experience. An alternative hypothesis is that the woman and the man really had had some relationship in a former life, as in their present one, and that common memories lay behind the shared experience. We will return to the question of hypnosis.

As these cases demonstrate, it is difficult to verify adults' experiences indicating earlier lives. Usually they contain only isolated pictures or scenes, like frames clipped from a film. Children's experiences are often more complete, containing longer sections from "the film."

The dreams of the cowherd's cottage (in Case 18) could be mentioned in this context. It is striking that these dreams were enacted in the place as it (really) looked several years before the dreamer was born. Perhaps the content of the dreams is a mixture of a school girl's fantasy and her unconscious memory of a former existence as a farm girl. In any case, no further conclusion can be reached by speculating about that case.

Sometimes only a certain type of behavior in children may indicate such memories. A small child, for instance, may reveal an inexplicable fear, start to cry or run and hide every time he hears or sees a plane in the sky before he has ever seen pictures of planes in a terrifying context, as for example, on television. In some cases, too, when they are old enough to talk, children have said that they have been shot at from a plane before.

Cases like these have made certain psychiatrists consider the possibility that a cause for a patient's difficulties may sometimes be found in experiences "outside of chronological time," that is, in an earlier life. Some believe outright that "the study of parapsychology will be the next important development in psychiatry [6]."

It proves most profitable to study children who have recollections indicating earlier lives, if this can be done while the memories are fresh. The psychiatrist Ian Stevenson, at the University of Virginia, is the pioneer in this field and has studied hundreds of cases. Children with memories indicating earlier lives are found in particular in Ceylon, India, Turkey, Alaska, and some areas in Lebanon and Syria. Isolated cases exist in many other countries, even in Europe and America, but they are most common in areas where belief in reincarnation is widespread. Hence it is only fantasy, argue the skeptics, for obviously the child will chatter on about reincarnation if belief in it is common. But what if what the children report sometimes corresponds convincingly with situations and details in a deceased person's life, facts which the child could not normally have known? Such examples have yet to be explained.

On the other hand, it is possible that belief in reincarnation does not make it easier for children to discuss their memories. This can be supported by known cases of verified memories [7]. The children's accounts of earlier lives are very seldom happily or indulgently received. In certain areas, for example in India, it is commonly believed that a child who can remember former lives will soon die. This may cause people to try to hush the children up, sometimes using very drastic methods such as beating them or stopping their mouths with soap. Yet some children persist in telling more, which indicates their strong identification with the other (former) personality.

As illustrations, here are two cases which Stevenson has studied, one which more closely resembles possession and one which indicates reincarnation.

The Case of Jasbir

It is the spring of 1954 in the village of Rasulpur in Uttar Pradesh, India. The family Jat had one son, Jasbir, age three and a half. He is very ill with smallpox and one evening his father believes that the boy has died. The father goes to his brother and asks him to help him bury his son. But it is late at night, and he is persuaded to wait until the following morning. Several hours later weak signs of life are noticed in the boy, and he slowly regains consciousness. Several days pass before he can talk again and more weeks before he can express himself clearly. But then he reveals a remarkable change in his behavior. He insists that he is the son of Shankar in Vehedi, and wants to go there. He refuses to eat his family's food because as a Brahmin he belongs to a higher caste. A Brahmin woman who lives in the neighborhood hears of Jasbir's refusal to eat and devotes herself to cooking for him. The father furnishes her with the foodstuffs which she then cooks for Jasbir in the Brahmin way. This continues for more than a year, but his family tricks him, sometimes giving him food which is not cooked by the Brahmin woman. He discovers the betrayal, and that, together with pressure from his family, wins him gradually to eat their ordinary food again. His way of talking has also changed. He uses considerably "finer" words, such as are heard in the higher social circles the Brahmins frequent. He has lost all pleasure in his toys and isolates himself from other children.

As the crow flies, Vehedi village lies only about thirty-five kilometers from Rasulpur, but both villages are remote from highways and scarcely any communication at all exists between them. Jasbir's family has never been there, only heard the name. For several years, in fact, no inhabitant of Rasulpur has visited Vehedi. But Jasbir talks more and more about his "life" in Vehedi. He describes in particular how he ate poisoned sweets during a marriage procession, fell from the carriage, hit his head, and died some hours later. He said his name was Sobha Ram. He felt he was an adult, said he was married with children.

The news of Jasbir's remarkable behavior becomes well known in the village. A woman who was born in Rasulpur, but married in Vehedi, is recognized by Jasbir when she comes to visit in 1957, her previous visit had not been later than 1952.

The woman tells her family in Vehedi about this. It appears that Jasbir's facts about "his" death and the other relationships correspond exactly with the known facts of a certain Sobha Ram, son of Shankar Lil Tyagi, in Vehedi. He died aged twenty-two in May 1954, about the same time as Jasbir's illness. [Information regarding the dates of Jasbir's illness could not be ascertained, since no one had noted it down.] Sobha Ram's family comes to visit Rasulpur. Jasbir recognizes them and announces each of their true relationships to Sobha Ram. Later Jasbir is able to travel to Vehedi, where he is put down at the railroad station and shown the way to Tyagi's home. He finds it without difficulty and reveals detailed knowledge of the Tyagi family and their life. He thrives in Vehedi and returns to Rasulpur most reluctantly. He visits Vehedi several times, identifying himself very strongly with the Tyagi family, and would prefer to live with them than with his own parents. In Rasulpur he is lonely and isolated, virtually rejected by the other children.

Stevenson investigated the case in 1961 and 1964, visited both villages, and interviewed all the relevant people. He gathered thirty-nine facts which Jasbir had mentioned of Sobha Ram's life before he went to Vehedi. These were verified with one exception: there was no proof, but ample suspicion, that Sobha Ram had been poisoned. Jasbir even named the alleged murderer.

The Case of Imad Elawar

A two-year-old boy and his grandmother are walking down the street in the village of Kornayel in Lebanon. A completely unknown man comes toward them. The boy suddenly rushes over to the man and hugs him. "Do you know me?" the man asks, astonished, and the boy answers, "Yes, you were my neighbor."

The boy is Imad Elawar, born in December 1958. As soon as he could talk, he made strange allegations. He states he has lived before and mentions events and people in that earlier life. The first words he said most often and distinctly are "Jamile" and "Mahmoud," two names which do not exist in his own family. He mentions Jamile especially often and compares her beauty with his mother's more modest appearance. He tells of an accident in which a truck runs over a man, crushing both his legs; the man dies immediately thereafter. Imad maintains that he belongs to a family called Bouhamzy in Khriby, a village situated a good thirty kilometers from Kronayel, linked with it by a single poor mountain road without regular traffic. He nags his parents to let him go to Khriby. Little Imad also expresses unusual joy at being allowed to go. He repeats over and over how happy he is that now he can go there.

Imad's family belong to the Druse, an Islamic sect whose members now live in Lebanon, Syria, and some villages in Israel. Belief in reincarnation is part of their religion. Imad's parents do not find it difficult to understand what the boy means. But his father doesn't like that kind of talk and scolds Imad for his "lies." Imad stops talking to his father about these things but continues to tell his mother and his paternal grandparents. He also seems to talk in his sleep about his "memories." The man who had been run over on the street had really lived in Khriby, and that even caused Imad's father to start wondering and puzzling over it. But the parents themselves do nothing positive to verify this information. Imad names several people he knew in his former life, and his parents try to connect them with names in a family. But then it is later revealed that Imad didn't mean that the accident had killed him, he merely described it very vividly. Nor had he said that Jamile really was his wife, he had just talked about her very often. Imad's father visits Khriby for the first time in December 1963, when Imad is five years old and has been talking about his "former" life for more than three years. But during this visit his father does not come into contact with any members of the Bouhamzy family in Khriby.

In 1962, Stevenson met a young Lebanese in Brazil who told him that in his hometown of Kornayel there were several children who said that they remembered earlier lives. He gave Stevenson a letter in Arabic to his brother in the village, and, this letter his only introduction, Stevenson arrived in Kornayel on March 16, 1964. He found that the person to whom the letter had been addressed had moved to Beirut, but when he talked about the purpose of his visit, he heard about Imad. It appeared that the letter was addressed to a cousin of Imad's father. Stevenson was invited to Imad's home, and that same day, in the evening, the parents described (with the help of an interpreter), among other things, Imad's unusual information, mentioned above, and the conclusions they had drawn from it themselves.

Stevenson decided to visit Khriby the following day. He discovered there that a person with the name Imad had mentioned had lived in the village. He also found out that a Said Bouhamzy had died in July 1943, after having been run over by a truck which crushed his legs. He had been operated on but died immediately afterward. But the facts Imad gave did not fit with Said's life, and Imad's description of "his" house did not match Said's.

A member of the Bouhamzy family found that *both* Imad's facts about events *and* descriptions of the house corresponded exactly to the actual situation of one Ibrahim Bouhamzy, cousin and close friend of Said. Ibrahim's house lay only a hundred meters from Said's and he had a very beautiful mistress called Jamile. They lived together but never married, something which had caused a scandal in the village. Jamile had moved from the village after Ibrahim's death. Ibrahim, aged twenty-five, had died of tuberculosis, in September 1949. The last half year of his life he was bedridden and couldn't walk, which he often complained bitterly about. He was a truck driver and had been in at least two driving accidents himself, and his friend Said's death from the accident had affected him deeply. An uncle of Ibrahim was called Mamoud, and the other names which Imad had produced were also found in Ibrahim's family. The man from Khriby whom Imad had embraced on the street had been Ibrahim's neighbor.

On March 19, Imad, his father, and Stevenson returned to Khriby and visited the house where Ibrahim had lived. Imad proved to know the interior of the house and could answer questions about the fittings and fixtures as they had been at the time of Ibrahim's death. The house had been locked up for several years and was opened specially for the visit. Imad's knowledge could therefore not have been produced from inspection from outside but only by some-one who knew the interior of the house.

Before the first visit to Khriby, Stevenson had noted down forty-seven different facts given by Imad pertaining to his "former" life. Of these statements, concerning facts and situations in Ibrahim's life, forty-four were verified as absolutely correct. During the automobile drive to Khriby, an additional ten facts were noted, of which seven were completely correct. The remaining three were produced by Imad in the heat and excitement of the moment (he had, after all, been nagging his parents for years to let him go to Khriby), mixed in with memories from his present life, perhaps under the impression that the guest expected more of him. During the visit to Khriby, Imad produced another sixteen facts about Ibrahim's life and house, of which fourteen were totally correct. Of the accurate information, several involved highly personal matters; Imad repeated, for ex-ample, the last words Ibrahim had said in his deathbed.

There was, moreover, remarkable conformity in personality characteristics between Imad and Ibrahim, as described by Imad's parents and Ibrahim's surviving family. Imad had correctly stated that Ibrahim owned two rifles, one of which was double-barreled, and he also showed where Ibrahim had hidden one of them in the house. Ibrahim was a very enthusiastic hunter, and Imad's interest in hunting was remarkable for a five year old. Ibrahim had served in the French army and spoke French very well. Imad was very advanced in

French for his age, which no one else in his family spoke. He learned it very quickly in school and corrected his elder sister. Imad, like Ibrahim, had a fiery temperament and got into arguments very easily. Finally, until he was four or five years old, Imad had pronounced fear of trucks and buses.

Fraud, ESP, Reincarnation?

Here we have seen a short summary of the broad facts in two of the cases which Stevenson describes and discusses in detail in his book *Twenty Cases Suggestive of Reincarnation* [8]. The account of Imad's case alone takes up forty-eight pages.

It would be absurd to explain these and all similar phenomena as simply involving coincidence, for the agreement of facts is too consistent and too complex. The parents might be suspected of perpetrating a hoax. This would involve their teaching the boy such facts as could be verified later. In the case of Jasbir they would have had to force him to refuse to eat their own food, or spread false reports to that effect, while instead, all indications are that Jasbir's father had actually tried to keep the whole matter secret as long as possible, because he was ashamed of Jasbir's behavior. A hoax in both cases would also necessitate an extensive connection, with more than twenty people involved, between two villages where very poor communications existed. A hoax for what purpose? Jasbir's family faced only difficulties and problems and sorrow as a result of his behavior. Nor did Imad's family receive any benefit from his case, if you leave aside the attention which Stevenson gave them. But he appeared on the scene completely unexpectedly and unannounced; he didn't even know about the case in advance. At least in Imad's case we can also rule out completely the usual explanation that we could have misconstrued the child's facts and then, consciously or unconsciously, arranged them to fit the verification. Here Stevenson himself could actually note down the facts before any verification was made. It was also proved that the parents' own interpretation of Imad's facts did not correspond at all to the verification. They had pictured Imad in his former life as a respectable father of a family, and then found out that instead he had been a rowdy fellow and a lady-chaser of dubious repute. The hoax hypothesis is very poorly founded in both cases.

But then, could the children in some normal way have received information about these other people's lives, and then forgotten it until it was recalled in a personified form, that is, as *cryptomnesia?* But Imad began to talk about a former life as soon as he could talk at all, and before that, the child had usually (as was always the case in Imad's milieu) not been out of sight of some family member. With this we return to the fraud hypothesis. And in Rasulpur it appeared that no one knew anything of Sobha Ram's life before Jasbir started talking about it. Cryptomnesia can be considered as an explanation in many cases of adult memory indicating reincarnation, but in these particular cases it would appear that the hypothesis could be ruled out. It seems certain that Imad's knowledge of Ibrahim's life, and Jasbir's of Sobha Ram's were acquired paranormally.

But then could it have been a question of ESP? Thus Imad, through telepathy, clairvoyance, or retrocognition, would have received knowledge of events in another place ten years before his birth, and lived in it so that it was experienced in a personified way. Jasbir similarly would have had to receive knowledge of events in Vehedi before his illness. But children with such memories very seldom demonstrate any indication of ESP when it involves facts other than those which are "clipped out" from the alleged former life. Imad knew nothing about the life in Khriby *after* Ibrahim's death, and Jasbir showed no indication of ESP. Their only "abnormality" was that certain pictures and events connected with alleged former lives stood out in their consciousnesses. They clearly experienced these pictures and events in the same way they and others experience memories from their present lives. Like "normal" memories, they can be released into consciousness by certain exterior events which give "resonance." The hypotheses of hoax, cryptomnesia, or ESP cannot totally explain the very strong emotional reactions which often appear when the child meets members of his "former" family; reactions and sympathies which may be so strong that they cause a crisis in the child's present family. We could maintain that Jasbir's memories of an earlier life were wishful dreams for a better life. When he visited Vehedi the wish-fulfillment dreams were realized. But this hypothesis really does not explain his paranormal knowledge of Sobha Ram's life. Furthermore, his "wish dreams" led him to become almost an outcast among his contemporaries in Rasulpur, and his life as a whole was scarcely happier as a result of his memories.

Stevenson emphasizes that, broadly speaking, these children developed completely normally and showed no greater indications of psychic disturbance than any other children. The only distinguishing feature was their memories of an earlier existence.

Cases of Jasbir's type are very seldom reported. They represent what could be called possession with a sudden and profound personality change and a strong identification with the deceased person. Similar cases have been described, however, even in adults [4]. In Imad's case, as in the majority of cases indicating reincarnation, the present person develops normally in spite of the fact that he carries memories which he associates with an earlier existence. As a rule, the detailed memories begin to fade away when the child reaches school age, but the strong emotional bond with the former family may last for a long while.

Stevenson has now collected about one thousand cases indicating reincarnation. The majority were assembled during the sixties, and have gradually been investigated thoroughly [18]. The most remarkable are those in which the present person's body has a unique, specially formed birthmark which in position and appearance correspond to a remembered scar, the result of an injury, which the former person received in connection with his death.

There have been attempts to explain cases of reincarnation by the theory of super-ESP together with personification [9, 10]. But support for the theory of super-ESP is weak [11], and in no case does it explain the birthmarks. Another proposed theory is that the former person felt a strong desire for his feelings and thoughts to live after his death. This would then cause a powerful "telepathic transmission," which, after an interval of up to ten years—but time is a relative factor in paranormal contexts—is then taken up by someone available, a child organism not "stamped" or impressed by a distinct personality, and then, through personification, this gives rise to a "divided personality" strongly identified with the former personality [12]. According to this theory, the former personality would have been the active agent and the present person only the passive receiver. But this hypothesis again does not explain the unique birthmarks.

But there is a hypothesis which explains all aspects of these cases, without contradictions. We may call this the reincarnation hypothesis. This means that in Imad's case, Ibrahim Bouhamzy's death did not involve his total annihilation. His consciousness and personality, or some aspect of them which we cannot yet identify but which could be called the psi-component, survived the death of the body and continued to exist on some other plane of existence. The interests and inclinations, the main personality characteristics which he had developed during his earthly life, were preserved in some way in this psi-component, which could be thought of like a wave or energy beam which cannot be picked up or registered by any measuring device to date. When the time was ready, in this case after about ten earthly years, contact was established between the psi-component and the fertilized egg cell that would divide and grow into Imad Elawar's body. This means that certain hereditary traits influence the whole course of his future development. By some form of resonance, contact was achieved with this one egg cell and not any other, this one answering the requirements of this particular psi-component more precisely. This psi-component, which formerly had come to be seen as Ibrahim Bouhamzy, on an earlier plane, now presents itself as Imad Elawar, a new personality with a new potential for development, but with a link of association, a bond backward in time, in the form of memories.

In the case of Jasbir, the way the mechanism operated would be apparently different, rather a form of accident or misfortune, unlike the "normal" process of this psi-component hypothesis. Here, an already developed body, not an egg cell or a developing foetus, is involved. No one knows whether Jasbir was actually dead during his illness, whether his heart stopped and his body was therefore "free" or "vacant," or if his earlier personality in some way was forced out while the body lay unconscious. It is also possible that the "change" of personality happened over a long space of time, during the weeks which passed before he could talk clearly once again.

Children with memories like Jasbir's and Imad's give similar kinds of information in regard to their former life, information which can in many cases be verified in detail. They say that they were a person who died young, usually in painful or dramatic circumstances. The interval between death and birth is seldom more than ten years. Cases in which a child announces that he was a person who died in old age have been very rare for many years. Perhaps one prerequisite for memories of a former life coming into consciousness is that they must be intensely imprinted, as memories of death would be if death happened in painful or dramatic circumstances. A bodily injury involving death would then give an especially strong impression and would later be expressed as a birthmark on the present person. Moreover, if the interval between death and birth is short, then the possibility exists that events in the new life can, in certain cases, rouse the memories to consciousness through the process of resonance. Perhaps what is abnormal is not the fact of being born again but rather the ability to remember the former life.

As an argument against the concept of reincarnation, it is sometimes said that when people maintain that they remember a former life, it is always that of someone great and famous—many can say that they have been a Roman emperor, but no one remembers the slave who whispered in his ear. But this statement does not correspond with the facts. The examples cited are typical of such memories, and in none of them do the memories involve anyone famous. On the contrary, in many cases indicating reincarnation, the former person cannot even be identified at all. Of course, the reason could be that he never existed, but it could also be due to the scanty and uncertain information known about him. In the vast majority of cases which can be verified, the memories involve a person whose life was known to only a small group of people: his relatives, friends, and colleagues at work.

It is more difficult to investigate cases in which the alleged memories involve an earlier life as a historically well-known person. Then the researcher faces a dilemma: either the memories cannot be verified, that is, they do not fit known facts and, therefore, are not genuine; or else the memories can be verified, indicating that they agree with what is known about the person, usually from written documents. But then the possibility exists that the person who says he remembers could have received knowledge of these written facts in a completely normal way or through ESP. Consequently nothing definite could be said about the origin of the memories in this case either. Perhaps facts about the person are not all collected in one place but must be combined from many different sources. Perhaps essential information exists in family archives which no outsider would have access to normally. In such a case, the memories would suggest the reincarnation hypothesis more emphatically, just as "drop-in communicators" indicate the spirit hypothesis. On the other hand, if the alleged memories involve a Napoleon or a Walt Whitman, then the problems of pursuing a thorough investigation are virtually insurmountable. If reincarnation does occur, someone alive now could, of course, conceivably be the reincarnation of either of these men and might recall something from one of their lives—but he who experiences such memories behaves wisely if he keeps it to himself.

Suggestion, Hallucination, and Déjà Vu

According to some critics of parapsychology, all so-called paranormal phenomena depend on various combinations of suggestion, auto-suggestion, hypnosis, hallucinations, déjà vu, fraud, or self-deceit.

This viewpoint might well be commented on at this point in our study [13].

Déjà vu is sometimes mentioned as an explanation in cases which may indicate reincarnation. An imaginary example to illustrate the concept: I come with a friend for the first time to a little town in a country I have never visited before. While we walk down the street I suddenly have a powerful feeling that I have seen the street before and *have already experienced the whole situation and events that are taking place at the moment.* This experience is known by the French words déjà vu ("already seen"). It is a rather common phenomenon which may be experienced during certain illnesses as well as by healthy people, especially if they are very tired. Déjà vu is therefore not a diffused memory of having experienced something earlier, nor is it a feeling that "I am experiencing what I believe is a memory." Déjà vu is a sudden, abrupt feeling or certainty *that the situation which I am experiencing right at this very moment was experienced earlier.* This feeling has, strictly speaking, no proper bearing on parapsychology, except possibly in connection with dreams such as the one in Case 19.

Now imagine instead that I think I have a memory of having been in the town before, and that I tell my friend what we will see when we turn the corner of the curving street, that I describe the way to a certain house which I can also describe in detail both inside and out. We walk down in that direction and arrive at the house. It turns out that my description corresponds somewhat, but certain details are inaccurate. We ask someone who lives there, and with the help of old pictures, he can confirm that many years ago the house looked exactly as I described it. This is the sort of possible paranormal knowledge we are looking for when investigating conceivable cases of reincarnation; compare Cases 18 and 51.

"*Concerning the phenomenon of reincarnation in India it must be pointed out clearly that starvation in India possibly may increase the occurrence of both hallucinations and the déjà vu phenomenon.*" Still, the case of Imad was not a question of either déjà vu or hallucinations but of what appears to be paranormal knowledge of incidents in the deceased's life, facts first noted down and later verified. Perhaps some people might rather wish to assert that Imad had spoken and Stevenson hypnotized all of Ibrahim's relatives to give answers which would agree with Imad's information.

Apparitions can also be thought to be explained as déjà vu to some extent by the assertion: *Those who receive the news of the death of a close relative may naturally be shocked by it, which causes*

*a déjà vu phenomenon, a sense that they have already had a vision
of the deceased."* But, for example, Hart's investigations of apparitions were built only on cases in which the vision had been talked
about *before* the news of the possible instance of death came.

Through suggestion, possibly under hypnosis, hallucinations may
be produced. But the fact that an experience can be designated as a
hallucination does not mean that it cannot provide knowledge of
events in some other locale in what seems to be a paranormal way.
During a complete ESP-projection, we can certainly say that the
projector and the percipient each experience his own hallucination—
but that does not explain how they can receive knowledge about what
the other is doing through their hallucinations.

*"If a person experiences something 'supernatural,' is it not more
plausible to assume that this experiencing mechanism has become disordered through suggestion or hypnosis—something that we know
may occur—rather than to decide that our common, ordinary perception of nature must be altered drastically on the basis of this 'supernatural' experience?"* Yes, if only one or a small number of people
had experienced something "supernatural," then there would be no
parapsychology to discuss. But the field exists because through the
ages a great many people have had "supernatural" experiences which
have not been completely formless or unstructured, but on the contrary, seem to indicate intelligent conformity to some laws and connection with other conditions and circumstances in nature.

Of course, an account of, for example, separation or memory
indicating an earlier life may be lightly dismissed by saying that "the
experiencing mechanism has become disordered." But then you also
deprive yourself of the possibility of investigating the condition more
closely and of perhaps learning something from it. Perhaps the experiencing mechanism has not merely got out of order but also
changed so as to admit experiences of commonly unknown but nevertheless existent aspects of reality? It could simply be thought that our
ordinary perception of nature is not complete but rather, gradually,
must be drastically altered, among other things, on the basis of the
material which parapsychology studies.

Hypnosis and Reincarnation

A conceivable way to learn about possible earlier lives is to visit a
medium who believes she can tell who another person has been (as

in Case 3). But it is obvious that this information has no value as proof if it cannot be verified, no matter how strongly the person "feels" that the medium is telling the truth. Often this feeling can, of course, stem from the medium's unconscious perception of the person's wishful thinking. The fact that several mediums, independent of each other, give similar information, has no greater value as proof. The first medium's information becomes incorporated in the listener's consciousness and memory, and thus may be accessible to later mediums.

Sometimes sensational cases are described in which someone has been led back to a "former life" through hypnotic suggestion. Such experiments are easy to make with any subject who can achieve sufficiently deep hypnosis [14]. The person describes a life as another person with great intensity and may even speak in a different, foreign language. But later, when the material is analyzed, it is discovered as a rule that the new personality is nothing more than a persona from the unconscious, eagerly created to satisfy the curiosity of the hypnotist. But paranormal information may be produced, and also, in a few isolated cases, material has resulted which actually does indicate memories of former lives. The case of Bridey Murphy has been actively and hotly debated [15]. Most, but not all, the information which that case has produced could be explained normally [16].

If the subjects in such hypnosis experiments have already had earlier spontaneous experiences which do indicate reincarnation, as in Cases 46 through 51, then the situation appears different, to some degree [17]. For then, from the start, some material exists which has not been produced by the wishes of the hypnotist, and therefore it is more likely that additional material might be forthcoming that perhaps could be verified later. This is particularly true of children and young people. Those who have diffused memories that cannot be associated with their present lives, might be led in this way to remember in more detail, for we may assume that their memories lie more "superficially," less deeply imprinted, than is the case with adults. Another question remains: is it desirable to release such possible memories? The individual's psychic stability and personal wishes must be determined and considered.

Survival after death can be thought of as taking several forms; reincarnation is only one. It could be thought to happen to everyone or only in certain cases to certain people. The fact that one person might survive beyond death does not necessarily imply that the same person will be reborn. The opposite however is certain: if a person has been reborn, then he has survived death. The crux of the matter is therefore to confirm the identity shared by the past and the present individuals, the continuing personality. "A person" may be defined in several ways. One way is to say that a person (or a personality) is his history and his memories: what distinguishes one person from another is the experiencing of different events and the linking of different memory chains. But memories and the information they give are only one aspect of the cases of reincarnation, others are a feeling of identity with the former personality and the resulting emotionally laden connection with that person's milieu and family. Unique birthmarks are a further aspect. An "ideal" case would contain all these aspects to such a degree that the identity shared by the former and present personalities could be firmly established. Such a firm case has yet to be found.

One single white crow would be proof enough for the assertion that white crows do exist. But no single "ideal" case indicating reincarnation would offer sufficient proof that it occurs, though it would make it highly plausible that it had occurred in just that one instance. But if the cases of what appear to be paranormal knowledge implying an earlier life are something more than coincidence, if they have a common denominator, then we can anticipate that eventually other similar cases will be found, provided that outward conditions do not change to complicate or obstruct the reporting of cases. And in fact, the collections of testimonies are accumulating steadily. The best-studied cases to date are solid witnesses to the existence of paranormal knowledge. In my opinion they also point strongly to the hypothesis of survival beyond death.

14

Speaking Unknown Languages: Xenoglossy

We do not believe everything. But we believe that everything must be investigated. LOUIS PAUWELS AND JACQUES BERGIER

An eighteen-year-old student in Stavanger, Norway, Ingebjørg Ekkersen, was severely injured in an automobile accident some years ago. She lay unconscious for a long time. . . . When she regained consciousness, she did not remember anyone in her family and didn't understand a word of Norwegian. A Finn who lived in the same district recognized the language the girl was speaking—it was Russian! But Ingebjørg didn't know any Russian and had never been to Russia.

It was through an interpreter that Ingebjørg explained to her family that her name was Nina Tashowitz, that she lived in St. Petersburg (Leningrad), and that she was born on March 17, 1897.

The doctors had their own explanation: Ingebjørg's brain had been injured and the poor girl had gone slightly crazy. They couldn't explain how a person who did not know Russian could suddenly speak the language, but they obviously implied that they believed she had known Russian before the accident occurred.

A journalist heard about this and thought it might be a case of reincarnation. . . . He traveled to Leningrad to look through the church registers. He found, to his astonishment, that Nina T. really had been born on the date stated by Ingebjørg and that she had died in 1916. He also succeeded in digging up two surviving sisters, one of whom had a photo of Nina at eighteen. When Ingebjørg was shown the photo, she cried out, "That is I!"

When I read about this highly interesting case, which seemed to have been forgotten, I immediately asked a Norwegian friend to find out more about it [1]. Later, it appeared that Dr. Stevenson had investigated the case several years earlier and discovered that it was completely fabricated. It had been published in a German periodical by a gentleman who seems to have been moved to invent cases of reincarnation [2]. Some cases are obviously too good to be genuine.

Xenoglossy

The above-mentioned case is an example of something every investigator of alleged paranormal phenomena meets with occasionally, namely, hoaxes and lies. But we may also admit the possibility of the phenomenon called *xenoglossy*. This term indicates the ability to express oneself in a language which one does not normally have any knowledge of. If the case of I. E. had been one of xenoglossy, if it had been genuine, it would mean that she had talked Russian, when she normally could only understand Norwegian.

Xenoglossy is not a completely unheard of phenomenon. It can be produced rather easily under hypnosis. A deeply hypnotized person may be given the suggestion that he is another person in another country, or that he will return to an earlier life. Then, in successful instances, he may talk or write in a foreign language. As a rule, this proves to be a language which he had had a remote contact with much earlier, or perhaps it is impossible to identify the language at all. In these cases, it would technically not be called xenoglossy, for this term implies that the language which is spoken really exists, or at least is known to have existed.

A Forgotten Experience: Cryptomnesia

A patient under hypnosis begins to talk a language which the doctors do not understand. He is asked to write, and jots down three lines which are completely incomprehensible, even to himself. Later investigation proves that they were written in a language which was talked in Italy around A.D. 200. But the patient in a waking state had not the remotest comprehension of antique Italian. How then could he have written these three lines?

By a special technique of questioning, one can cause him to recall an earlier experience. One day he sat in a library trying to study for an examination. But his mind wandered, preoccupied. Instead of concentrating on his books, he thought about his girlfriend, who had just agreed to meet him. His glance wandered from the book he should have been reading to another book, which happened to be lying open on the table and presumably belonged to another student. It was a grammar book of a certain ancient language. On the open page was printed a curse of Vibia, a name which reminded him of his girlfriend's nickname. Without actually being aware of it, he "photographed" the printed strophes he later reproduced under hypnosis word for word. This is a beautiful example of *cryptomnesia,* a "forgotten memory." Moreover, the patient was completely honest when he denied knowing anything about the language—the experience had, in fact, never reached his consciousness. It does not matter how long the time span is between the experience and the hypnosis; it may very easily be several years [3].

Responsive Xenoglossy

Cryptomnesia is a conceivable explanation for many psychic phenomena. But all cases of xenoglossy cannot be explained so simply, especially when they involve *responsive xenoglossy.* This refers to occasions in which the person, the patient in our example above, can not only mechanically repeat a few words or sentences in a foreign language but can also use the language actively, that is, hold a conversation and give adequate answers to questions. Such knowledge of a foreign language, for example, of Spanish if you are Swedish, comes only from learning it, either by studying it in a course or by traveling, staying in a Spanish-speaking country. You cannot acquire it simply by having happened to look at one page in a Spanish grammar or by hearing Spanish on one occasion or by listening to someone who often recites Spanish poetry. If a person reveals such knowledge of a foreign language as could be called responsive xenoglossy, and he proves never to have learned or heard more than a few words or phrases of it in his present life, then there is good reason for us to suspect a paranormal background for xenoglossy.

The Case of Rosemary

The best-known example of responsive xenoglossy is the case of "Rosemary [4]." An Englishman, Dr. Wood, was acquainted with a young woman whom he referred to by the pseudonym Rosemary. In 1927 she had started automatic writing spontaneously. She didn't like doing this and turned to Dr. Wood for advice, since she knew that he was interested in parapsychology; she herself did not share that interest initially. Wood began holding seances, with Rosemary as a medium. During a seance in 1928, a communicator appeared who called herself "Nona" and said she had been a woman who lived in Egypt under Pharaoh Amenhotep III, that is, *ca.* 3,300 years ago. Nona said she communicated her thoughts telepathically to Rosemary, who then formulated them into English, verbally or on paper. But Nona also began to express herself directly in her "mother tongue," ancient Egyptian. According to her own statement, Rosemary "heard" words clairvoyantly and repeated them aloud. The seances were, of course, held long before the invention of tape recorders, and Wood wrote down the words in a phonetic transcription as best he could.

During the seances, which were held over several years, Nona expressed about five thousand words and phrases in ancient Egyptian through Rosemary. From Wood's phonetic transcription of the first eight hundred phrases, an Egyptologist, Hulme, could identify and translate the words. He found that the phrases were expressed with real continuity and intelligent thought, and that they were adequately related to what was under discussion at that moment in the conversation. To be able to reply to criticism from other Egyptologists, Wood subsequently began to study ancient Egyptian and was gradually able to translate the phonetic transcriptions himself, which he had only written down before without understanding.

The Egyptian hieroglyphs represent only consonants. There is, therefore, no way definitely to prove or disprove whether the vowels Rosemary enunciated were actually those used by the ancient Egyptians. But the theory that they were genuine is supported by the fact that they were used consistently in thousands of phrases and that Rosemary's language in all essentials was correct compared with what is known about consonants and grammar of the ancient language.

Nona maintained that Rosemary was a reincarnation of "Vola," a contemporary and friend of Nona. Rosemary described individual "memories" of her life as Vola in Egypt during the many seances. But the majority of these "memories" were of such a nature that they could neither be confirmed nor rejected. Responsive xenoglossy is the essential feature in the case of Rosemary.

A medium can sometimes be questioned in an unknown (to the medium) language during a seance and will give adequate answers in her own mother tongue. A conceivable explanation is that the medium picks up the desired answer telepathically. Such experiments fail if the questioner does not understand the language the question is asked in [5]. But in the case of Rosemary, the roles were reversed: Wood asked in English and Rosemary answered in a language completely unknown (at least in the beginning) to both of them. We will return later to the question of how this case could be explained.

The Case of Jensen

A case of responsive xenoglossy especially interesting to Scandinavians has been investigated by Stevenson [6]. Because it has yet to be published, I will give only a very brief summary of it here.

In an American family, which we will call A, both the husband and the wife were interested in spiritualism, and they were in the habit of holding seances with several friends. Mr. A hypnotized different people who then functioned as mediums. Now he wanted to try to summon the memory of an earlier life from Mrs. A under hypnosis. She was a good subject for hypnosis and responded easily to his suggestions. During one seance, she produced a male communicator who called himself "Jensen." Mrs. A identified herself with him; she therefore referred to Jensen as "I." But Jensen said some words in a language no one present could understand. The seances were recorded on tapes, and it was later confirmed that the language Jensen spoke was Swedish.

Jensen appeared in a total of eight seances, but during the first five, no Swedish was spoken except for isolated words. During the last three seances Swedish-speaking people were present, and most of the material came from these seances. Questions were asked in Swedish, and Jensen could answer in Swedish. Usually his answers were very laconic; sometimes he only repeated the question. But most often the answer was adequate for the question, and Jensen himself introduced Swedish words that none of the questioners had used. His active Swedish vocabulary was, nevertheless, limited to a few hundred words. The questioning was done by different people and, unfortunately, not very systematically. (Possibly more material would have been produced had the questioning techniques been better.)

After the hypnosis, Mrs. A had no recall of the contents of the seances or of Jensen. But then once, when she lay down to rest after a seance, she sank back into a spontaneous trance state and Jensen appeared again. Mr. A became frightened that Jensen would continue to come unbidden and "possess" his wife. Therefore the seances were stopped and Jensen did not return. These events took place about ten years ago.

Stevenson made a very scrupulous survey of Mrs. A's whole life. He considers that he can rule out the possibility that she had ever had sufficient contact with Scandinavian people in her present life to be able to talk as much Swedish as Jensen.

As of the date of this book, the analysis of Jensen's language has not been published. But it is noteworthy that Jensen speaks a mixture of Swedish and Norwegian, and also adds a few Danish words. But he is not at home in the present era. He lacks words for present conditions and new objects, while, on the other hand, revealing a striking knowledge of objects from the seventeenth century which were borrowed from a museum and shown to him. He talked about a certain "Hansen," who was his "right hand man." He had been up in the mountains and knew someone called "the Oslo man." He hated war and was afraid of the Russians. He lived near a place which he called "Häverö." But information about the time and place was too imprecise to pin down with any certainty where Jensen might have lived, and it could only be determined that he most probably lived during the seventeenth century.

How Can Responsive Xenoglossy Be Explained?

How can cases like that of Rosemary and Jensen be explained? In principle, the same possibilities would apply to them both: we will proceed with the case of Jensen.

If Mrs. A did not learn Swedish normally, and Jensen's language therefore did not originate with her, where did it come from? It is improbable that she could have picked up his language telepathically from someone now living, since there was an old-fashioned style to Jensen's language and he lacked words for common modern occurrences and objects.

Jensen could have been a split personality which Mrs. A fantasized or produced completely unconsciously. But that assumption does not explain his ability to talk a language unknown to Mrs. A.

By retrocognition, Mrs. A could have known Swedish words which someone in the seventeenth century had expressed. But that too would not explain her ability to use the language actively. It is completely unheard of for anyone to learn a language telepathically, clairvoyantly, or through retrocognition. Through ESP one can receive knowledge of matters and events in past, present, and future time. But no experiences are known which indicate that a person has ever acquired a skill through ESP—and the ability to speak a language is precisely such an acquired skill.

But if Jensen's language awareness cannot be explained as cryptomnesia, or as a talent existing in a split personality within Mrs. A, or as ESP, then we must consider a hypothesis which involves some form of survival after death, that is, (a) reincarnation or (b) possession.

(a) This hypothesis implies that Mrs. A, in an earlier life, probably in the seventeenth century, was a man called Jensen. Under hypnosis she was in some way put into contact with her memories from that time. But her contact with these memories was incomplete —perhaps comparable to when you try to understand words spoken on a very old and worn 78-rpm record—and therefore the language became imperfect, defective. In large collections of alleged memories of former lives, changes of sex between the two lives are said to occur in about 10 percent of the cases. That Jensen and Mrs. A are of different sexes is therefore consistent with what one knows from other alleged cases of reincarnation.

(b) This hypothesis involves Jensen being a "drop-in communicator" who came unbidden to the medium, Mrs. A, during the seances and temporarily possessed her. According to this hypothesis, fragments of memories from Jensen's own life were then communicated.

So far we have not referred to a concept which is sometimes brought up in connection with retrocognition and cases indicating reincarnation. In different doctrines, a "cosmic reservoir of memories" is mentioned, sometimes called the Chronicle of Akasha [7]. In this, the "memory" of all events is said to be stored and available to someone who is able to attain the necessary level of consciousness. Thus, in cases like those of Rosemary and Jensen, the medium would be said to have in some way made contact with a certain person's memory out of this reservoir, and then by personification experienced it as his own. The same explanation would fit all cases of memory implying earlier lives, and the cases, thus, need not indicate survival. But doctrines which include the Chronicle of Akasha assume as fundamental that both survival after death and reincarnation do exist. It is also said that contact with the Chronicle of Akasha, as a rule, cannot be achieved until after death. The cosmic reservoir is therefore no argument against survival.

The hypothesis of survival can be made more or less credible by examining experiences people have in the earthly existence we all share now. The conception of a cosmic reservoir is, on the other hand, more a matter of faith and cannot be discussed in the same way, and therefore we need not refer to it further.

A related theory is that *genetic memory* could explain these cases. This assumes that a person's experience in life is stamped in some way into the genetic code and thus passed on to his descendants, producing "memories" which were actually experienced by ancestors. This hypothesis goes far beyond what research into heredity considers remotely possible. Even if this would support some other material, it would only explain a small minority of cases indicating reincarnation, namely, those in which the present person is a direct descendant of the former personality. Cases like Jasbir and Imad, in which no relationship exists, cannot be explained by genetic memory.

It would be interesting now, ten years later, to make new experiments to contact Jensen. But the family A refuse to allow this, for easily understandable reasons, and therefore the puzzle of Jensen will never be completely solved as long as hypothesis (b) is not true and Jensen does not return in the future through another medium. The material in the cases of Rosemary and Jensen are scarcely sufficient to make a definite choice between the hypotheses of possession and reincarnation.

The cases of Rosemary and Jensen do, however, point strongly to some form of survival of the dead. A "something" which can use a language to exchange meaningful communication can, according to our present knowledge, scarcely be called anything other than a personality: talking robots and computers are still not yet possible. If we can rule out the possibility that the talking personality is identical with the medium's personality in her present life, or with the personality of any other living person (which can probably be done in both these cases), then the only possible remaining alternative is that the personality belongs to someone else—someone who has survived beyond death.

We have now surveyed the experimental results of parapsychology and some groups of experiences and impressions which have bearing upon the question of consciousness and death. Many details have been mentioned. The rest of the book attempts to integrate these details into an overall view and thus achieve a synthesis. In Part Four we will first discuss the connection between paranormal phenomena and altered states of consciousness.

Part Four

AN ATTEMPT
AT EXPLANATION

15

Altered States of Consciousness and ESP

It is self-evident that a very great part of our mental activity—yes, for most of us the predominant part—is in one way or another connected with the material world, but our inner conscious reality, however, extends over other, infinite areas, and sooner or later it is here that we must look for the real basis of our perception. CARL HØEGH

What is ESP actually? Under what conditions does it function best? Could anyone learn to produce it at will? Do paranormal phenomena fit into our world picture? Is it really conceivable that some aspect of an individual's personality can survive beyond death, and if that is the case, which? These are only some of the questions raised by the preceding chapters. In this section, we will consider some of these questions more closely and look at the answers which people have tried to give. Many hypotheses have been put forth, here only a few will be mentioned.

We may begin by asking under what conditions ESP functions best. Here we have the experiences drawn both from experiments and from studies of spontaneous cases. As the preceding pages have indicated, ESP is something more than just a "sense" functioning basically the same way as sight or hearing. The definition "the sixth sense" is therefore completely misleading. We have seen that there is a connection between personality and the ability to demonstrate ESP in experiments. But the situation, the environment and atmosphere in the laboratory are also important. In a relaxed, friendly atmosphere (which need not necessarily rule out strict scientific procedure), the chances are best for getting positive results. The more skeptical or hostile the attitude of the subjects or the researcher, the less likely the chances are for demonstrating ESP. The same holds true for experiments with mediums: a hostile investigator can anticipate less paranormal material, and chances are increased that the medium, consciously or unconsciously, resorts to sensory cues or even fraud to satisfy the investigator. But the more a medium makes a conscious effort to produce paranormal information, the worse will be the results.

Altered States of Consciousness

This leads us to the question of certain states of consciousness which are particularly conducive to the demonstration of ESP or paranormal experiences. Figure 4 summarizes some states of consciousness which will now be described; several others also exist. Flowing transitions occur between many of these states, difficult to define precisely, as is also the case between the broader groups of states. Since some of these states are not as commonly known as others, a brief survey may be helpful here [1, 2]:

1. *Normal daytime consciousness* is the usual state, identified by goal-oriented activity, logical cause-and-effect thinking, and by the feeling that one is in control of one's mental activity. Thinking is reflective; one is conscious of oneself as experiencing a complexity of impressions, stimuli from the outside world. One's own physical body is included in this world.

States numbered 2 through 12 are distinguished by the fact that experience of stimuli from the outside world is diminished to some degree. States 2 through 9 characteristically produce vivid, lifelike visual imagery despite the fact that the eyes are closed.

2. *Daydreaming* is indicated by quickly changing thoughts which need not be related to outward surroundings. If the eyes are closed, images may still be easily experienced, and EEG may indicate rapid eye movements similar to those of night-time dreams (number 6).

3. *Trance* defines a powerfully increased suggestibility (the tendency to react to suggestions). There is general disagreement as to whether, during a trance state, EEG indicates that alpha waves are present or not [1]. Nevertheless, a trance is not a passive state; the conscious condition remains, but attention is concentrated on a single stimulus. The eyes may be open or closed. Trances may be induced by the suggestion of a hypnotist, but mediums and others can delib-

FIGURE 4

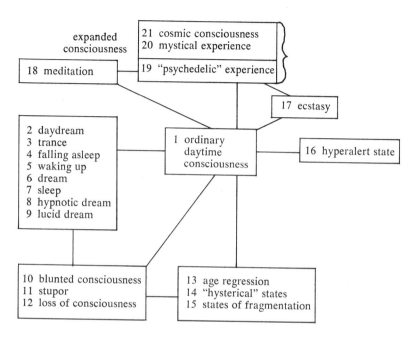

erately induce the state in themselves. It can also be produced by visual or auditory impressions or movements which are repeated in a monotonous way: "brainwashing," certain rituals, rhythmic dance or music. Furthermore, a trance may be induced by activities which demand attention but in which the stimulus varies very subtly, for example, driving on a monotonous road with one's eyes fixed on the median line. If the trance has been deep, a total loss of memory of what happened during the trance may occur. Automatic activity, for example, automatic writing, may be induced easily in a trance. Paranormal experience may occur.

4 and 5. *Hypnagogic* and *hypnopompic* states are transitions between sleep and being fully awake. During both, visual and auditory impressions may be experienced, but mental activity is different from that which is experienced during sleep or dreams. The experience of falling asleep, the hypnagogic state, varies considerably. Some people cannot recall any experiences at all in this state. Others may experience it as a pleasant period which they enjoy prolonging, a state full of lively visual and auditory impressions which can be heightened and intensified to the point of hallucination. In this state, conscious con-

trol of the psychic functions slackens (ego-regression) and the images may become fantastic, bizarre, and symbolic. Hypnagogic states can also occur during the day, unconnected with sleep periods. Paranormal content may appear [1, 3, 4].

6. *Dreaming* can be identified objectively by EEG as the presence of rapid eye movements. Paranormal content may occur.

7. During ordinary, "dreamless" *sleep*, EEG has a distinct pattern different from that which occurs during dreams. If a person is awakened from this state, he will often report a dream, but it will be short, plain, and meager, markedly different from the dream reports which are received from state 6. However, this does indicate that mental activity continues even during regular sleep.

8. An *hypnotic dream* may be induced during a trance through suggestion, and resembles ordinary dreams according to the EEG reading. Paranormal material may occur [1].

9. The *lucid dream,* in which one is conscious of dreaming, may possibly be a distinct state of consciousness [5]. But we do not know yet whether the EEG for this state differs from that of ordinary dreams. It is unclear whether out-of-the-body experiences (separation) represent a distinct state either; as we saw in Chapter 8, separation may occur in several different physiological conditions and circumstances.

The states mentioned so far are all consistent with a normal physiological state without any indications of illness. The following six states appear more often during various conditions of illness. The first three, numbers 10 through 12, are indicated by an increasingly diminished ability to receive outer stimuli. This may be due to medicines and poisons or the phase of an illness, or brain damage, or, as in number 10, also by great stress.

10. *Blunted consciousness,* lethargy: slow, sluggish, phlegmatic mental activity.

11. *Stupor:* strongly diminished ability to react to impressions from the outer world.

12. *Loss of consciousness, coma:* the inability to react to outer stimuli.

13. *Age regression.* A behavior which does not correspond to the individual's physiological age and condition. Can be produced experimentally under hypnosis and may be the result of illness [6].

14. *Hysteric states* are characterized by intense feelings and overwhelming agitation. The state is experienced subjectively as unpleasant and negative. It can be induced by rage, jealousy, envy, panic, fear, violent mass activity (e.g., lynching).

15. *States of fragmentation* are characterized by a loss of connection between the main facets of the total personality. This is expressed as psychosis, severe neurosis, multiple personality, dissociation, loss of memory, periods of dazed bewilderment and confusion. It may be caused by drugs or suggestion under hypnosis, by physical injury, stress, or illness.

16. The *hyperalert state* involves the intensification of mental activity. This occurs, for example, during war and other activities which involve danger to life, and can also be induced by drugs which stimulate the central nervous system.

17. *Rapture states, ecstasy,* related to state 14. Like the hysteric states, these are characterized by intense emotion and overwhelming inner turbulence, but experienced subjectively as pleasant and positive. They can be induced by sexual stimulation, rhythmic dance in quick tempo, various rituals, religious activities (conversion, "salvation").

Rapture may resemble the mystical experience (number 20) but is characterized by a stronger and more uncontrollable "emotional storm" and may leave the individual in a state of bodily exhaustion [7]. While the state is being experienced, the person demonstrates very little possibility of being reached or influenced from the outside. Reports exist of people in ecstatic states who can expose themselves to fire and poisons of various sorts without any indication of the injuries or harm which would normally have been expected [8]. Schwarz studied members of an American sect who commune with poisonous snakes, thrust their hands into flames, and eat strychnine without any resulting injury [9]. Walking through flames and other remarkable behavior is also reported in connection with magic, as was mentioned in Chapter 6. Probably rapture can be induced by certain magical rites.

Here we should also mention the state which is called *inspiration.* Possibly it should be counted as a separate state of consciousness, related to trance and rapture but identical with neither of them. Inspiration is characterized by a precipitous access to usually unconscious psychic material in connection with strong impulses to creative activity. Artists, mathematicians, and inventors can, under inspiration, experience a problem which they have worked over earlier and perhaps abandoned as insoluble, and find the solution is obvious, clear; all the person needs to do is carry out the solution in his working material with his technical skills, whether this involves words or pictures or other notations. Obviously he had continued to work on the problem unconsciously until the solution was reached. Then, later, the solution was presented to his consciousness when circumstances were favorable. In other instances, inspiration may be experienced as a purely automatic activity, which allows the individual to experience himself as the instrument for powers from a source beyond, outside himself. In this state he can produce creations which stand far superior to what could be expected from his "ordinary" personality. Between the inspired poetry in case 42b and Mrs. Curran's automatic authorship (pages 139–140) there is only a difference of degree, of quality. Spiritualist circles easily tend to overrate the result of inspiration. Indeed, they hold that such writing comes from deceased relatives, higher masters, or other beings "on the other side" and the products are therefore sacred to them—not a word or sign must be changed. The artist, on the other hand, limits and refines the results of his inspiration critically in order to further intensify, if possible, the experience which he wishes to convey, and the inventor must make tests to see whether his inspired findings actually work [9].

18. The *meditation* state is clearly distinguished from all the preceding ones. It is the antithesis of trance and the related states 2 through 9, which may involve lively visual experiences. Meditation is a minimal mental activity with an absence of visual impressions, and the state is characterized by EEG readings of continual alpha waves. This may be induced through training in certain methods and is described in more detail on page 224.

Finally, states 19 through 21 could be grouped together under the general definition "expanded consciousness."

19. The *psychedelic* state can be induced by hypnosis [10, 11] or by meditation, but in the West is usually induced by the so-called psychedelic drugs, for example LSD, psilocybin, or mescalin. It may be considered from four aspects [14]:

1. From the *sensory* aspect, the psychedelic state involves an altered experience of time, space, and one's own body, often accompanied by lively experiences of beauty in vivid colors.

2. *Analytically,* it presents the individual with new thoughts and ideas about the world and his role in the world.

3. *Symbolically,* the individual in this state identifies himself easily with other people, ideas, or symbols.

4. *Integration* may appear as a fourth aspect: a religious-mystical experience of wholeness, unity within the totality. This is the most desirable aspect of the psychedelic experience, but it is achieved by only a few among all those who take these drugs.

It is now commonly known that the influence of LSD involves

certain risks. LSD and substances producing similar effects seem, among other things, to weaken the defense mechanisms and "barriers" we all have and which to a certain extent are essential for everyone in order that we can all live together. The result of this weakening may be destructive activity, and, in unfortunate circumstances, behavior which is not only completely foreign to the individual normally, but also vitally dangerous to himself and others may occur, for example, attempts at murder or suicide. This is mentioned mostly to emphasize the fact that references to and inclusion of LSD and other similar drugs in the following pages does not imply any recommendation to use them. The use of these substances is, moreover, forbidden now in many countries, among others, in Sweden and the United States.

20. The fourth aspect of the psychedelic experience may become the dominant feature of a state, in which case it is referred to as the *mystical experience*. This is very important in any attempt to explain ESP and will be described in greater detail in Chapter 17.

21. *Cosmic consciousness* is a hypothetical state which could be described as the permanent result of a mystical experience. This will also be treated in Chapter 17.

Minus-functions and ESP

Complete agreement does not exist as to which of these states of consciousness is particularly conducive to psi-phenomena. Spontaneous experiences are quite commonly reported in ordinary daytime consciousness, but as we have seen they are also often conspicuous during dreams. The psychoanalyst Ehrenwald discusses "minusfunctions" and means by this, among other things, states 2 through 9, which involve diminished contact with outward reality [15, 16]. Thus, in these states, access to unconscious material is facilitated, and this material easily presented in a disguised, symbolic form. Psychoanalysts who study telepathic communication in working situations often also indicate that this telepathic material is experienced in a symbolic form in connection with the patient's psychodynamic situation.

The minus-functions in fact mean that the five senses' ability to convey impressions is reduced. The fact that ESP then appears to be intensified may indicate that it is a "need mechanism," that is, seen from the viewpoint of development, a more primitive way of receiving information, which the organism resorts to when the more sophisticated senses are not functioning at their peak. During one investigation, patients suffering the effects of brain injuries gave indications that their ESP had increased. On the other hand, ESP is not noticeably increased in patients with Parkinson's disease, nor does the brain operation usually done to relieve symptoms result in any improvement in ESP. The negative findings in this instance may therefore be due to the rigid, stereotyped conjectural patterns of these patients, a behavior which is a consequence of their illness [17].

ESP signals do seem to come more easily into consciousness when contact with the outer world is cut off. The signal appears first to reach the unconscious layer of the personality and is treated there in the same way as other unconscious material before it is allowed to surface into the consciousness. This may indicate that ESP-stimuli are being continually received, but that normally they cannot compete with the stream of impressions from the senses which must be picked up first of all and worked upon immediately. The extent to which ESP signals reach the consciousness depends, among other things, upon the strength of the so-called defense mechanisms, as was mentioned in Chapter 7.

ESP and PK

Thouless and Weisner regarded ESP and PK as, respectively, the sensory and motor aspects of the same phenomenon [18]. This view was carried further by Ehrenwald, who considered psi in relation to the psychoanalytic personality model [16]:

The ability of the self to register stimuli from the outside world is greatest in the retina, but the sense of touch is best developed in the fingertips. Turning to the back of the hand, the sense is already appreciably weaker, and the soles of a person's feet are relatively unfeeling. Hair can be cut without it being felt at all. Here the limit of the body is reached, and, according to current information, the ability to receive impressions ceases there. The odds against any impression being received thus increase enormously when the limits, the boundaries, of the body are passed. To the extent that any impressions are registered, for example in ESP experiments, they prove indistinct, and like the darts a poor dart thrower has aimed, spread all around the target. But the appearance of clairvoyance demonstrates that, far from the body, stimuli can still be registered.

As far as motor abilities go, control is greatest in a person's hands. It is not difficult to execute finely graded movements with your fingers, but only a few people can wiggle their ears. Even fewer can influence their heart beats at will. When the body's limits are passed and a person attempts to influence the fall of dice through PK, then the odds are immediately increased against success. Nevertheless, laboratory experiments demonstrate that such influence is possible to a limited extent.

This personality model is not final and limited; it is hypothetical, open. The possibilities of the I-self observing and acting diminish abruptly with increased distance from the conceived center of self, but the potential does not suddenly cease at some specific point, rather, it diminishes gradually.

ESP and Memory

According to Ehrenwald's theory, ESP and PK are, therefore, not supernatural but only extensions of ordinary sensory and motor abilities, even though they cannot yet be explained in these terms. ESP is a completely natural, biological process. In line with this reasoning, Roll's theory adds that conscious ESP impressions consist only of associations with details from the percipient's own memory, his "memory traces [19]." The ESP signal merely causes him to remember something he had learned earlier. Therefore, this aspect of the ESP process resembles a completely ordinary psychological and biological mechanism. Only if memories and associations emerge which are related to some outer circumstances that the percipient could not normally know, would we talk of paranormal phenomena. In an instance of telepathy, the stimulus might then sometimes be memory, namely, the agent's. Roll mentions a medium who was requested to describe what an absent person had just done. Instead, she related in great detail what that person had done the preceding day, that is, what was in his fresh "memory bank." Through psychometry, it is obviously possible to also read the "memories" or psi-traces of inanimate objects, by making contact with their psi-fields, as was mentioned in Chapter 3.

Synchronicity

C. G. Jung was interested in paranormal phenomena and had many such experiences himself. He advanced the concept of *synchronicity,* which he defined as a "time link between two out of several causally unrelated events [events which lack a causal connection] which have, however, the same or similar meaning." Synchronicity is an "intellectually essential" principle which, according to Jung, should be included in the known triad of time, space, and causality as the fourth concept. It would then apply only when a causal explanation is inconceivable [20].

The concept of synchronicity is, by its very nature, such that it cannot be proved or disproved. It is, therefore, not suitable for experimental work in which one seeks definite causal factors. A useful theory or hypothesis, from the point of view of being objectively provable, must include both laboratory experiments and spontaneous cases and must also be possible to test in experiments.

Hypnosis

Let us now return to the states of consciousness in Figure 4. Suggestion under hypnosis (numbers 3 and 8) has often been used to facilitate ESP [21, 22]. Hypnotic dreams may contain telepathic material, just as ordinary dreams do [1]. Separations, ESP-projections, and shared dreams have been produced with varying success under hypnosis or as a result of post-hypnotic suggestion [23]. The possibilities of demonstrating ESP under hypnosis are considered greatest when the subjects are trained to summon visual impressions during a trance, if the relationship between them and the hypnotist is positive and if the material used has some personal or emotionally laden significance (for example, cards with the names of people close to the subject) [24].

Meditation and Alpha Waves

Meditation is the state of consciousness which has drawn ever greater attention. Like states 2 through 9, it involves an alteration of perception of the outward world, but as was mentioned, in a very crucial way it is more precisely the antithesis of these states, for it is characterized by an absence of fantasized visual imagery. The state is characterized by EEG readings of continuous waves of a certain type, the so-called alpha waves. Such waves are produced from time to time normally, as recorded by EEG, in a person who is resting with his eyes closed. The state of meditation can be induced through training in certain methods, for example yoga (meditation with closed eyes) or Zen (meditation with open eyes) [25]. When ordinary subjects, whose EEG indicates alpha waves, are subjected to certain outer stimuli, such as repeated flashes of light or sudden sounds, the alpha waves, at least momentarily, cease and are replaced by other types of waves. But no one has succeeded in breaking the pattern of alpha waves of yogis in meditation by using such disturbing interference; they appear to be completely unconscious of the outside world. The yogis who sat with one hand in ice cold water for forty-five minutes also indicated continuous alpha waves, suggesting that they could prevent the nerve impulses of their hands from actually reaching their consciousness [26]. The state of meditation appears to have profound physiological effects [27].

During meditation with open eyes, visual impressions come as a matter of course, but the attention is concentrated on a point or a certain object, for example, a blue vase against a neutral background. The fact of the object is merely registered, not analyzed or associated with. Thoughts and associations are obliterated until the experience of the vase finally comes to fill the whole consciousness [12].

This state of meditation appears to be conducive to ESP. A group of people studying psychology made a short ESP experiment which produced random results, and then they listened to a lecture on meditation and breathing given by a yogi. They followed this with a short attempt at the breathing exercise. A new ESP experiment after the exercises revealed significant results ($p=0.01$) [28]. After a two-week course in "psychic development," which, among other things, involved training in relaxation, another group obtained better ESP results [29]. In card guessing experiments, some with closed and some with open eyes, results were more positive in those experiments during which EEG indications revealed a high percentage of alpha waves [30]. In attempts to cause separation by will, alpha waves were registered in the preparatory stage, while the experience itself appeared to be accompanied by EEG which indicated REM sleep. (See Chapter 8, Note 17.)

This suggests possibilities for further experimentation. An EEG apparatus could be conceived of with a tone generator which gives off a certain sound when the EEG registers alpha waves, by which the subject is rewarded when he succeeds in producing it. Thus, the subjects could easily be trained to produce alpha waves themselves for long periods. The state is described as relaxed and very pleasant [31]. ESP experiments in this state have been made [30].

Group experiments could be done before and after meditation, following different methods.

It is not known in what way meditation and related states facilitate ESP. One explanation could be that ESP signals are received more easily in this pleasantly relaxed and passively concentrated state. States 2 through 9 can be difficult to make much use of under formal experimental conditions; the easiest to test are numbers 3 and 8. It appears to facilitate ESP most markedly if unconscious material is made more readily accessible, so that unconsciously received "ESP transmissions" are allowed to become conscious. But the most rewarding and successful ESP experiments in the laboratory appear to be related to a sensory state which is relaxed and passive, without any imagining or fantasizing, in which attention to outward stimuli is reduced [30]. This is precisely the state which can be reached through meditation [39].

Psychedelic Drugs and ESP

The occurrence of ESP has also been studied in subjects under the influence of psychedelic drugs. However, one difficulty has proved to be that subjects often sink into their own private drug experiences and stop taking part in the experiment [32]. Spontaneous paranormal experiences have also been reported in the psychedelic state.

Is There Any Explanation?

The nature of ESP signals in themselves is completely unknown. They appear not to be of an electromagnetic nature. Experiments made with subjects placed in Faraday cages, which cut off electrical signals, have given significant results; in fact, Faraday cages surrounded by an electrical field seem instead to facilitate ESP [33, 34]. Transcontinental experiments have been made to investigate the influence of distance on ESP, but the results are not completely conclusive [35].

The "channel" which conveys ESP signals is thus completely unknown [36]. A rich flora of speculation abounds. Some have considered a "psychic ether" as the medium for psi [37], and include psi in cosmological models. We exist, thus, in a universe in which we perceive three dimensions in space, and include time as the fourth.

Perhaps further dimensions exist which we cannot perceive but which are essential to an explanation of psi. Hart believes that spontaneous psi experiences are acted out in a fifth "psychic dimension." (See Chapter 9, Note 5.)

The physicist Mach, who at the beginning of this century debated the fourth dimension of space as a purely mathematical concept, thought that the sudden appearance or disappearance of objects would be the best indication that such a higher dimension exists. If an object can move in this fourth dimension, there is indeed no possible way to lock it in: it should be able to disappear suddenly and pop up again in a completely different place in three-dimensional space. And abrupt popping up and disappearance of objects through what appear to be solid walls and locked doors are precisely what are reported, the so-called *apports* in spiritualism, as well as in connection with RSPK occurrences, as was mentioned in Chapter 10 [38].

By studying the mystical experience in Chapter 17, ESP will be illustrated from a new point of view. But first, in the next chapter, we must investigate the relationship between the brain and consciousness and elucidate what we really mean by these concepts, materially and psychically.

16

Consciousness, the Brain and Death

Our bodily physique, with its center in the brain, is an instrument for the spirit. This is clearly apparent when we are faced with a human being. Then we experience that it is not the physical which is most important, though that does play a role. What is essential and what captures us is the spirit, which makes itself known in a radiance from the eyes, in speech, in facial expression and in behavior. Without that a person would be like a wax doll with life—but without spirit. —CARL HØEGH

We have touched on different human experiences which suggest that survival beyond death could be possible. But perhaps all this is a delusion? If by logical methods we could prove that survival is impossible, or if, with the support of neurophysiology (the science of the workings of the nervous system), we could prove that consciousness is only (and cannot be anything other than) chemical processes in the brain, then the whole matter would be settled once and for all. Survival would then be impossible, and we would have put ourselves to all this trouble in vain. All the material we have gathered and gone through must in that case have other explanations. In this chapter we will investigate whether such proof does exist.

Here the different theories of the relationship between the brain and consciousness will not be treated in detail. But I will mention several important viewpoints emphasized in particular by the philosopher C. J. Ducasse [1].

Attitudes Toward Survival Beyond Death

The most important attitudes to the theory of survival beyond death may be summarized thus [2]:

1. Survival of the dead is logically impossible.

2. Survival is logically possible but impossible to experience (empirically), or at least utterly non-credible.

3. Survival is both logically and empirically possible.

4. Survival is logically possible and empirically believable, at least more plausible than implausible.

5. Survival is not only logically possible but also empirically confirmed.

6. Survival is logically necessary.

When Are We Conscious?

Faced with these different options, we must first emphasize that each and every one of us has always been *conscious* as long as each of us can remember. We can never experience total loss of consciousness—to do that would involve being conscious of being unconscious, which is self-contradictory. It is true that in certain circumstances, under the influence of narcotics, to some extent, and in sleep, we are what is called unconscious. But this only means that our ability to react to stimuli from our surroundings is greatly limited. Sleep does not involve complete loss of consciousness; to some degree we can react to certain outside impressions. A sleeping mother may be awakened by a sound from her own child, while she will sleep on undisturbed by other, significantly louder noises. During sleep she may have lively experiences in the form of dreams. In a coma or loss of consciousness, caused by other circumstances, for example, narcotics or brain injury, our ability to react to outward stimuli is even further reduced; we cannot react no matter how loudly someone shouts our name. Yet, nevertheless, under certain conditions we can have lively experiences of separation (Cases 29 and 32). It has also been demonstrated that people in narcosis can perceive meaningful sounds, like conversation, in their surroundings [3]. Those who nurse patients who remain unconscious for long periods of time, for example, after traffic accidents, sometimes sense that the unconscious person may actually be picking up something of what is happening around him. Perhaps he, like the patients under narcotics, can perceive what is being said, though as a result of being unconscious he cannot communicate. (Through mediums, communicators have decribed how they experienced their own deaths. As a rule, it appears that hearing is the sense which receives impressions from the physical plane the longest. According to these sources, the dying can hear and perceive long after they have become "unconscious.")

We cannot observe this loss of consciousness any better than we can observe other psychic states. All we can observe is that the ordinary indications of consciousness are lacking. The conclusion that we are not conscious at all during these moments is only a hypothesis, which attempts to explain the fact that under these conditions we cannot communicate and usually cannot remember any experiences. But lack of conscious memory is no proof that a person was not conscious. In that case we would actually be unconscious for a large part of our lives. Indeed, we can only really remember a small segment of everything we experienced in our lives, despite the fact that the majority of these experiences were actually received in "full consciousness."

Material, Living, Psychic

Next we must define three concepts: material, living, and psychic.

Material (physical, bodily) includes, according to Ducasse, every phenomenon, occurrence, thing, event, action, process, etc., which is or can be made *perceptually public*. That is to say, materials are all those phenomena like stones, plants, gases, living beings' bodies which at a certain point in time can be perceived by more than one person. Material also includes those elements in material objects which as a result of their smallness or other reasons cannot be perceived directly (for example, molecules or atoms), but the existence of which can be deduced from knowledge of the material phenomena.

Living means, *biologically*, that all of certain criteria are fulfilled and functioning, like growth, metabolism, increase, and adaptation to environment. But *living—in the psychological sense of the word—* implies consciousness. Biologists know that signs of life in a biological sense cease when the body dies, and thus they draw the conclusion that the consciousness also dies. But that is not necessarily the only conclusion that can be drawn from the known facts. It has not been proved that all aspects of consciousness are involved in bodily processes.

Psychic (mental, spiritual, of the soul) phenomena are all those processes, actions, etc., which are *private,* that is, which each person can only observe directly within himself. These phenomena, such as thoughts, feelings, ideas, wishes, drives, needs, states of mind, moods, mental images, etc., can be described as *contents of the consciousness.* In this way, what is revealed through observation of the self—introspection—can be made public, through actions like talking, writing, gesturing, or other means of expression. By saying "I am afraid," I can cause another person to think about the conscious content in his consciousness which is "afraid" as if he experienced it himself, and he may believe that it is the same as what I experience when I say "I am afraid." But in itself, the very state of being afraid, which is expressed by these words, is not public in the sense that the words are. The state is private and belongs to the person's history, no one can directly investigate it in any person other than himself. The expression caused by the state may be investigated in other people. "The behavior appearance of fear," that is, the behavior which experience has taught us that a person usually demonstrates, is public, but the fear itself is private and something other than behavior.

Just as "material" includes not only those phenomena which can be observed publicly but also those elements of them which for different reasons cannot be observed, so also "psychic" indicates aspects of consciousness which cannot be observed directly through introspection, that is, those which are called "unconscious."

What Is a Psyche?

A psyche, or mind, according to Ducasse, is a complex of capacities or dispositions [4]. A *capacity* is defined here as a connection of cause and effect between certain events. For example: sugar has the characteristic, or the capacity, of being dissolved in water. This means that sugar is such that if event A occurs (sugar is placed in water) then this causes event B (sugar dissolves). In a similar way, a person has the characteristic, for example, of being irritable. This does not mean that he experiences the emotion called irritation continually, but rather that certain events which can produce the feeling of irritation in the majority of people will also produce it in him. These different capacities in the psyche may be gathered under three main headings:

1. psychosomatic: a psychic occurrence causes a material or somatic (bodily) occurrence,

2. somato-psychic: a somatic occurrence causes a psychic occurrence,

3. psycho-psychic: a psychic occurrence causes another psychic occurrence.

These three groups may be represented schematically:

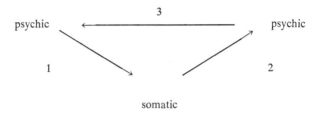

If a psyche continues to exist after the body's death, we may dispense with both groups of capacities involving the body, that is (1) the psychosomatic and (2) the somato-psychic. Only (3) the psycho-psychic remains.

A psyche is, therefore, a complex of capacities made up of these three kinds combined into a *personality*. The fact that a psyche *exists*, or is to be found for a certain time, indicates that it *exercises* some of these capacities during that time. As a result, a series of occurrences takes place. The existence of a psyche, therefore, indicates not only a certain nature, but also involves a certain history consisting of a chain of such events, the result of these released, activated capacities.

Just as material objects consist of parts combined in a certain way, so also a psyche consists of smaller units of capacities. As in a material object, one part can be separated out and may function more or less independently, in a way that will distinguish it from the functioning of the totality. We have seen examples of such dissociation in the chapter on spiritualism. The unity of a psyche is thus not a question of all or nothing, but rather a matter of more or less.

A psyche can, like a material object, be analyzed as a complex of capacities and dispositions. The psyche could be said to have a structure, thus to consist of some sort of psychic "substance," just as a material object consists of material substance.

Are Thoughts Identical with Brain Processes?

One theory put forth quite often is that thoughts and other psychic processes are nothing other than chemical or electrical processes in the brain, that is, that the psychic and the electromagnetic processes are *identical*. The concept that "thoughts are fundamentally nothing other than chemical processes" cannot be disproved, but not because it is true, rather because it is absurd. It is equally absurd to say "iron is fundamentally made of wood." The concept that psychic processes and brain processes are identical is untenable, because it totally disregards the fundamental difference between material processes in the brain and psychic processes in the consciousness. The material processes can, in principle, be observed directly and are objectively demonstrable, while the psychic ones may be observed only by individual experience through introspection and may only be described to others. We mean by fear, for example, a type of experience, a psychic process, and not a reaction in the blood vessels, a material process. Even though the latter reaction always follows the former, it is still not identical with it. What advocates of the doctrine of identity basically mean is probably that thoughts and emotions are *produced* by these chemical courses of events in the brain, the view which we will now examine.

"The Brain Excretes Thoughts As the Kidneys Excrete Urine"

Another common conception of the relationship between the brain and consciousness is that psychic processes are not identical with, but always *caused by,* material processes in the brain. This view is known as *epiphenomenalism*. According to this conception, consciousness is only a by-product of the brain. Therefore, only the somatopsychic capacity is thought to exist; the others are illusory. Survival of the dead in this case is not conceivable either, since the only existent functioning capacity ceased with the death of the brain. This is described by such analogies as consciousness is nothing more than a "spark lit by the machine."

But this analogy mixes and confuses material and psychic occurrences. The spark, like the machine, is a material phenomenon, while consciousness is a psychic phenomenon. What is really meant is that changes in the brain's material state cause changes in the psychic state or content of consciousness but not the opposite. The psyche is conceived of as a "substance" like the brain, though the substance is different. There is no compelling reason why the process could not work in the opposite way so that alterations in the psychic substance would cause alterations in the material substance. In particular, epiphenomenalism argues that a causal relationship can be found between such radically different phenomena as the material and the psychic—but only operating in one direction. According to Ducasse, there is, in fact, no theoretically binding obstacle to prevent the causal relationship functioning in the opposite direction as well [5].

Epiphenomenalism states, for example, that the material process of burning a matchstick against the skin causes a psychic process, the experience of which is called pain. But other factors can be interpreted equally well in the other direction. Thus, a psychic process, the wish to lift your hand, causes a material process, you lift your hand. That all psychic states without exception are caused by chemical states in the brain is not a proved fact but only a hypothesis, an assumption based on a fraction of the known facts. Other facts can contradict the theory.

Telepathy is just such a fact. It does appear that a mental occurrence—a certain emotion or experience within the agent—causes a material occurrence—a certain effect in the percipient, for example, to visit the agent or to choose a specific card. A convinced epiphenomenalist would perhaps explain away the majority of laboratory experiments and spontaneous cases as pure coincidence and the rest as fraud. But if he himself visited a medium anonymously, and that medium described his deceased relatives and personal relationships in great detail, details which could not have been known normally, then perhaps he would turn to the telepathic explanation simply to avoid the spirit hypothesis. If he is faced with the cases which give the best indications of reincarnation, his need to turn to the telepathic hypothesis or even to "super-ESP" becomes even more compelling. If he studies paranormal tape recordings, he may be forced to resort to the hypothesis of psychokinesis to avoid the spirit hypothesis. But psychokinesis does imply, like telepathy, that psychic phenomena cause material occurrences, and by acknowledging this he has contradicted his own doctrines.

Epiphenomenalism, therefore, builds untenable concepts and is not consistent with all known facts. The consequence of epiphenomenalism, if it were true, namely, that psychic activities *cannot* be produced after the brain's death, has not been proved. In other words, at least certain functions of the consciousness after death are completely possible theoretically and are not contradicted by known facts. We have thus rejected the first of the alternatives mentioned on page 229, and the weight of the empirical evidence which exists must determine our choice between the remaining possibilities (with the exception of number 6, which is an article of faith). As Binkley [2] stated, it is obviously difficult to find a conception of the relationship between the body and the psyche in which survival was not conceivable. "Even the grossest materialism would have to allow that it is conceivable that the seat of consciousness and personality is not the physical brain after all but an 'astral' brain that can survive the death of the physical body." The possibility exists, and only experience can tell us anything of the real relationship.

Reciprocity Between Psyche and Brain

But do the facts speak for the brain really producing the consciousness? It has not proved possible to localize consciousness definitely anywhere in the brain. It does not appear that nerve cells have intrinsically any different physiological properties than other cells. Furthermore, there does not appear to be any crucial positive difference between nerve cells in the spinal column (which is not thought to carry consciousness) and those in the brain cortex (which is sometimes considered to bear the higher forms of consciousness). The contact between adjacent nerve cells, brought about by chemical substances, seems also to be similar in nature throughout the entire nervous system. We shall not build our entire argument on these observations; neurophysiologists are not of one mind as to how these observations should be viewed. But it is interesting that prominent neurophysiologists have begun to concern themselves increasingly in the problem of the brain's relation to consciousness [6, 7]. Some consider that the brain definitely produces the conditions necessary for conscious activity, but they add that this does not cause consciousness itself. A comparison with a television set might explain what is meant: the television set itself is essential for people to be able to see a program, but it does not cause the program, which is there even if the set is turned off. In the same way, the brain could be considered to intensify impulses from a mental energy field, impulses which are too weak for all available measuring devices but which do, nevertheless, exist.

The brain would thus, in other words, function as a two-way sender-receiver, transmitting communication between the body and this mental field. Certain occurrences in the brain, caused by stimuli from the outside world (for example, a burning match stick against the skin) or by states of the body, cause certain psychic occurrences, namely, perceptions of different sorts. But on the other hand, certain psychic phenomena (irrespective of how these themselves are caused) cause material occurrences. Example: a wish to lift your hand leads to nerve impulses which release movements in certain muscles so that the action is carried out. Naturally, the machine, in this case the brain, must function so that this reciprocity may be completed. But the brain and the psyche's acting on each other in this way does not exclude their ability to act independently. It is true that the formation of the psyche throughout a lifetime is for the most part dependent on this reciprocity between the brain and the psyche, but this does not exclude the possibility that the psyche, after the brain's death, might be able to continue to exist and use at least a certain number of its abilities, namely, the psycho-psychic.

This theory of reciprocity, this interaction between the psyche and the brain, does not mean that we have taken the position that the psyche survives beyond death. We have only established that survival is conceivable. Otherwise, the question is left open, to be settled by the existing empirical evidence [8].

If, then, survival is possible, the question remains of what does survive and how does the survival come about? If it is impossible to form a comprehensible picture of a life beyond death, then it would really be meaningless to argue the matter. As we will see in Chapters 18 and 19, such a picture is completely possible. But first we must look more closely still at another human experience, namely, the so-called mystical experience. The interpretation of this can, in fact, have consequences both for our understanding of ESP and for the interpretation of the function of the brain and life after death.

17

The Mystical Experience and the Psychic Field

Our thoughts are free, they may appear unattached, in any pattern whatsoever, and it has been demonstrated that through apparently inexplicable spiritual impulses, the mind can grasp reality intuitively, because, in fact, we are ourselves a part of this reality. CARL HØEGH

Included as states of consciousness in Figure 4 on page 217 are number 19, "psychedelic experiences" and number 20, "the mystical experience." As mentioned, the mystical experience, one of "unity with totality," can be an aspect of the psychedelic experience or may appear completely independently. (The word mystical therefore means "mysterious, strange, enigmatic," but it is used here only in the above sense, indicating an experience of unity.) The contents of the mystical experience may be illustrated by the following two examples:

52. As a child . . . I was very unhappy that I had been born on this earth. I heard Father argue with neighbors and friends that God does not exist. To lie in bed listening, especially late at night, after alcohol had had its effect and the discussions grew rather loud, made my existence even worse. I must have been about six years old, when one cold night I decided to make an end to this unbearable existence. I crept out of the house, dressed only in a nightshirt, and lay down in the snow. The freezing cold was severe. In that snowdrift I said out loud to myself, "I'm going to die here tonight if I don't receive any proof that a God exists." How well I remember those words. Then something happened

which changed my life up to this present moment. Everything in that dark night became illuminated. The stars grew bigger than usual. From the stars and the planets I saw chains, and from these stars and planets the chains extended down into the earth too. All these chains ran on cogwheels and behind it all there was a power, like a kind of dynamo. There was also a sound, muted, as from a great activity of machines. After this experience, I felt that there were powers in the universe and I called them God. After that, life on earth became much happier. I felt connected with the universe. I experienced many events which cannot be explained. Even so, I taught myself to keep silent about it and tell no one about my experiences, since they were only received with scorn and I was told that I was only deceiving myself with fantasies.

53. I was about ten years old. Early one beautiful morning I was sitting listening to the birds and enjoying the scent of the newly unfurled birch leaves. Suddenly I was conscious that everything had become silent all around me, the birds hushed. I heard nothing; I grew frightened. Then I heard a voice from somewhere. It was not a voice, but another's thought with the power of a voice: "You sit here enjoying all living things, yet you feel sorrow because it dies down in winter. There is no difference between living and dead—everything is living." Then my glance was caught by a gray stone sticking up out of the grass. It suddenly became like a shining mist, slowly altered itself and changed into a whole world of shining stars, stars with space between them. It changed form again and the stars turned into bright streaks which moved swiftly—white, red, blue, green—like shining, moving streaks, fast, fast. Some went straight, some arched like a bow, some like waves, and in the midst of all these one swirled in a spiral, more slowly and more deliberately, as if it was weaving everything together. You could not imagine anything more lively and vibrant. Slowly the vision left me, and the stars came again, and then, later, the mist, and finally there was the stone, as if inanimate. But it wasn't really inanimate any longer. I also got the feeling that "humans are not foreign beings in the universe. Everything is of the same spirit." . . . I was the happiest person, the birds sang again . . . but my mother explained that the sun had shone and the stone glittered and it had reflected back into my eyes. I took it as a little manifestation . . . anyway until I saw that my parents would never understand what I had seen, and people shake their heads and look askance at people who "see" things like that, saying: "they end up in the nut house. . . ."

As these examples suggest, experiences of this sort often have profound and long-lasting effects on the individual. The young age of the percipients is noteworthy: as a rule these experiences come to adults. Usually the effects are described as very positive, and this is yet another reason why these experiences should be investigated more thoroughly [1].

Mystical experiences may, therefore, appear totally spontaneously and unexpectedly. A psychedelic and possibly mystically colored experience may also appear as an element in a psychosis, that is, a mental illness, with altered perceptions of reality [2]. Finally, such an experience can be induced in three different ways:

1. by the so-called psychedelic drugs [3]
2. by suggestion under hypnosis (See Chapter 15, Notes 10–11.)
3. by contemplative meditation (See Chapter 15, Notes 12–13.)

Expectation Directs the Experience

It should be emphasized that a person's expectations and his circumstances at the time of taking drugs like LSD seem to determine to a great extent what sort of experience he will have. When the drug is taken illegally (which is still the only way in, for example, America and Sweden), with the fear of being caught by the police or, despite every precaution, of having unpleasant effects, the chances are increased of undergoing a disagreeable experience, perhaps accompanied by long-lasting negative side-effects. If, instead, the drug is taken while participating in an experiment concerned with investigating the appearance of the mystical experience, under expert direction in a suitable milieu, in an atmosphere which encourages feelings of devotion, spirituality, solemnity, and tranquility, then obviously a person has much greater chances of really achieving an experience of a mystical nature. Thus, the experience is to a high degree anticipated [3].

One difference between spontaneous and chemically induced mystical experiences is that spontaneous ones are, as a rule, very brief, lasting seldom more than a few minutes, often only seconds. But during this brief period, an incredibly rich content may be experienced. (Using certain techniques under hypnosis, the perception of a period of time can also be "prolonged," so that an extended course of events can be experienced subjectively in several seconds [4].) On the other hand, the peak, the high point, of a psychedelic experience can be extended over a few hours. Whether, therefore, drug-induced mystical experiences should have a more profound and long-lasting positive effect on the individual is controversial. There is also a dispute as to whether mystical experiences under the effects of drugs are of as "high quality" as those produced in a religious milieu. Religious people have feared the possibility that chemical means would offer a shortcut to the peak experience which many deeply religious individuals have achieved only after subjecting themselves to years of discipline and self-denial [5, 6].

The Characteristics of a Mystical Experience

Common characteristics are easily discovered in different individuals' testimonies of mystical experiences. Pahnke [5] proposed nine basic characteristics of the mystical experience as a result of his research.

1. The experience of unity of both the outer surrounding universe and the "inner" world. The self appears to die or else fade away, while "pure consciousness" paradoxically remains and appears to expand, to become an extensive "inner world."

2. Objectivity and reality: the feeling of *knowing* and *seeing* what is *real* contributes a strong conviction that the experience is one of reality. This insight is experienced as more fundamental and profound than any which may be achieved in everyday experiences or through the most vivid hallucinations and dreams.

3. Time and space are bridged (transcendence). Time and space are experienced as meaningless concepts, despite the fact that the individual may occasionally see back over "total history" during the experience, back into his own and mankind's ancestry.

4. A feeling of solemnity, exaltation, holiness, sanctity, which is experienced more profoundly, more fundamentally, than any philosophical or religious concept which the individual had ever experienced before.

5. A deeply felt *positive state of mind:* emotions of joy, love, well-being, and peace.

6. The experience is *paradoxical:* the essential aspects are experienced as true despite the fact that they contradict ordinary logical conceptions (for example, consciousness despite "the death of the self").

7. The experience is *indescribable:* impossible to describe satisfactorily with ordinary language symbols.

8. *Transience:* the experience lasts only seconds or minutes, in chemically induced cases, up to a couple of hours.

9. Positive changes in attitude and behavior. The experience is followed by a long-lasting and profound alteration: increased personal integration, a feeling of greater personal value, a diminished need to take refuge in habitual defense mechanisms.

Other writers have described similar characteristics. Maslow's [7] "peak experience" is basically the same as the mystical experience. Several of these mentioned characteristics are to be found in the following experience, which a twenty-four-year-old nurse had some years ago:

54. A May evening, I am outside, strolling along Lake Mälaren. Seabirds splash and chatter down in the reeds. The sun has set, it starts to grow chilly, but I don't really want to go home until I've sat down and enjoyed the view for a while.

Suddenly I notice that everything has become completely silent around me, as if everything has stopped in a kind of solemn expectation. I feel astonished and wonder what is about to happen. Soon I'm not freezing anymore. I feel I'm growing, though I'm still just sitting there; I try to get up but can't. Instead I feel as if I've left my body, flowed out of it, and merged with the grass, earth, and everything close around me.

Such peace I have never experienced before: I think this must be the very kernel of reality. Wish that I didn't ever have to return to my self again, but I worry a little that my body is still completely visible. I don't see it but I know it's still there on the ground. If people find it, it will be an unnecessary nuisance for them. I'd prefer if it could disappear too. After a little while longer, this worry leaves me too and everything that exists is complete, a *unity*. How long this wonderful feeling fills me, I don't know, perhaps about half an hour, but when I see my surroundings again, it has become completely dark. It feels a little bit like waking up from a very deep sleep, I work my way up out of it—and I do it though I don't really want to. Then it takes a good long while before I function well enough so I can walk home again.

Since then I've had similar experiences a few times, but they are never as intense as that first time. More like a reminder so I won't ever forget.

Mysticism and Psychosis

One basic difference between a mystical and a psychotic experience is the duration. The spontaneous mystical experience lasts only seconds or minutes, in individual cases longer, the drug-induced ones up to several hours. A psychosis, on the other hand, is long lasting: hours, days, weeks, or months, though during this time the state may vary. Aaronson (see Chapter 15, Note 10) has been able to produce mystical as well as psychotic states in his subjects through hypnotic suggestion concerning the alteration of space and time perception. A suggestion of reinforced depth perception, that is, stronger than stereoscopic vision, produces a psychedelic, mystically colored experience, while suggestion which obliterates depth perception (no stereoscopic vision at all) is responded to by transient psychotic behavior. Aaronson believes that the mystical experience may be characterized precisely by this intensified depth perception in contrast to the psychotic experience's flat space perception. In the mystical state's experience of depth, objects in the outer world are not perceived as isolated but rather as connected with each other, while the unclear and flat depth perception of psychosis conveys uncertainty about the relationship of each object to all others and to the individual's self.

Deikman [8] taught his subjects a simple meditation technique and found that after a short period of "experimental meditation," psychedelic-mystical experiences occurred. He emphasizes, in particular, five characteristics of the mystical experience: intense conviction of reality, unusual perceptions (indicating that "liberated psychic energy" could be perceived as sensory impressions), unity with the universe, ineffability, and the fact that the experience exceeds all ordinary sensory experiences, ideas, or memories. He considers that these qualities of the mystical experience are dependent on a "de-automatization of hierarchically ordered structures." This means that the ordinary apperceptions which build a sensory impression—chosen in each case always because of special needs and combined into acquired, learned patterns—are broken down into their constituent elements. When, for example, you see a landscape, you do not necessarily have to combine the different elements—houses, roads, meadows, water, woods, mountains—that make up the landscape into the concept "landscape." This is done automatically, due to training acquired from birth. But a person who has been blind for thirty years, and then regains his sight following an operation, is not able to perceive in the same way: he must learn all over again how to combine separate elements into a totality. He sees the world "new and fresh," which is a feature of the mystical experience (but only one feature, other aspects are missing).

In a later article, Deikman [8] views the altered perception to be the result of an altered focusing of consciousness in relation to the surrounding world. The states of consciousness in Figure 4 could be seen as examples of variations of three basic attitudes, approaches, or positions held by the individual. Numbers 1 and 16 represent what Deikman calls the outward directed action mode of consciousness, in which the intention is to manipulate, to control your surroundings. Numbers 18 through 21 represent the opposite attitude in its most pronounced form, in which the purpose is to experience, to assimilate, to take in: the receptive mode. Numbers 2 through 12 represent a third position (not mentioned by Deikman), in which the external world is, in some important respect, screened off, shut out, from consciousness. This may occur as the result of an act of will or from physical or psychic illness. States 13 through 15 and 17 have elements of all three positions, in varying degrees, which may result in a chaotic experience.

In this article, Deikman considers the possibility that the mystical experience can supply knowledge of aspects of existence which we are usually unaware of. The existence of ESP is just such an indication that there is a reality in addition to the one our senses perceive. It could be thought that, compared with the mystic, we are as the blind compared with the sighted. Someone born blind is perhaps inclined to take what a sighted person says about "another reality" as pure fantasy or a beautiful story.

William James [9] characterized the mystical consciousness as "pantheistic and optimistic, or at least the opposite of pessimistic." But what authority does this consciousness have? James gives the answer in three points:

1. The mystical state is usually perceived by the percipient as absolute authority, that is, as absolute truth, and with good reason.

2. But these experiences have no intrinsic authority which could make it obligatory for any outsider to accept their content uncritically.

3. Nevertheless, the existence of the mystical state overthrows the claim that the non-mystical state alone shall dictate what we are to believe. The concept of the mystical state does not deny any known facts but rather enriches them with "metaphysical, transcendental meaning." It breaks down the authority of the non-mystical, or

rationalistic, consciousness, which is based only on sensory testimony. It demonstrates that this is only one kind of consciousness among several. It opens up the possibility of other aspects of existence. It must remain an open question whether or not the mystical state can be a "window through which the psyche can see out over a more wide-reaching and all-embracing world."

Two Ways of Experiencing Reality

Physicists teach us that light behaves sometimes as a wave movement and sometimes as a stream of particles, but neither of these ways of behaving seems to cancel out the other. Perhaps reality is also a unity including two such dimensions which seem to exclude each other and yet do not? This would mean that we could not be conscious of both of them simultaneously.

Psychic experiences confirm this assumption. The world picture which becomes evident from mediums' experiences has been studied, in particular by LeShan [10]. According to him, each individual experiences reality (by which we mean the outer world, "that which exists outside of oneself") in two completely contradictory ways. The ordinary, "normal," sensory perception gives a *sensory individual reality,* S-IR. In addition to this, a medium may experience what LeShan calls a *clairvoyant individual reality,* C-IR, the essential characteristics of which it shares with the mystical experience. These two windows through which existence can be experienced will be referred to as sensory reality, or S-IR, and clairvoyant reality, or C-IR. These, then, are the two opposed "individual realities" which an individual can experience. Briefly, following LeShan, we can describe these ways of experiencing:

SENSORY
INDIVIDUAL REALITY, S-IR

Things and events are primarily individual and separate. Secondly, they can be combined into a greater unity.

S-IR MAY BE DESCRIBED
IN GREATER DETAIL:

The senses are our only reliable

CLAIRVOYANT
INDIVIDUAL REALITY, C-IR

Things and events are primarily parts of a pattern, which is part of a greater pattern, and so forth until everything is included within the great pattern of the universe. Individual things and occurrences do exist and happen, but their individuality is something secondary; their identity as parts channels of information. Time is divided into the past, the present, and the future. An occurrence or action can be good, neutral or bad, even if its consequence often cannot be known until long afterward. Actions can be made on the basis of will in a desired direction, if they are not blocked by space or time.

of a pattern is the most essential fact.

MORE DETAILED:

The information of the senses is only illusory: real knowledge is experienced directly. Time is a unity; past, present, and future are illusions. Events take place in an "eternal now." What exists is neither bad nor good but part of a total harmonic plan of the universe, which exists beyond good and evil. A person cannot act actively, but can only observe the pattern. (Active deeds involve the person's returning to S-IR.) Observation cannot be directed; knowledge comes from the state of being within the pattern, not from the wish to receive specific information. Neither time nor space hinders the exchange of energy or information between two individual objects or beings, since distinctions of time and space are illusory.

LeShan goes on to point out that to survive as a biological being, it is necessary to live in and be conscious of S-IR. To live consciously in C-IR uninterruptedly for any length of time would result in the individual's not being able to survive on the physical plane. But he who is never conscious of C-IR does not live as richly as he could. S-IR and C-IR could be thought of as the opposite ends of a scale. Only the completely convinced materialist lives continually in S-IR. Those mystics who seek to isolate themselves from the sensory world to attain the mystical state, who live apart from worldly things, are always close to C-IR. The consciously psychic person lives mainly in S-IR but can "attach himself" to, link up with, C-IR. Only in exceptional cases could a person be conscious of and in both planes at the same time, as in Case 21, page 93.

LeShan emphasizes that the aspects of C-IR which have been mentioned are only part of the mystical experience. The mystic's C-IR is more than the medium's C-IR, as we will see.

The Psychic Field

LeShan suggests in his book that clairvoyance, precognition, and psychic experiences can be seen as the result of a temporary adjustment from S-IR to C-IR. Starting from his premise of the two windows through which the universe may be viewed, we may now proceed toward a hypothesis which would embrace and integrate ESP, PK, psychic, and mystical experiences.

Suppose that the mystical experience is not only a psychological adjustment, as Deikman [8] believes, but is rather a consciousness of another existing dimension of reality, as LeShan [10] and others believe. We could call this dimension or aspect "the psychic world" or *the psychic field*. Then suppose that the brain, as defined in the previous chapter, functions as a two-way sender-receiver, transmitting information between the psyche and the body. We could picture the brain as a transformer station, a device which transforms "low-tension" physical energy to "high-tension" psychic energy, or the reverse. It is probably more precise to picture the brain as a transducer, a device which transforms one kind of energy into another, for example, a photocell which transforms light into electrical energy. But the picture of the brain as a transformer station is more clearly illustrative and is used for that reason here. So, then, the brain is the intermediary mechanism between a field of psychic energy and a field of material energy. Figure 5 demonstrates this in a crudely schematized form.

In the diagram, C-IR has been placed above the dividing line, S-IR beneath. This does not imply, however, that C-IR should be considered *identical with* the psychic world and S-IR identical with the material world. The relationship is better expressed by saying that C-IR is the *experience of* the psychic world, while S-IR is the experience of the material world. To the extent that both S-IR and C-IR have to do with experiencing, they are both psychic occurrences. But they have been placed on either side of the dividing line to define the differences between them and their respective relationships to the psychic and material fields.

The psychic world is a broad, general term for everything psychic

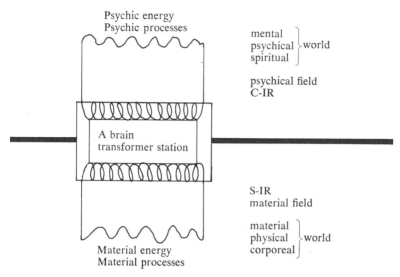

FIGURE 5

or mental according to Ducasse's definition (see Chapter 16, Note 1), and the material world includes everything material. We can thus refer to a psychic and a material field. In the material field we find "concentrations" in the form of atoms, molecules, and physical bodies built of them. In the psychic field as well, the energy of which is for the present of an unknown nature, we find "concentrations" in the form of individual consciousnesses.

This would mean that the psychic, which according to Ducasse (see Chapter 16, Note 1) is "private," is private only in relation to an observer who is operating in S-IR. In C-IR everything exists as a unity, and all "private" systems are only local energy fields or concentrations in an all-embracing field. Also, presently, we cannot attain sufficient contact with C-IR to be able to experience that unity in anything other than exceptional cases, for example, during a mystical experience.

According to this conception, the brain's task is not to create consciousness—the individual's consciousness exists in the psychic field independent of the brain—but rather its task is to limit and define the consciousness to those quantities and qualities which are consistent with life in the physical plane [11]. Therefore, over thousands of generations, we have been trained above all to connect sensory impressions with S-IR, the reality of the senses. We have done this despite the fact that from the very beginning perhaps we have had an equally great possibility of being conscious in C-IR, the metaphysical reality. But for most of us, C-IR is suppressed so effectively that at its peak it only appears as occasional isolated paranormal experiences, when conditions are particularly conducive. For some reason, some individuals' consciousness of the psychic world is so powerful that it cannot be suppressed. These people, in the best instances, are able to teach themselves to choose between S-IR and C-IR, so that they know which impressions come from the psychic, and which from the physical, universe. They are called psychics or mystics, depending on the degree of their contact with C-IR. Finally, there are others who also receive impressions from the psychic universe, but who, for some reason, cannot distinguish these impressions from others which belong to S-IR. These people are called mentally ill, psychotic, or schizophrenic. I do not mean to imply by this that *all* cases of psychosis have this cause, but only that *some* of them perhaps might concern the inability to distinguish between C-IR and S-IR.

People with this inability are what Bendit [12] defines as *negatively psychic*. They experience a stream of impressions from the psychic world against which they cannot defend themselves because they don't know where these impressions come from. They cannot, like the medium, cut off their contact with C-IR more or less at will; they are helpless victims of all "psychic storms" which may rage in their vicinity [22]. The impressions need never even reach the consciousness. Barker's and Rhine's "projection of pain" (see Chapter 7, Notes 17 and 18) might be caused in this way.

> Bendit mentions a "highly intelligent and sensitive" woman who walked into an empty room. She felt as if she were coming out onto a battlefield and was being bombarded from all directions. Overwhelmed by panic, she rushed from the house without carrying out her errand, and immediately afterward she was violently ill. When she telephoned to apologize for her behavior, she was told that a short while before she entered the room a violent argument had taken place there. She was completely unprepared for the "violent emotional storm which was still active in the atmosphere." [12]

To use an image, the *positive psychic,* as distinguished from the negative one, can pull on a coat to shield himself from a psychic storm, use the coat to protect himself from unexpected bad weather.

By introspection, increasing his consciousness of the reality of the psychic world, and by training, the negatively psychic person could, according to Bendit, develop himself into a positive psychic and thereby make his sensitivity a quality which could enrich his life rather than make it inexplicably miserable.

To be unable to distinguish between information from S-IR and C-IR would create anguish in a medium and make it impossible for the medium to function at all. Perhaps that is why so many mediums put themselves in a special state, such as a trance, or use techniques like automatic writing when they seek paranormal information [10]. They know or believe that information received in this way is more likely to be from C-IR.

The Psychic Field and Psi

Consciousness of the psychic world can be induced in several ways:

1. On the one hand, clearly innate factors may produce an unusually profound sensitivity to stimuli from the psychic world, and the child with this sensitivity becomes psychotic or psychic depending on whether or not he can learn to distinguish between S-IR and C-IR.

2. On the other hand, the attention is consciously focused and directed to C-IR through different forms of meditation, following Zen, yoga or other systems, by various techniques for relaxation, through hypnosis, or by a religiously oriented hermit or cloistered life.

Thus, the degree of success in laboratory ESP experiments depends upon the extent of the contact with C-IR that can be established. This may explain the connection between alpha waves and success in ESP experiments. (See Chapter 15, Note 30). Possibly stimuli from the psychic universe are received all the time, but worked over unconsciously and not able to reach consciousness. In meaningful situations, for example, a person's death, the energy conversion in the psychic field could be thought to be especially strong and to cause an unusually powerful "transmission" which, under the right conditions, will become conscious as a telepathic occurrence. Under similar conditions, energy transformation in the psychic field could be experienced as an apparition. This does not mean that it must be present in material space, but nevertheless it may be something which is not merely created by the percipient [13]. Astral and etheric bodies can be seen as phenomena which belong essentially to the psychic field, but which under certain conditions are able to draw physical matter to themselves, and so become totally or partially materialized, in the same way that force lines around a magnet which are made visible by the positions of iron filings are affected by the magnetic field so that they move in a certain way.

3. Changes in the transformer, that is, the brain, may cause "short circuits" between the two energy fields. These changes may be thought of as being caused by chemical processes which are not completely understood (during certain psychic illnesses) or by the addition of chemicals like LSD.

4. Finally, the experiences of the psychic universe may occur completely spontaneously, but even in these instances it appears that certain controlling factors are to be found.

Psychic-mystical experiences of a similar kind can thus be produced or induced in several different ways, among others by the conscious concentration of attention or by chemical changes in the brain. (It is also possible that chemical changes follow the altered behavior during, for example, lengthy meditation.) The content of the experience and the effect on the percipient thus depend on his expectations, his religious bent, and, not least of all, on his ability to manage and direct these "high-voltage" energies.

Newspapers quite often mention people who jump out of high windows under the influence of LSD or other chemicals. Possibly such actions have been caused by panic or deliberate suicide. But occasionally the circumstances have indicated that the person was convinced that he could fly. Feelings of ease, independence, and freedom from the laws of gravity are completely identical to those experienced during separation in C-IR. But when the same sensation is caused by chemical influences, it affects the body, which is still in the material world, and these unsuccessful attempts to fly could be seen as drastic examples of the dangerous risks of not being able to distinguish between S-IR and C-IR.

The "inner world" or "psychic ether," which Hart describes (page 122), could be considered essentially the same as the psychic world. It is conceivable that the projector's consciousness during an ESP-projection really is moved through material space, but more probably this movement is illusory and the "transportation" occurs in the psychic field, in a "psychic fifth dimension."

PK could in this sense be thought of as the motor aspect of ESP. It could be seen as the "whirling motions" of psychic energy, which under presently unknown circumstances and conditions, may induce "motions" in the material field as well, and which may cause inexplicable movements of objects. Here, too, an obvious gradation exists, from neat and precisely measurable effects or phenomena produced in a laboratory experiment to the more stormy occurrences of RSPK, depending on the quantity of psychic energy which has been applied.

The unity of everything within the psychic field would indicate that animals also share ESP capabilities, which, in fact, several experiments indicate [14]. According to certain experiments, plants also have a form of "ESP [15]." Other experiments indicate that both plants and animals are sensitive to "psychic storms" and negative suggestions [16]. Grad's (see Chapter 6, Note 9) experiments with mice and the influence of thought on the speed of growth in seeds suggest that animals and plants are also sensitive to positive psychic climates. These results may be compared with the custom of priests blessing the sowing of seeds and with the folk belief that cows produce milk better and potted plants bloom more beautifully if you "talk in a friendly way" to them.

This model of reality is an attempt (inspired by LeShan [10]) to summarize psi-phenomena and psychedelic-mystical experiences and to see them as different gradations of the same phenomenon, namely, the conscious focusing of attention on the psychic world. Demonstrations of ESP and PK in laboratory experiments involve a rigidly limited contact with a small part of the psychic world, namely, that part associated with target objects, whether they are ESP cards or a Geiger tube which is struck by electrons. (Inanimate objects could also be thought of as having correspondences in the psychic world, and for lack of a better term, we will call them etheric bodies, as Hart does. Essentially, then, etheric bodies are only developed to the extent to which they have ever been associated with a consciousness. An object which has never been associated with any form of conscious activity would therefore not have an etheric correspondence, or "double." See further on page 122.) In such circumstances, the contact we can have with C-IR is tentative and uncertain, doubtful and diffused. It is partly the nature of C-IR that attention cannot be focused consciously, a person is able only to put himself in an attitude in which he may receive contact and then experience whatever information may result. Naturally, it is easier to direct attention of subjects to target objects which are meaningful to them, for example, to cards containing names of people who mean something to them.

Spontaneous and psychedelic experiences involve contact with the larger "sphere" of the psychic world, but are still limited—not because the psychic world is limited, but because our capacity to make contact with it is. Finally, mystical experiences of different intensities include contact with a very much greater "area" of the psychic world, up to the highest mystical experiences which can be perceived as an all-embracing unity.

Figure 6 is an attempt to represent schematically what has just been said. In the material field the direction of the communication is defined by arrows. In the psychic field there is neither a "from" nor a "to"; everything is mutually interdependent and connected, as the lines indicate. This figure does not include pre- and retro-cognition: that would require a three-dimensional presentation. In that case, imagine a plane stretching through the demarcation line at right angles to the paper. This plane would represent the time dimension with the present moment at the intersection between the plane and the page of the book, the past time being behind the page and the future in front of the paper. The lines linking "telepathy" and "clairvoyance" would thus be seen as directed forward or backward in time (pre- or retro-cognition) in relation to the object (in this diagram, the envelope) or the people (here, the faces).

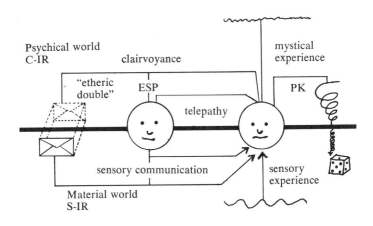

FIGURE 6

Cosmic Glimpses and Cosmic Consciousness

Deikman [8] considers the "lower" mystical experiences to be colored by the percipient's religious disposition and expectations, while the "highest" experiences are without any specific content as pictures or ideas. Cases 52 and 53 then would be "lower" experiences and the more "imageless" experiences in Case 54 would be "higher." But any grading of such experiences must remain completely subjective; there are no objective criteria to date. For example, the following experience, which Ruth Dahlén, a Swede, had in 1946, when she was in her forties, cannot really be called "lower," although it is characterized by images and ideas [17]:

> I had my gaze directed toward an unusually beautiful snowflake which had landed softly on a spruce needle. Suddenly something happened to the spruce needle, it dissolved into flickering flames of light. . . . The light waves seemed to move incredibly fast into . . . spiral forms within the needle, which still all the while kept the form and character of a spruce needle. It was as if I suddenly had before my eyes a magnifying glass which enlarged millions of times . . . soon the whole spruce was one single pillar of flame. For a second I was incredibly frightened—was my brain in some way deranged?—soon the woods were a whole ocean of the same living light . . . my hands were of the same transparent luminosity. All of creation vibrated with these incredible, quick light waves, but in there you could also clearly distinguish each individual light beam, you could see it function.
> . . . I saw the cosmos function like a five dimensional geometry . . . with the three dimensions of space, time as a fourth, and, added to these, a fifth dimension as well, the constructive, unifying, harmonic dimension, the innermost mystery of the universe, love . . . this is a poor, weak attempt to find words for *something which I really saw with my own eyes,* something absolutely real and clearly manifest. Perhaps the image of an incredibly complicated clockwork mechanism with a dizzying number of wheels would be a better image, but the five dimensions must absolutely be included . . . more and more I turned into light, until I saw myself functioning as a beam phenomenon, vibrating on the same wave length as the "fifth dimension." I saw the events take place as in a powerful film, a film which clarified not only the historical course of life but also *cause and effect.*
> . . . Before I even managed to formulate a question, the answer was already there. I was in some way *omniscient.* Then, gradually, all memory of any earthly existence ceased, I was in Eternity, in Paradise, in an existence of harmony and beauty sensible and rational above all. . . .
> [Slowly she became conscious of her earthly self, and everything became as it had been, but yet not as it was before. . . . The experience returned in the same place again four, five days,

but increasingly diffused and pale. She still felt an afterglow of the white light around her for a long while. . . .]

For a comparison, let us extract from the descriptions of an experience which a thirty-six-year-old Canadian doctor, R. M. Bucke, had in a carriage in London one spring night in 1872 [18]:

> All at once, without warning of any kind, I found myself wrapped in a flame-colored cloud. For an instant I thought of fire, an immense conflagration somewhere close by in that great city; the next, I knew that the fire was within myself. Directly afterward, there came upon me a sense of exultation, of immense joyousness accompanied or immediately followed by an intellectual illumination impossible to describe. Among other things, I did not merely come to believe, but I saw that the universe is not composed of dead matter, but is, on the contrary, a living Presence; I became conscious in myself of eternal life. It was not a conviction that I would have eternal life; but a consciousness that I possessed eternal life then; I saw that all men are immortal; that the cosmic order is such that without any peradventure all things work together for the good of each and all, that the foundation principle of the world, of all the worlds, is what is called love, and that the happiness of each and all is in the long run absolutely certain. The vision lasted a few seconds and was gone; but the memory of it and the sense of reality of what it taught has remained during the quarter of a century which has since elapsed. I knew that what the vision showed was true. That view, that conviction, I may say, that consciousness, has never, even during periods of the deepest depression, been lost.

Dahlén compares her own experiences with chemically induced ones and with Bucke's [19]:

> The similarities to my "creative vision" were in many ways astounding . . . everything was giddyingly clear, near, and holy. I was "omniscient" in a way inconceivable to human reason. I don't know much about being high on narcotics but in the . . . descriptions I have read or heard . . . I have always felt myself to be lost for a moment in my vision—the experience of a completely new, undreamed of dimension of the cosmos which I called the fifth dimension, saw it gather the cosmos into a unity. I have called this dimension Love.

Bucke began to study other people's accounts of related experiences and, in 1901, collected his observations in a book, *Cosmic Consciousness* [18]. He gave special emphasis to the following characteristics of what he called the cosmic experience:

> The experience comes suddenly and unexpectedly. Without warning the individual receives a feeling of being in the midst of flames, and in the next instant he is filled with intense joy, heightened to ecstasy. Equally suddenly, an intense intellectual clarification of information comes over him, which involves *knowledge* of mankind and the eternal life of everything, the unity of everything, and the identity of the universe with life, which is permeated with what could be called love. In these seconds, the individual learns more than during years of study. With this certainty of individual immortality, all fear of death disappears. The experience comes, as a rule, between the ages of thirty and fifty to people of "good intellect and high moral qualities." It has a profound influence on his remaining life. He now has *cosmic consciousness* and can never really return to the state of consciousness he had before the experience.

The essential characteristics of Bucke's description appear in Dahlén's account, from which only a short excerpt has been given here. It is easily understandable that such an experience could alter a person's experience of life for his remaining years. The cosmic experience itself lasts only seconds or minutes, and if it does return, it is as a rule less intense each time. Consciousness cannot endure such intense contact with the field of psychic energy for more than a very short period of time. What Bucke refers to as cosmic consciousness slowly fades away, but the person's remaining lifetime is illumined by the memory of it.

Experiences such as those Dahlén and Bucke describe seem to me to indicate a more intense and profound contact with the psychic field than those described in Cases 52 and 53 and in the more "imageless" Case 54. Or is the distinction simply one of ability to describe these experiences? It is still possible to imagine a difference of degree even in these experiences. Perhaps the term *cosmic flash* would be more appropriate for experiences of Bucke's type, for it suggests both their cosmic nature and their short duration [24]. The term cosmic consciousness could then be reserved for the permanent state of consciousness which is the result of such cosmic flashes, primarily in the few cases in which the individual can willfully re-establish contact with the content of the cosmic flash, that is, the psychic world. Actually, then, cosmic consciousness should provide the ability to willfully establish contact with desired aspects of the psychic world. This is a state which surpasses C-IR, in which, according to LeShan [10], attention cannot be focused but rather is directed and determined by whatever information is forthcoming.

Cosmic consciousness is a provisional hypothetical state; as long as we have no opportunity to experience it ourselves or to study it easily in others, we cannot either prove or disprove the conviction that it occurs. The criterion for the quality of this state must remain the accounts of those people who say that they have experienced it. In cosmic consciousness two different grades of experience may be pictured.

Figure .7 is an attempt at visualizing the different grades of consciousness of the psychic world: from the "everyday consciousness," or sensory experience, S-IR, to the humble level of C-IR, which is probably produced in ESP-experiments, on to a higher grade of C-IR in spontaneous paranormal or psychic experiences, on through different degrees of mystical experience and cosmic flashes, up to, finally, the cosmic consciousness. The curve does not, of course, intend to express any materialistic connection, only an attempt to sketch relationships which have been discussed here.

Inspiration refers to an intense contact with the psychic field and

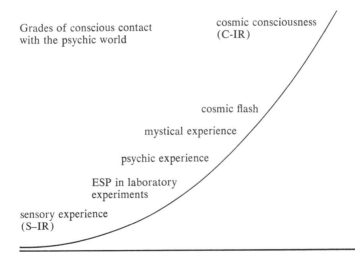

FIGURE 7

may be placed in Figure 7 between the psychic and the mystical experiences. The highest states, cosmic flashes and cosmic consciousness, are, on the other hand, rather dependent on access to another quality of consciousness, namely, *intuition*.

Only a very few reports exist of people who can establish contact with the cosmic consciousness by will. The Danish author Martinus describes, among other things, the following account of his experience in 1921, at the age of thirty [20].

> . . . Then it happened that one day, as a completely untutored and ignorant thirty-year-old man, I came to a total stranger's home to borrow a theosophical book. A friend in the office where I worked had recommended this man to me. . . . I never got to read the book in the end. The little I did read was what lead me to meditate on God. And then one evening, just when I was trying to do that, the following experience occurred, whereupon, for purely psychic reasons, it was completely impossible for me to continue reading the book, for my consciousness from that moment in time in itself had become an unfathomable eternal source, which made the study of any kind of literature superfluous.
>
> *
>
> Following the instructions in the book I had borrowed, I tried to meditate one evening on the concept of "God." And suddenly, without any idea of how, I found myself the center of a kind of incredible exaltation. . . . I looked right into a figure of flame. A Christ-being of mixed sunrays now moved with raised arms as if to include me in his embrace. I was completely paralyzed. . . . But the figure continued to move forward, and in the next instant it entered my own flesh and blood. A wonderful, astounding elevated emotion seized me. The paralysis was over. The holy light which had come to abide in me gave me the ability to see out over the world. And behold! Continents and oceans, cities and countries, mountains and valleys bathed in the light from my own interior. In the white light, the world became changed to "God's kingdom."—The holy experience was over. I was faced with physical reality again, the details of my room, my humble position. But "God's kingdom" continued to glow and glitter in my brain and in my nerves.
>
> Then the next morning when I made myself comfortable on my meditation chair, and had scarcely prepared myself, when I was elevated once again to my godly light. I saw within it a shining blue sky, which was drawn aside in a way, whereby a new and even more shining heaven came into view. This

went on until a heaven was revealed of such incredibly blinding golden light and of such swiftly vibrating matter that I felt here I had reached the limit of what my organism and my consciousness could endure. . . . But in the fraction of a second that manifestation lasted, I experienced a universe of unity, purity, harmony, and completeness. I found myself in an ocean of light. It was not, as in my first manifestation, white as snow, but on the contrary, appeared the color of gold. All the details were gilded fire. . . . Throughout everything, small golden threads vibrated. . . . I knew this was God's consciousness, his own thoughtsphere. It was the substance, the all powerful, the greatest living power, through which the godly Self directed and led oceans of worlds, winter streets and multitudes of stars, in the microcosm as well as in the macrocosm. I was completely overwhelmed. The godly fire vibrated within and without, over and beneath me. . . . I felt as if I was bathing in . . . love. I was the origin of all love, saw the godlike perfection; I was one with the Way, the Truth, and the Life, was one with the great Father.

An earthly organism is not yet able to bear such an overwhelming concentration of God's highest being itself, and therefore I had to cut off this divine vision quickly. But even though the supernatural experience had to cease, I could never return completely to the physical world again. A change had come over my consciousness. I had been born into a new world, had become conscious in a new body. And from that instant, the world which lay beyond all physical phenomena was permanently part of my daily consciousness. The golden light had left me in a state of conscious immortality, with the ability to see that only life exists, that darkness and suffering are only camouflaged love, that God's being is present in each and every one of us.

. . . let me emphasize that the experience occurred when I was completely awake and in conscious control. It came . . . as soon as I sat on my meditation chair. It was not a question of my first falling asleep, going into a trance, or losing my waking consciousness in any other way. . . . I instigated and broke off the experience myself completely of my own volition and in relation to what my organism could endure [23].

*

. . . such an elevating occurrence is always a personal, private experience, completely and totally dependent upon the way it takes place, and, of course, it can never be proved an absolute fact, for anyone other than the person involved. The pure outer details . . . are seen only as signs for myself and can neither confirm nor deny the truth of my mission.

The spiritual visions I have had, therefore, would have no

significance in themselves had they not left behind them . . . the capacity to observe available effects. There are, in fact, many people who say that they have had spiritual images, visions, or manifestations, but most of these alleged experiences have not left behind them any outward visible sign, any change in their emanation, discernible by other people. And the identity of those experiences can therefore not be determined to be either fantasy or reality and so has no intellectual value. These visions may be accepted only by people who are able to enjoy "faith" and therefore demand neither intellectual nor scientific understanding. Thus they constitute no foundation for scientific knowledge at all; they are merely released moments for the creation of "faith."

If these visions are not real, but rather mere illusions, "the faith" becomes identical with "fanaticism" and the "believers" with pure "fanatics." Consequently, great risks are involved in believing in manifestations, which have produced no visible effects to be investigated by the intellect, and the identification of which as reality might be made factual for others.

The essential aspect for the reader is, therefore, not the spiritual visions in themselves which I have had, but the results they have created, for these can, more or less, be investigated by an honest, impartial person acting as a free agent.

*

One circumstance also worth noting is that after these experiences it was completely impossible for me to read. The very thought of reading a book was enough to cause an apprehension in my brain as though it were about to shatter. And from the time that I went through these spiritual processes up to when I had fundamentally and thoroughly created a world vision and manifested it in visual form, I was then not in contact with any book or any other form of theoretical guidance at all, just as I must furthermore say that before the awakening of my cosmic capabilities, I had been a totally unlettered, unread man. I had never studied deeply, only received the ordinary public school education which, in my case, since I was born in the country, only happened three hours twice a week in the summer and somewhat longer in the winter. . . . Hence, with the exception of my "learning as a child," I had not been in contact with theosophy, anthroposophy, spiritualism, or any other of the current foremost spiritual movements until after I had myself experienced the whole vision of the universe and produced it in the forms of my own symbols and drawings. Thanks to these happy circumstances, I can now be a living proof that a state really does exist in eternal development in which one can come

to the highest wisdom and knowledge—through completely
personal observation—absolutely independent of books or other
means of receiving theoretical knowledge, in which one can
achieve, can be elevated to, an eternally explicit, lucid existence
in the midst of a temporal physical existence.

The description of this cosmic experience shares essential characteristics with those of Dahlén and Bucke. The basic differences seem
to be that the access to cosmic consciousness could be controlled by
will. The visible results of Martinus' experience have been an extensive and unique body of literature, which we will return to in Chapter 19.

Thus we conclude our summary of the twenty-one states of consciousness defined in Figure 4. By the hypothesis of two aspects of
reality, S-IR and C-IR, the material and the psychic fields, the psi-
phenomenon can be included in a total vision together with the mystical experience. LeShan [21] has also carried out experiments to test
certain aspects of his hypothesis of S-IR and C-IR.

A concept which aims at being comprehensive always involves
a simplification of the reality it attempts to describe. If the concept is
very simple, it is easy to understand but gives an "untrue" picture of
that reality. The more complicated the concept, the nearer it may
come to corresponding to reality, but the more difficult it will be to
understand. The image of material and psychic energy fields with
the brain as a transformer is a very simple one. It may be objected
that this image merely replaces an old question mark with a new one.
It doesn't actually explain very much as long as we still do not know
what "material energy" and "psychical energy" really are. Yet the
hypothesis of the two fields can be useful, since it offers a common
frame of reference for these phenomena which appear so different:
psi-experiments in the laboratory, spontaneous psychic experiences,
mystical and cosmic experiences. Perhaps the theory might eventually
be developed in greater detail and possibly contribute to a better understanding of paranormal phenomena.

The hypothesis of the material and the psychic worlds implies
that some form of survival of the dead is possible and likely, though
not definitely determined. In the following chapter, we will see how
we might envisage this hypothetical survival.

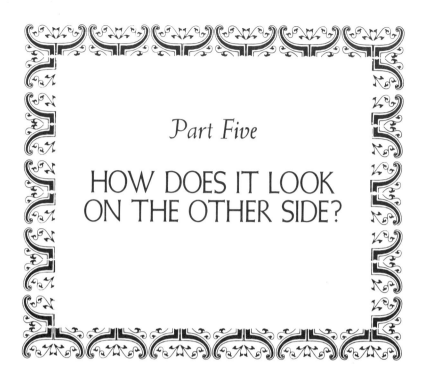

Part Five

HOW DOES IT LOOK
ON THE OTHER SIDE?

18

How Can Life After Death Be Pictured?

Perhaps we've stopped a fleeting moment here
While on our way to quite another sphere.

Perhaps we must profoundly be debased
Before in honor elsewhere we'll be raised.

Perhaps our death which heightens all our fear
Will, with annihilation, turn to cheer.

Perhaps our lives are only obstacles
En route to where there are no earthly shackles.

HJALMAR GULLBERG

The phenomena and experiences described in Chapters 8 through 14 are all consistent with the hypothesis of survival of the dead. In many of the best-studied cases, the survival hypothesis is actually the *simplest* explanation, and it can explain all of them without our having to enlarge or alter the hypothesis with additional theories to fit each separate group of phenomena. In as much as the hypothesis assumes survival of the dead, it appears to be rejected from the start by many in our culture. Any other theory, however muddled it might be, is preferable to them, yet the alternative hypotheses have drawbacks. They assume "super-ESP" and other miraculous abilities, the existence of which is not confirmed by any of our evidence except those very phenomena which indicate survival.

Then why do so many people prejudge the survival hypothesis?

One reason is because it is impossible for us to offer any conception of what an existence after death might be like. Furthermore, of course, no one has come back and told us about it.

But this assertion is unfounded. There does, in fact, exist a rich corpus of accounts describing "the other side," partly from mediums who declare that they have contact with the deceased, partly from people who state that they have made short visits to "the other world." Nor is it so difficult to describe a conceivable form of after-existence. Naturally, we are working with guesses and suppositions; the only way to ascertain their truth definitely would be for someone to check them himself after his own death, to the extent that this is possible. We shall consider more closely some suppositions which can be made from the existing collected evidence.

Five Forms of Survival

Ducasse [1] mentions five different possibilities for imaginable survival:

1. The psyche might be conceived of as existing in a "sleeping" form, such as we assume it has when the body is unconscious. Thus, at its peak it is able to function automatically, mechanically, and can be conscious of vague associations with names and ideas from its earthly life. The great mass of "greetings from the deceased" during spiritualistic seances scarcely indicate much more than this.

2. Another possibility is that some of the psyche's abilities are not only preserved but may also be utilized more actively, but without critical control. This defines psychic life in the same way that ordinary dreams or daydreams are psychic life.

3. A third possibility is that psychic life after death might consist of a reviewing glance back over experiences from earthly life, made with the intention of achieving perspective and of learning something from them. (How this new survey could be used later is another question.)

4. The fourth possibility is that the psyche is able to function with intelligent control and goal-directed, creative thinking. This psychic life would consist of such activities as, for example, mathematicians, poets, musicians, and philosophers carry out during their earthly existence, occasionally completely undisturbed by and unconscious of their surroundings.

5. A fifth possibility is that psychic life also consists of an ability to make contact with other psyches in the same state through telepathy, and may also, under special conditions, contact psyches which are still bound to an earthly body.

As Broad [2] has pointed out, these possibilities need not exclude each other. Different stages of development could also be considered to exist in life beyond death. Psychic life, in its wider sense, means that at least occasionally possibilities 3, 4, and 5 could perhaps be realized. The better indices of life after death, for example, the cross-correspondences (page 149), also imply the fifth possibility.

The Next World

Life after death must mean that the psyche is cut off from sensory stimuli, since the sensory organs no longer function. The psyche has, therefore, no contact with the material world but finds itself instead in what Price [3] calls the "next world." This world could be thought to resemble the world in which our dreams take place. As long as a dream lasts, it is actually very vivid and real to us, as real as the outside material world. In dreams, we move about through houses, down streets and roads as real as the material ones. We are able to see bright colors, experience intense smells and taste sensations. We can handle objects and communicate with other people. Yet we know that these experiences do not depend on sensory impressions from the outer world but have other causes (even if isolated stimuli from the outer world can be perceived during sleep and incorporated in dreams). The dream's events are played out in the *inner world*. This is a world of mental images, but need not consequently be an imagined world. Objects in dreams are absolutely real to us as long as we do not awaken from the dream. These objects could be said to exist not in the material sense, but this does not mean that they do not exist at all. But the world in which they exist obeys other laws than those of the material world. If "the next world" is similar to the dream one, then it can also be experienced as vividly as the present material one.

Then each psyche could be thought to build its own world after death from memories, wishes, and needs, just as these influence dreams during earthly life. Consequently, many "next worlds" could exist, one for each psyche, but to the extent that different psyches share similar interests, wishes, and memories, they would communicate telepathically and, during this phase, have access to each other's worlds. Ducasse's (see Chapter 16, Note 1) concept of the "private" psyche could also be found here. But as several psyches have common interests, they could also have a common world, public to them.

Does this mean that all wishes are fulfilled? Yes, this could be considered the case, but it does not mean that this existence becomes automatically happy, in a banal way, or free from problems. This environment which the psyche experiences consists of these wishes and needs: these could be said to become materialized in the psyche's environment. But if the wishes and needs are not beautiful or pleasant in themselves, then the surroundings will follow suit. A world consisting exclusively of our imaginings and dreams, materialized in the outward surroundings, would not automatically turn out to be happy and positive—any more than our imaginings, wishes, drives and needs are positive in reality. Moreover, if the state after death involves the elimination of the borderline between consciousness and unconsciousness, then even greater possibilities exist for unpleasant psychic content becoming visible and manifest in our surroundings.

The fact that very different descriptions of the next world have come from mediums in different cultures need not argue against the existence of such a world, since different psyches could be thought to construct common surroundings, depending on their common conceptions of surroundings. Similarly, groups of individuals with different conceptions of existence after death could have experiences of these particular conceptions verified. The "heavenly city," with thousands of pious citizens, would indeed be thought of as a common milieu for psyches sharing similar concepts, built completely according to their own expectations and wishes. The Viking's Valhalla, the Indian's Happy Hunting Ground, could also have a real existence for a number of psyches. The convinced materialist could experience the total emptiness he anticipates after death; the only essential difference would be that he finds himself still psychically living and conscious. If possibilities for telepathic connection with psyches in earthly bodies (that is, mediums) exists, then, as a matter of course, two mediums could establish contact with two completely different "lands" or "cultures" in the next world and therefore give what seem to be completely different accounts. But by studying these, we may still expect to find basic common characteristics, as typical for the next world as they are distinct from our present one.

At the Border of the Next World

Now, how do these guesses about the nature and geography of the next world relate to the facts? It can be established that many communications through mediums describe conditions very similar to those suggested here. But these communications presuppose that a next world really exists. Two types of experiences, which do not assume a concept of the next world, have been studied by Stevenson [4], among others. These are the experience of separation and the state of being "near death."

Separation has fascinated researchers who have seen in it a short visit to the next world. Persons who have experienced many separations sometimes describe how in that state they have had contact with and observed people who were also in a separated state. They could still, however, see them completely clearly and vividly, just as distinctly as individuals are seen on the physical plane. They concluded, or felt instinctively, that these other people were what is called dead, though they still had "bodies" and could be observed as living [5]. Noteworthy also is how often people after separation have described an experience of psychic clarity (despite the fact that in certain cases their brains have been severely injured). They often describe a feeling of peace and freedom from ordinary cares, occasionally a sensation of unity with other beings and with totality, which approximates the mystical experience.

Dying people, like dreamers, have less control over their thoughts than people who are completely awake. Occasionally they are in a state similar to what is called delirium, in which thought processes resemble those of the dream. (Another common cause of delirium is lengthy and ample consumption of alcohol.) Thinking becomes less abstract, richer in imagery. A stream of images comes to the consciousness and can be projected into outer reality and thus can be perceived as hallucinations. Analysis of the content of hallucinations under delirium has revealed them to be largely determined by the person's ordinary thinking [6, 7]. A patient in delirium can perceive the hospital bed as his car and the ward personnel as his relatives or the people he works with. His customary ways of thinking largely determine what sort of hallucination he experiences: his thoughts become materialized. A dying person in this state actually finds himself already at the borderline of the next world, and should his psyche survive, then possibly his experience after death will also be dependent on his habitual ways of thinking. This conception, which is based on observations of dying people, is completely in accord with certain Oriental teachings of the state after death. For example, *The Tibetan Book of the Dead* [8] clearly states that each person's next world will be determined to a great extent by his customary thoughts and wishes.

The Difficulty of Communication

Then, if survival does exist, why do we have such scanty communication from that sphere? People who are interested in the problem of survival state before they die that they will communicate if they can. They die, and nothing is heard from them—or, through a medium some very meager messages appear, not at all of the quality to be expected from them. (Still, exceptions do exist, very intimate personal communications, for example, the cross-correspondences.)

Many people immediately conclude that no extensive communication is forthcoming because survival does not take place. But this is not certain. The explanation might be that the conditions in the next world virtually exclude connection with psyches in earthly bodies. Perhaps communication demands very strong motivation and great effort to be effected at all, and perhaps it cannot be achieved in any way we have been considering before death. Perhaps also the motivation diminishes because the psyche is involved in new experiences and interests, despite the promise and the intention to communicate. This condition might, as Stevenson [9] mentioned, be likened to the chemically induced psychedelic experience. The subject may be ever so purposeful in his intention to participate in the way desired, but nevertheless becomes absorbed in the drug experience and sinks into it: his motivation slides away from him.

Stevenson [9] indicates that perhaps we are expecting the impossible of potential communicators from the next world. We cannot demand of them that they identify themselves by name, social security number, and most recent address. To be able to do this, they must recall these facts. But the imprint of memory depends partly on the intensity of the experience, partly on its repetition. Moreover, the results of parapsychology indicate that signals of strong emotional content are those most readily perceived. A person who does not write his name professionally very often may not have his name so deeply imprinted. A surname in particular is, for most people, seldom connected with experiences of emotion. Communicators do actually seem to have difficulty giving their surnames; instead, they identify themselves by their first names. Address and date of birth have even less emotional significance, and we cannot expect that they would be so deeply imprinted.

Moreover, what communicators perceive to be essential is different from what is essential to us. If we wish to increase the possibilities of communication, contact must first of all be sought in such areas as are emotionally meaningful to the communicators. Ordinarily, in spiritualist seances, the survivors' wish to communicate is more often completely egotistical and directed to what is emotionally meaningful to them rather than what is meaningful to the deceased communicators.

Comments on the difficulties of communication itself also often appear in the messages produced by mediums. Little else could have been expected. Our language is actually perfectly adapted to conditions in the material world. We cannot expect that the same concepts would also be suitable to describe conditions in a non-material or psychic world. Indeed, mediums often describe the communications as moods, feelings, or images rather than words, or trains of thought. The communicator "shows images," which the medium tries to receive. This is a reasonable technique to use when disturbances are very powerful in connection with signal intensity. Perhaps the point worth making is not that the communication is scanty but rather that it occurs at all. The most detailed communications have also usually taken place using techniques in which the communicator could be thought to work through a part of the medium's body more directly, for example, in automatic writing.

These guesses concerning the conditions in a possible next world (anything more than guesses they cannot be) have been based on the reports by people who have been near death and on observations of the dying. These are, so to speak, observations of the next world from outside, from the borders of our world. Furthermore, accounts of people exist, who, during separation, say that they have made short visits to the other world, and these descriptions point in the same direction. Communication through mediums represents alleged communication directly from inhabitants of the next world, more or less accurately deciphered by mediums. Still another channel to the next world is conceivable. The mystical experience could possibly involve direct contact with conditions in this next world, in so far as it is identical with the psychic world. Therefore it is of interest to hear what a present-day mystic has to tell us about this world, and such is the theme of the next chapter.

19

A Contemporary Mystic's Description of Life After Death

So long as one flower exists, the recollection of a higher world cannot be erased.   MARTINUS

Modern Western man, brought up with a materialistic vision of life, believing only in "science," looks upon phenomena like mysterious and mystical experiences very suspiciously and dismisses them from the start as not worth knowing about at all. But, as Chapter 17 indicated, mystical experiences need not be at variance with the image of reality we receive through our senses and their different extensions in the form of technical devices. What you see depends on your viewpoint: a person who views the surrounding world from the bottom of a mine experiences it differently from one who sees it from a mountain top. In fact, the content of mystical experiences does not contradict the testimony of our senses but rather illuminates it from another point of departure, gives it supersensual, metaphysical meaning. Mystical experiences may possibly be only illusions caused by psychological mechanisms. It is also possible that they provide genuine information about another dimension of existence, a dimension which cannot be perceived by the five senses. The occurrence of ESP speaks strongly for the latter possibility.

I want to emphasize that the perception of existence after death which will be treated now does not claim to *prove* anything or to represent "the truth." The mystical experience carries with it its own absolute wisdom and certainty for the individual who receives it, but this does not affect anyone other than himself. Each of us must judge the content of the vision in the same way we judge other hypotheses, namely, by its own inner logic and by its outward conformity to known facts. But if we find the conception logical and unified in itself, and if, moreover, it is more consistent with known facts than other hypotheses, then nothing prevents us from accepting it as a working theory. The next step will then be to try to find ways to prove it through experiences and experiments.

Several religious movements in our time give information about existence after the death of the body. Different teachings within Hinduism and Buddhism offer separate concepts of the question. *The Tibetan Book of the Dead* (see Chapter 18 Note 8) contains detailed information concerning the state after death and instructions on how the dead should conduct themselves. Oriental teachings have inspired the bases of doctrines such as Theosophy [1] and Anthroposophy [2, 3], which also describe life after death. These descriptions agree fundamentally but can be distinguished one from another in many details.

A Present-Day Mystic

None of these doctrines will be discussed here; each has its own brilliant and capable spokesmen. Instead, I will turn to a less well known present-day mystic, the Danish author Martinus Thomsen (whose pen name is Martinus), born in 1890. His work is an example of how a mystical or cosmic experience can totally alter a human being. At the time of his "cosmic initiation" in 1921, he was working as an accountant in an office in Copenhagen. He had a positive, open attitude toward religion and felt vague dissatisfaction with his work because it gave him no opportunity to do anything for others. He was completely ignorant of spiritualism, theosophy, and similar movements. A friend at work, noticing his interest in spiritual questions, introduced him to a well-read man who lent him a theosophical book. Martinus went home and began to read the book. After a few pages, he read that if a person wanted knowledge, he should sit and meditate on the concept of God. Martinus did this, and had the experience that has been described in his own words on pages 257–260. Afterward he found it impossible to read any further in the book. It was, moreover, unnecessary; he found himself now in a completely new state of consciousness which he called cosmic consciousness. He had conscious and will-controlled access to the path of knowledge which he called *intuition*. (This can be defined as "direct insight, which is not preceded by analytical reasoning [4].") As soon as he established contact with this intuition and thought about spiritual problems, the answer was immediately there, in the form of absolute *knowledge*. But it was a knowledge without words, and his real work followed afterward: to express this knowledge in words and to make it comprehensible to others. This knowledge involved spiritual areas, for which suitable words do not exist in our materially oriented language.

The new state of consciousness produced paranormal experiences as well: telepathy, clairvoyance, and separations. He experienced other people's illnesses vividly, palpably, as pain in his own body. He had to refrain from separations completely, when he found that they hindered his basic work. After a long and initially trying adjustment to this new state, he could begin to express his intuitive knowledge as a systematic and inclusive world view or cosmology, which now appears worked out in a series of books and symbols. The inner logic and beauty of this world view and its compatibility with natural scientific facts have inspired others. The description of life after death is therefore only a small part of this total image of how our existence is ordered [5].

"Death Is in Reality God's Greatest Surprise for Mankind"

The point of departure for the following is that earthly man, according to Martinus, consists not only of the material body, but also of a psyche which interacts with the body through the intermediary of the brain, basically as was suggested in Chapters 16 and 17. The more detailed structure of this psyche is described in Martinus' work, but we cannot discuss it in greater detail here. What happens during the process we call death is that the psyche's contact with the physical body is broken, and it is now obliged to live only in the psychic world. (A certain limited contact with the physical world may still occur for a short while. The dead person is able to receive diffused impressions from conditions around his body for a few hours or some days after death. Actually, this contact occurs through clairvoyance or telepathy, and it soon ceases completely.) From now on the expression: "(the living) being" will be used to refer to a person who through death has lost contact with his physical body.

The Mental Life Space and the First Sphere

The world which greets the being after death is therefore, in Martinus' terms, the spiritual, and the state during the time immediately following the body's death is called *the first sphere*. The physical world is one of *time and space,* but the spiritual is of *time and condition.* It does not, like the physical world, consist of matter which the being experiences as heavy, stable, or difficult to handle. The spiritual world is one of easy, light, transient, *"spiritual matter"* which has also been called "astral material" or "psychic ether." This spiritual matter becomes visible only in so far as the being itself concentrates and forms it. Matter obeys the least wishes of the being. As soon as the being conceives, wishes, or needs something, it is immediately present. When the concentration on a certain material form ceases, it dissolves and fades away.

After death a being cannot make contact with physical matter. Instead, it experiences details in what could be called its own *mental life universe,* that is, everything the being has knowledge and experience of, all the concepts and memories that are imprinted on his consciousness. The stronger and more emotionally emphatic these concepts are, the more they contribute to the formation of a mental life universe and thereby the surroundings of the being. This means that the surroundings immediately after death are not remarkably different from the surroundings immediately before death. The difference is simply that the surroundings are now constructed solely by the being's own conceptions.

Thus, the being experiences an environment of pure hallucinations, very like a dream experience. Actually, according to Martinus, the dream takes place in the spiritual world and thus the dream—especially the lucid dream—gives an indication of how the state after death will appear. However, in a dream a person is still biologically alive and retains primary consciousness, day consciousness, on the physical plane. The dreamer is only a temporary guest in the spiritual plane. Impressions from the physical world can be received and worked into the dream. After death the bond is broken with the physical world and then day consciousness exists only on the spiritual plane. For a short while after death the ability to evaluate experiences critically is, as a rule, ineffective, just as it often is after an ordinary dream.

The tangibility and reality of spiritual matter can be illustrated by

Case 21, on page 93. But after death there are no more light switches behind mountain sides: the hotel room cannot be experienced any longer, for now only the grotto represents "reality."

Martinus points out that the being in the spiritual world actually does not move: instead, the surroundings come to the being. An example from a lucid dream can illustrate this:

55. I became conscious of a dream while it was happening. The dream consisted of my climbing up a gigantic pile of telephone poles, stacked in a square, two by two, so that there was just enough space to put one's foot in between them to climb. I clambered up very high, and the pile seemed to grow even higher. When I approached the top, I thought, "What if the whole pile should begin to sway?" And in the next instant it began to shudder. "Now it's going to crash down," I thought, and then it crashed, and I fell to the ground. But while I was crashing down I could notice that I was still lying on my bed calmly. It was very simply a foreshortening of perspective which produced the sensation of falling down. It was not I who moved, rather the piles and the ground, totally illusionary. [Compare with Case 23 on page 95 from the same dreamer.]

Just as in a lucid dream, a person can experience matter obeying his will after death, but in this state it would happen always and completely. In a lucid dream, the dreamer is most often so rooted in the concept of being in the physical universe that he cannot make up his mind to use his dominance over matter. It is the same here: the being behaves in his hallucinated physical world precisely as he did before death. He continues to live as usual, uses tools and machines to shape matter; walks, drives cars or takes trains, collects money, eats and sleeps. Existence resembles his physical one so much that a long time may pass before the being even realizes that he has died and is no longer in the physical world. But sooner or later he attempts to contact some person who is still in the material world. Perhaps he may hallucinate a "phantom" which resembles this person, but his emotional contact with this phantom will not be real; something about it doesn't ring true. The being notices afterward that a radical change has taken place, but some more time may pass before he fully perceives the nature of the change. A being with strong spiritual interests, prepared for conditions after death, may obviously come to understand his situation more clearly and quickly.

Contact Only "On the Same Wave Length"

According to Martinus, the spiritual world consists only of "super-physical" rays and wave movements. Beings who want to make contact with others can only do so by literally "getting on the same wave length," or contacting those with common interests and inclinations. While in the physical world we are surrounded by people who have other interests, in the spiritual world, two beings cannot basically even make contact with each other if in some way they do not share a common mentality. As long as this common wave length is present, they will be in contact and experience each other in the bodies which they themselves choose to present themselves in. But if one of them shifts his attention to another area of interest, and thereby alters his wave length, he will then contact beings on that other wave length exclusively. The process is similar to that of twisting a radio dial: with each change in frequency, contact with a certain station is lost but other stations may be picked up.

All Wishes Fulfilled

An existence in which your slightest wish is fulfilled, in which matter obeys messages from the will, and in which you can only contact beings who share your own interests, could be thought to satisfy the most banal dream descriptions of a blissful life after death. But reality may be somewhat more complicated.

A successful businessman, whose main interest has been to amass a fortune and property, dies and comes to the first sphere in the spiritual world. He continues his activities with greater success than ever; riches heap up around him with a speed that quite takes his breath away. Naturally he starts thinking of the possibility that he may be robbed or ruined—and immediately robbers appear, and he is subjected to gangster exploits worse than anything he has seen on television. His fantasy takes hold of what has happened and works upon it, suggesting even more terrible hazards which are all immediately reality to him. His situation deteriorates because now he can only contact beings who are on the same wave length as his, that is, beings who also are only interested in making money and who therefore see him as a competitor. But at the same time they are all just as clever as he: no one is impressed by his successes. He is totally alone, surrounded only by competitors and those thieves he produced by his own suggestion. As long as this conception drives him, he will remain bound by it, and he will be less likely to get onto any wave length through which he could alter his condition. He finds himself in a state that could only be characterized as a nightmare or hell, one hundred percent real but also totally of his own creation.

This is only one example of a conceivable course of events. It is not difficult to imagine a corresponding course of events for a person who dies full of hate and bitterness or who is caught in some form of narcotic addiction or other destructive way of thinking and acting that takes up a large part of his mental life universe. These individuals would also live their conceptions worked out in their surroundings, and would also only be able to contact other beings so inclined. They would literally be closed in a mental prison which they experience as absolute reality.

Another example is the religious believer who has been impressed by preachings on the existence of hell and damnation. Horror-laden wondering as to whether perhaps hell exists after all would immediately cause it to exist in all its gruesomeness. Next, such a person might wonder about his own fate in such a setting, and immediately the whole situation is suggested. One factor strongly contributing to a realistic experience of hell is that all time perceptions are now completely subjective. Here there are no regulating clocks. The being gets the impression that what happens now will continue for all eternity, and this greatly intensifies his experience.

The First Sphere As Hell and Paradise

These are only a few examples of how complete fulfillment of all wishes and expectations, together with the impossibility of making contact with beings who do not share your own inclinations, could lead to a very tormented existence. Martinus calls this state *purgatory*. According to him, it is essential, but is usually passed through quickly on the way to higher states. But it is also possible that, from the very beginning, the first sphere may appear like paradise rather than hell. A being who lives totally in a religiously conceived world of a positive nature would have such an experience. An Indian convinced without any doubt that he will go to the Happy Hunting Ground will experience it as he has imagined it. There is a paradise for every mental inclination which is *free of conflict*. But the modern person's view of death (and his view of existence as a whole) is seldom free from conflict. If he really would like to believe in a future life, he may still face scorn and irony from more materialistically oriented fellow men. If he suffers from embracing the total materialism and longs for something more, there may be uncertainty behind the convictions to which he gives lip service. If he turns to established religions, he may encounter the doctrine that hell awaits a person who breaks certain rules. Whatever type of direction he embraces, it probably will not be free from conflict. Wishes and needs that are entirely egotistic can make the experience of the first sphere into a hell. Few people are completely free from both conflicts and egotistic wishes and needs, and therefore to some extent most of us would face purgatory as a very vivid reality. But a person who is basically motivated by the wish to help others, and who has a relatively conflict-free attitude toward death, will meet this reality for a considerably less prolonged period. He will find rich possibilities of increasing his interests in the first sphere. The same is true for those who are primarily interested in art or knowledge, whose interest in these subjects is of a spiritual nature, not egotistically motivated. ("Egotistic," in this context, means the cultivation of an individual's own interests without concern for the interests of others.)

But what happens to beings who, at death, are met and helped across by their relatives on the spiritual plane? Many deathbed visions indicate this, as was mentioned in Chapter 9. Aren't they helped so that they may completely avoid purgatory? No, in so far as egotism is prominent in their concepts, the material for experiences of purgatory exists in them as well.

Purgatory and Guardian Spirits

In this way most people come into a highly realistic contact with the state of purgatory, and for many it soon becomes unbearable. In this situation, religiously inclined people have an easier time than convinced atheists, for a religious being reminds himself in time of need of the efficacy of prayer to the higher powers he believes in, and thus the way is opened to be released from purgatory. The atheist may wait longer before he perceives this way out, but sooner or later he too will pray [6]. Prayer involves a realization that an individual's capabilities are not sufficient; prayer is a turning to others for help out of an unbearable situation. Thus, a being would give up the attitude which has lead to the creation of a purgatory. A change of consciousness is involved, an altered wave length which leads to contact with other beings. These other beings are more experienced on the spiritual plane and are specially trained for the task of helping new arrivals out of their tormented state. Martinus calls them *guardian spirits*. They have always been there, awaiting an opportunity to intervene. But their opportunity first comes when, through prayer (a mental inclination rather than a prayer formulated in words) the being in purgatory alters his own wave length.

Thereupon the guardian spirits intervene, first by revealing themselves to the being in a suitable form. The naïvely religious person may see them as angels with white wings, the more skeptical as "ordinary" people. By showing themselves in a form which awakens both wonderment and belief, contact can be established. From then on, through a process of suggestion, the guardian spirit influences the being, aiming to divert his attention from those conceptions which held him captive earlier, to lead him to other conceptions. The method may be compared to the comfort an adult gives a weeping child, comfort which is also carried out largely through suggestion. Through this influence, the needy being's consciousness is gradually channeled in a new direction. But this can happen only as a result of experiences which the being underwent during the course of purgatory, leaving him with feelings of loneliness, helplessness, and insufficiency; above all, because he was disgusted by those qualities in himself which created the purgatory. Without these experiences, even the most energetic guardian spirit would be ineffective, because the being would not be disposed to let himself be influenced. He would instead tend to rely only on himself and continue to cultivate his own interests. This process might be explained as a form of "brainwashing:" the guardian spirits' suggestions result in the blocking or temporary paralyzing of certain wave lengths and corresponding abilities and inclinations in the being. Then, for the first time, the being enters a state in which he can endure light from the higher spheres he will now visit. Purgatory is, in other words, a melting pot, a crucible, essential for the psyche's "cleansing" from psychic "dross." The process involves limiting the consciousness and reducing the ability to experience life. The being is freed for a while from all incomplete, egotistically colored aspects of his consciousness. "Thereafter this consciousness moves only in the spheres which are already developed to such a degree that within them it can only experience and create light and joy, for others as well as for itself [7]." The being is now "clad in wedding garments," prepared for a solemn occasion, and gains access to a completely different form of experience, namely, that which is called paradise [8].

Summary

We can summarize briefly: the environment which the living being meets immediately after death, called the first sphere, is created totally by the being himself. This consists of a personal mental universe, habitual conceptions and thoughts, which become materialized here as a very vivid outer reality. On the physical plane, the being reciprocates with the psychic outer world, which can lead to concepts and thoughts other than those occupying it at the moment. Now the being is not in contact with any outer world which can spur him to other ideas, imaginings, or thoughts: he is confined in a "mental prison" created of personal needs and ideas. He cannot make contact with other beings unless they are on the same wavelength, that is, have the same inclinations. As a result of the indefinite perception of time, the being may easily feel convinced that this state will continue for all eternity. All this contributes to a more or less intense experience of hell or purgatory. This unpleasant experience causes the being to pray for help, after a shorter or longer period of time, irrespective of whether or not he believes in a higher power. The prayer indicates an altered disposition which makes contact with other beings possible, namely, the guardian spirits. These, through suggestion, rid the being of tormenting ideas and redirect his attention. Their suggestion also causes the being's consciousness to become limited, temporarily incapacitating those inclinations which created his purgatory. This alteration is necessary for the being to be able to endure contact with spiritual energies and spheres of higher quality. This process is called "the second death," and is at the same time a "birth" into a higher sphere.

Martinus emphasizes that no one need fear death because of purgatory. In purgatory the being experiences only his own thoughts, vividly materialized to constitute his entire surroundings, so that he may fully realize the extent of his development and the primitive qualities of his personality.

Paradise in the First Sphere

The being's existence in the first sphere, after the release from purgatory, constitutes the sharpest possible contrast to his existence in purgatory. In the first sphere's paradise, the being may carry on a physically oriented ideal existence in which he can develop his positive needs, wishes, and interests. He is able to experience an ideal existence in the highest form he could ever imagine or conceive of. Each and every one, needless to say, has the possibility of doing whatever he wishes. Here beings live for each other, in contrast to the purgatory area, where each and everyone lived for himself. Nevertheless, existence remains predominantly "physical" in its emphasis, which means that it functions more or less as it does on the physical plane: there is work, for example, as guardian spirits, and free time. Here there are also local "paradises" and "holy cities" for the various religious denominations; they are populated by people with common concepts and can be sought out and experienced by all those who share the same wave lengths. "In my Father's house are many mansions" (John 14:2).

Mystics and Parapsychology

Let us imagine for a moment that survival does occur according to the theory outlined in Chapters 8 through 14. Martinus' description of existence immediately after death has, as we mentioned, been formed from knowledge acquired directly through intuition, not after study of parapsychological or theosophical literature. And yet we find amazing conformity between Martinus' description and the guesses which were mentioned in Chapter 18.

Statements received from communicators through mediums often describe conditions which seem remarkably like the earthly ones. But this is really not surprising if they are created by the habitual thought pictures of the beings, and if the beings have not yet learned to make full use of all the possibilities on the spiritual plane.

Martinus points out that a being who, during its earthly life, had been dependent on, for example, alcohol, may contact an earthly alcoholic, in order to "sponge" on his drinking telepathically. A being who died full of thoughts of revenge against someone could seek to contact that person so intensely that his contact would be experienced as possession. This is illustrated by "Murray" and "Marvin" in Chapter 11. In both cases, Prince assumed the role of guardian spirit by indicating other options open to them. "Marvin" also confirmed that in the first sphere a being attracts those similarly inclined: "It was not only myself who tormented you. Others gathered around me, joining their efforts with mine and urging me on."

As was mentioned, the guardian spirits' suggestions result in certain capacities in the being becoming paralyzed. This means that thought forms and concepts and images linked to corresponding psychic organs are "cast off" by the being, much as you discard a worn-out suit of clothes. Some of these images, especially those belonging to the being's conception of himself as a physical body, are very strongly imprinted. Using Hart's expression (page 122) it could be said that these conceptions had built up a very deeply imprinted etheric body. This then will be "laid aside" at the being's second death, but it does not dissolve or disappear as fast as other creations of spiritual matter. On the contrary, it may exist for a while longer and also mechanically repeat certain parts of the original physical organism's habitual patterns of action. Under certain conditions, it may also become visible in the physical world as an apparition or a "ghost."

> An American officer who visited Hiroshima sometime after the atomic bomb, stood by the remains of a bridge foundation. Suddenly he saw before him the whole bridge complete and undamaged with a group of school children walking on it to a point where they suddenly disappeared. He looked on fascinated as the children came into sight again, walked on the bridge, and disappeared at the same point. The scene was repeated several times, as long as he could retain the vision [9].

A conceivable explanation of this experience would then be that the children, now on the spiritual plane, tried for the first time to come to some understanding of what had happened to them by repeating their last actions on the physical plane, namely, walking on the bridge up to the moment of the explosion. When shortly thereafter they were taken in hand by the guardian spirits, they laid aside their remaining coarse psychic structures, which then functioned robotlike for a while, until they gradually dissolved. What the man saw would then have been their discarded psychic "shells" repeating their last movements in the physical lives mechanically. According to Martinus, such "psychic robots" are what may become visible as apparitions of Hart's type A (compare Cases 40a and 40b). They could be called "psychic corpses" from the second death, but unlike a corpse, they are able to repeat a series of life impressions mechanically and soullessly. In order to be perceived on the physical plane they must remain materialized to some extent, and so there must be some substance present, which in spiritualist materialization seances would be called *ectoplasm* or *teleplasm*. This substance is produced, according to Martinus, by certain psychic persons. It is also produced to some extent by others through psychic activities expressed as faith in life after death, the spirit world, and other expressions. This could be considered an explanation of experiences of ghosts, phantoms, revenants, and all those apparitions which have been judged up until now not to be completely uncommon or unheard of, in any case, not in the country. (Naturally, a general belief in these phenomena may also produce other phenomena assumed to be similar, but which are not, in fact, apparitions at all.) The prevailing materialistic concept today views such theories with contempt, as pure superstition and naïve, gullible belief. This has resulted in a completely different psychic climate, obviously with poor consequences for materialization of the spirit world.

Through mediums, communicators have described experiences after death which could be literal illustrations of Martinus' basic concepts. Often a state of purgatory is suggested which includes a special being whose task is to help new arrivals in need. Raudive's tape voices describe a remarkably earthlike existence. They obviously have an intense telepathic contact with the experimentor on the material plane. Perhaps while in purgatory, which some of them describe very graphically, they experience this contact as a soothing comfort [10].

When communicators are asked whether rebirth occurs, they give very unclear answers. This is also to be expected, if they themselves are still in the first sphere and have no foreknowledge of their coming development in the spiritual plane. They mention beings from higher planes coming to visit their plane, and the possibility of development is indicated. But then the information ceases and the communicator himself is silent thereafter. As the being develops and moves away from the first sphere, clearly his ability to communicate diminishes similarly. But contact with higher spheres in the form of "pure inspiration" may still occur [11].

Evolution Through Higher Spheres

Martinus also describes development beyond the first sphere. This paradise of the first sphere might appear impossible to surpass, from our earthly viewpoint. Yet it is primarily composed of *physically* oriented activities. On the other hand, the spiritual world is more conducive to the development of *spiritual* interests, that is, such interests as art and knowledge, at first especially those activities in which a being occupies himself with material content and meaning and aims at controlling matter. Beings with primarily spiritual interests need only make a short visit to the first sphere. But even the others eventually tire of the physically emphasized activities there, and then direct their interest toward the spiritual aspect of existence. By this altered disposition, the being is gradually led toward new and fascinating zones, in which he has occasion to increase his purely spiritual interests to the full extent of his capacity. Martinus has described these zones and their ordinary inhabitants, but we cannot expand on this more fully here. The being exists as a marveling guest or "tourist" in these highly spiritual worlds and, according to his capacity, takes part in these activities. But sooner or later a time comes when he has exhausted his capacity to renew his life experience in this area. His capacity to handle spiritual energies is very elementary compared with the capacities of the regular inhabitants there. The being's primitive organ for experiencing and creating with this material begins, quite simply, to wear out, just as the earthly body is worn out by a long life.

This causes the being slowly to draw himself back from the company of his "hosts" in the high spiritual zones. He now begins to feel a need for a contrast to the light-filled experiences which have involved him for so long and which he has now almost tired of. The only conceivable contrast is . . . earthly existence. In a dizzying memory panorama, the being experiences his three or four previous physical lives. For he has lived several times on the earth (or on another planet). In his memory panorama, the being experiences the physical occurrences cleansed from all unpleasantness. Now he finds a perspective, an overview, and a meaning which he could not see on the physical plane. This memory experience fills the being with the highest joy, which has caused Martinus to name this state "the blessed kingdom." Here the being can see what plan and purpose the last life had followed. He considers that a new physical incarnation is necessary for his being's further development, and thereby the process begins which leads to a new physical life.

The Rebirth

As the being in the blessed kingdom nears his next physical life, which as a rule happens automatically and almost unnoticeably to the being, itself completely absorbed in his memory experiences, the physical beams or rays begin once again to approach the physical plane. This beaming is of a certain nature, which, for example, determines that the being can only be incarnated as a person and not as an animal. In this context, a fertilized cell (that is, an egg cell joined together with a sperm cell) can be thought of as a "receiver": the inclination to receive depends on the complex of genes and chromosomes which determine the physical organism's future development. Through a process of resonance, the being makes contact with the one fertilized cell of all those available which best corresponds to its own beamings; the rays beam out and join to this cell, and that is when the reincarnation takes place. Normally this happens at the instant of conception, but under certain special circumstances it could happen later. (The case of Jasbir, Chapter 13, could be seen most specifically as an example of a "failure.") But the being is still primarily conscious on the spiritual plane, thus he keeps his waking consciousness in the blissful kingdom; consciousness of the new physical life grows gradually and is not total until some time has passed following his physical birth.

This should indicate that infants are beings of high quality, coming directly from the spiritual world, with a high degree of insight concerning the meaning of their last lives as well as the one already begun. Why does this insight disappear; why doesn't the child remember his former life?

As we have seen in Chapter 13, there are children who do remember earlier lives. But most often these memories lead to trials and difficulties in their present lives. The pains and trials of one life at a time are sufficient. Even fewer people say they can remember the state between death and birth.

Daytime waking consciousness, minimal during nursing and infant stages, gradually draws them away from the spiritual to the material plane. The impressions of the blessed kingdom gradually fade away: stimuli come instead more powerfully from the physical world. During their first phase on the physical plane, children learn only very gradually to distinguish between impressions from their own inner worlds and stimuli from the outer world: between the "I" and the "not-I." The knowledge of the blessed kingdom remains with infant children as a series of dispositions which indicate the potential development of the new life. The primitive, unready, egotistically insistent part of the being's consciousness, temporarily not functioning because of the guardian spirits' intervention, awakens again; it can be influenced permanently only by experiences during physical life.

Reincarnation and Karma

The theory of *karma* appears in many concepts of reincarnation: a principle of what is "sown and harvested." What man sows in one life, he will, according to the law of karma, reap in the same or a later life. You "pay now—or later," but you must pay. Now, if reincarnation really exists, then it is simpler to imagine that there must be some meaning to it. A conceivable meaning is that the being gathers wisdom and experience through the workings of karma over several lifetimes, wisdom it can later use. Physical lives could be thought of as resembling working years in school, and the break in the spiritual world could be called "summer vacation." According to Martinus, this is an accurate simile. He has also described how karma functions, but we cannot go into that in greater detail here. It is only important to mention that the process of incarnations described here works according to karma principles. The radiance which the being has in the blessed kingdom is, among other things, dependent on this inclination and his activities during the last physical life. An activity like excessive use of narcotics has a highly negative effect on the psychic structures which give off this radiance. And this beaming, this radiance, determines which fertilized cell the being will be linked to. The fertilized cell's genetic code in turn determines the future development of the organism. The physical attributes shaped by the laws of inheritance are therefore largely determined by karma. The personalities of parents, the social and geographical milieu are other factors through which the karma operates. The mechanisms which direct the karma appear so subtle, according to Martinus, that they may actually be characterized by Jesus' words: "Are not five sparrows sold for two farthings, and not one of them is forgotten before God? But even the hairs of your head are all numbered." (Luke 12:6–7) [12]

Another question concerns the length of the interval between two physical lives. This varies greatly and depends partly on the individual's spiritual interest—since this determines the phase spent in the spiritual worlds after the first sphere—and partly on the length of the last life. A little child who dies has only recently been a guest in the spiritual world and so experienced as much as it required there. It has not been able to achieve very many new experiences in the physical plane this time, and consequently has little new to experience on the spiritual plane. It is taken care of by the guardian spirits immediately upon its arrival, passes through the spheres, and is soon born again. An old person who dies replete of days has, on the other hand, more to experience, especially if, moreover, he has pronounced spiritual interests. For him the interval between lives, counted in earthly years, will be perhaps as long as that of his last earthly life or longer.

Someone who dies young with his needs primarily focused on physical activities also passes rapidly through the spiritual world. His contact in the blessed kingdom will also be shorter. This may result in the last life's experiences not being completely or thoroughly "worked through." Instead, memories from that life may surface in childhood in the next physical life, as we have seen in Chapter 13. This is worked over more or less intensely for several years and then, as a rule, begins to fade away as the new physical life demands more and more of the child's consciousness and concentration.

This, in very rough outline, is the existence between two physical lives as described in Martinus' cosmology. It should be emphasized once more that this is not set forth here as absolute truth, but rather to give an example of the knowledge which can be experienced through intuition, independent of book learning. Regardless of what our opinions are of the experiences which have been described in Chapters 8 through 14, and which many consider indicate survival, we must agree that Martinus' description tallies completely with them and moreover puts them in a wider context. But then each of us must decide for himself whether he has got anything from this vision, or whether he prefers to see it as a pretty story, or as the invention of the devil. Even if we were to take Martinus' descriptions seriously, it would not, of course, make further research superfluous. On the contrary, it should greatly inspire us to begin such researches. Martinus himself points out that his world view provides only broad general characteristics and basic principles, later specialists in different areas must check the accuracy of the principles and enrich the picture with details. The conditions in the spiritual world are certainly not at all like those in our present material one.

Thus we have surveyed the state between two physical lives as described by a present-day mystic. Now only a few concluding remarks remain to be added.

20

The Conception of Death and Life

We have to imagine that everything in our universe, the physical as well as the spiritual, is bound by a universal law which includes the whole universe and all life to be found therein, a law which—were we to know it—would give us the solution to all problems, those of this world as well as problems of life, God, and the soul's immortality.

CARL HØEGH

The aim of this book was sketched in the preface: to survey the work of parapsychology and its findings, and also to view these findings in relation to the question of life after death. We have come to realize that the material parapsychology deals with, in and out of the laboratory, is many-sided and complex. It seems to me difficult, if not impossible, to deny, given knowledge of this material, that there are ways to attain knowledge other than through our known senses. The existence of ESP opens wider perspectives, for it means that people are something more than mere biological machines, that a person is even more mysteriously connected with his fellow beings and his surroundings. In Chapter 17 we have placed the psi-phenomenon in relation to two dimensions of reality, that of the senses and that of the mystic. The world of the senses is heavy and stable; everything has its place, isolated from everything else. The world of the mystic is an all-embracing unity, wholeness, totality, penetrated by life and forces. And yet the contrast is only apparent; these are two sides of the same reality. We could make a comparison with recent developments in physics. Modern physics tends to split up what appears to

287

be stable matter into a universe which is difficult to imagine, of beams, wave movements, and energy fields, a world which seems full of contradictions between "particle aspects" and "wave aspects [1]."

Parapsychology and Death

We have also described experiences of phenomena related to the problem of survival. The following phenomena have been investigated in parapsychology:

1. Separations and lucid dreams (Chapter 8).
2. Apparitions and ESP-projections (Chapter 9).
3. Communication through mediums, primarily of knowledge which neither the medium nor those taking part in the seance could normally know of (Chapter 10), sometimes in foreign languages (Chapter 14).
4. Behavior which indicates possession (Chapters 11 and 13).
5. Alleged memories of a former life (Chapter 13).
6. Paranormal taped voices which say that they come from "the other side" (Chapter 12).
7. Physiological changes at the moment of death, photography of the "etheric body" (Chapter 9) and "spirit photographs" (Chapter 6).
8. Deathbed visions, observations of the dying, reports of persons who have been near death (Chapters 9 and 18).

No material from any one of these groups is enough by itself to prove survival. But the whole body of this material of human experiences and empirical evidence is consistent with the survival hypothesis, and part of the material is explained better by the survival hypothesis than by any other. Thus, instead of one single kind of experience indicating survival, there are several groups of experiences, very different from one another, all of which point in the same direction and all of which can be explained harmoniously by the survival hypothesis. In other words, the hypothesis does not depend on one single group of phenomena but rather is supported by several groups.

Then could the survival hypothesis be proved someday? Yes, development in several areas, involving better working methods and new experiments could be imagined, work which would be better able to rule out more definitely other conceivable explanations. Cases of the reincarnation type and of xenoglossy in particular (Chapters 13 and 14) may be discovered which could give even stronger indications of survival than those described so far. The investigation of paranormal taped voices has scarcely even begun. One basic task is to develop the methods mentioned in group 7. If the existence of an "other body" could be demonstrated objectively after the physical body's determined death, then the survival hypothesis would have a major, valuable confirmation. Perhaps these are the directions that investigation and research must take to prove that some form of survival takes place. Material from communications through mediums and memories of earlier lives would then receive greater attention as means of gaining more detailed knowledge of the nature of life after death.

Even if the present material cannot, as has been emphasized, *prove* survival, it is nevertheless so rich and wide-ranging that it can indeed motivate a *rationally based belief* in survival. "Science" has not proved that death is the end of everything. Each of us must evaluate the material himself from his own viewpoint and judge the plausibility of survival, but no one can do this if he has tossed aside and dismissed the material as worthless before he begins. Even today, we can take survival as a respectable, "scientific" working hypothesis.

Outside of parapsychology as well, a great deal of evidence exists also indicating survival:

9. Descriptions received through mediums of the state after death (Chapters 18 and 19).
10. Reports from people who state that they have visited "the other world" during separation (Chapters 8 and 18).
11. Descriptions of the state after death in certain religiously oriented doctrines. This means primarily Eastern doctrines like Buddhism and Yoga together with their Western branches, Theosophy and Anthroposophy. These teachings are based more on the individual's "inner vision" than on communication of knowledge from a priest whom the individual must believe. Their descriptions of the other world share essentially similar characteristics, though there are distinctions and differences in many details (Chapters 18 and 19).
12. Descriptions of the state after death (part of a total vision) from a present-day mystic, who received his knowledge not through studies of any of these doctrines but rather through intuition, after a cosmic experience (Chapters 17 and 19).

Experiences from these widely separate areas of human life therefore argue in the same direction as parapsychological material: that individual consciousness survives beyond death, that the individual is fundamentally within and part of a greater unity.

Consequences of the Concept of Survival

Critics opposed to the concept of survival consider, among other things, that the concept is based only on fear of death and therefore represents pure wishful thinking. But Stevenson (see Chapter 18, Note 4) points out that millions of people, especially in Asia, believe in survival which they do not wish for at all. They do not long to continue spinning on the "reincarnation wheel;" the object of their strivings is to attain freedom and release, to reach Nirvana, which, according to the belief of many, means that individual consciousness ceases. Therefore, opposition to the survival concept probably also involves fear, not of death, but of surviving it. This fear, not clearly expressed and perhaps not completely conscious, concerns the state which might follow after the death of whatever constitutes consciousness.

The survival hypothesis has in itself no moral or ethical consequences, but these lie so close to hand that they are difficult to avoid. If consciousness survives death, then the purely mechanistic and materialistic explanation of existence, considered by many to be the only "scientifically acceptable" one, falls away. Other questions do remain: how this survival functions, what principles direct it, whether or not a higher power might possibly stand behind these principles, whether our present conduct has consequences for our existence after death. Perhaps the realization of this, consciously or unconsciously, lies behind part of the opposition to the survival concept and to parapsychology as a whole [2].

Several reasons could be thought of to explain why the survival concept is immediately dismissed by so many people. Upbringing and education in an industrialized and highly technical society focus such great effort on teaching people to think in technical and material terms. The church's earlier influence has diminished or ceased, and the laboriously won freedom of belief has, in many areas, given over to a new intolerance, one which defines the obvious spiritual aspects of existence as unscientific, ecstatic ravings. That which has been given the stamp of "unscientific" is considered altogether inferior; these arguments and experiences are rejected if not dismissed straightaway. (The growing interest in mysticism is perhaps an indication that this intolerance is now beginning to diminish [3].) But even in a materialistic culture death still exists and causes anguish. Therefore consciousness is restricted about death: it becomes taboo. People don't talk about death (see Chapter 1, Note 1). Doctors, too, feel anguished when faced with death, their own and that of their patients. They don't know how to handle it, they avoid the problem. They have no answers for the patients' questions; the patients notice this and the questions remain unexpressed.

The assumption that belief in survival by itself can give meaning to life is, on the other hand, exaggerated. Completely atheistic and materialistically oriented people without any belief in survival can certainly find rich meaning in another form of immortality: living on through their heirs or in the works they have begun during their lifetimes. The effort to set in motion as many and as positive action chains as possible gives meaning to a life. Then it is less important to that person if life ends with death: through the actions he has set in motion, he can live on, as ripples will spread out over a calm surface of water. But someone who, upon glancing backward over his life, finds that he has failed in almost everything and not accomplished anything tangible, perhaps cannot find such great comfort in this approach.

Materialism tends to explain all individual differences in terms of factors outside the individual. Some decades ago it was popular to explain glibly that all difficulties afflicting individuals were the result of their childhoods: their parents bore the "blame." Now the prevalent tendency is to consider that all evils come from "society." In another social situation everything would be different or better. But it is easily forgotten that the community consists of individuals. The possibility of survival beyond death places the individual's own responsibility for his personal development squarely in the foreground [2]. This naturally does not mean that all other factors are denied, or that people should be less concerned with making better social conditions. On the contrary, the concept of individual responsibility could strongly stimulate people to work in some area serving others, involving themselves in the wholeness of life. A positive, personal development must indeed move from egotism toward altruism.

The survival concept also has consequences for one's personal attitude toward suicide. It means that no one can avoid a painfully difficult situation by that act: a person would merely continue in a perhaps equally difficult situation on the other side. He must seek to work through the problem and "pay now, or later." This does not involve anyone's sitting in judgment over other individuals. Each and every one of us must choose his own way. Thoughtful consideration of the meaning of death is therefore fundamental for a person who must decide about the medical preservation of life and treatments of incurable illnesses [4].

A rationally motivated belief in survival beyond death can have positive meaning for personal development. It can also increase the possibilities for helping others who are tormented, suffering the loss of a dead relative, brooding over the nature of death, or simply afraid of dying. By becoming aware of the vast, copious material which exists supporting the survival hypothesis, these people are given the opportunity to construct a sound, personal conviction. This does not mean they should be driven into the arms of spiritualism. Those who feel that need must naturally feel free to take part in those activities, although too great a preoccupation with these phenomena is not totally without risk, as was indicated in Chapter 10. If the dead survive, then perhaps we should not constantly seek to contact them in our egotistical way. Perhaps by this sort of activity, we delay their development on the other side.

But, someone objects, it really does not seem at all as if a belief in survival beyond death could have any positive meaning. Among the millions in Asia who believe in reincarnation, there are perhaps just as many insensitive and egocentric individuals as we have among us here. And during the middle ages, when everyone believed that those who did not obey the church's teachings would face torture in hell, existence was scarcely better than it is now. In that time, too, no one could walk around safe from robbers. That is perfectly true, but there is a possible difference in the two forms of belief: on the one hand, belief in the doctrines of priests—a belief founded on a strong tradition, or impressed by fear during the Inquisition—and, on the other hand, a belief founded on an independent, personal assessment of material from existing testimonies [2].

A considered belief in survival beyond death can therefore have fundamental meaning for the experience of physical, material life. But death perhaps is also equally meaningful. Here we return to our point of departure in Chapter 1: if belief in a life after death enriches life, then it has fulfilled a great task. Then we have everything to gain and nothing to lose: if it is proved wrong, if consciousness ends with death, then, of course, we will never know that it is wrong. But if we should prove right, and consciousness continues, then perhaps it would be easier for us to manage on the other side if we are prepared beforehand.

Even greater perspectives are opened up if survival beyond death has the form of rebirth. This need not mean an endless chain of physical lives, an eternal whirling "wheel of rebirth" from which the individual tries in vain to jump. There are also other possibilities. In the works of Martinus and others, a dizzying perspective comes into view: a venturesome, strange, awesome, rich development within a universe full of life. Such a perspective on the survival hypothesis is suggested in this verse from Rumi, a Persian mystic of the thirteenth century [5]:

> I died a mineral and became a plant.
> I died a plant and rose an animal.
> I died an animal and I was man.
> Why should I fear? When was I less by dying?
> Yet once more I shall die as man, to soar
> With blessed angels; even from angelhood
> I must pass on. All except God perishes.
> When I have sacrificed my angel soul,
> I shall become that which no mind conceived.

Bibliography and Notes

The most important parapsychological publications are referred to here with the following abbreviations:

JSPR: *Journal of the Society for Psychical Research* (SPR)
PSPR: *Proceedings of the SPR*
JASPR: *Journal of the American Society for Psychical Research* (ASPR)
PASPR: *Proceedings of the ASPR*
IJP: *International Journal of Parapsychology* (ceased publication with vol. 10 in 1968)
JP: *Journal of Parapsychology*
ZPG: *Zeitschrift für Parapsychologie und Grenzgebiete der Psychologie.*

JSPR and *PSPR* are published by SPR, 1 Adam and Eve Mews, London, W.8.

JASPR and *PASPR* are published by ASPR, 5 West 73rd Street, New York, N.Y. 10023.

IJP was published by The Parapsychology Foundation (PF), 29 West 57th Street, New York, N.Y. 10019. In addition, PF published a *Newsletter,* which since 1970 has been replaced by the *Parapsychology Review,* which appears once every other month. PF also publishes *Parapsychology Monographs.*

JP is published by the Foundation for Research on the Nature of Man (FRNM), College Station, Durham, N.C. 27708. This is the institute founded by Dr. J. B. Rhine when the parapsychology laboratory moved from Duke University. FRNM is therefore a private institute, completely separate from the university.

ZPG is published by Institut für Grenzgebiete der Psychologie und Psychohygiene, Freiburg (a department within the psychology institute of the university). Address: D 78 Freiburg i. Br., Eichhalde 12, German Republic.

The Parapsychology Association also publishes *Proceedings* of lectures and discussions held during their annual meetings.

The Psychical Research Foundation, P. O. Box 6116, College Station, Durham, N.C. 27708, publishes *Theta,* a small pamphlet containing, for the most part, book reviews and references of interest to the survival question.

Those who would like to keep up with the scholarly parapsychological literature are referred first of all to *JASPR,* which is full of variety and rich in content. Articles in it, as in many of the other scientific journals, are, however, sometimes highly technical and difficult for the layman to grasp. More easily accessible information and current notices appear in the *Parapsychology Review.* Subscriptions to *JASPR* presuppose membership in ASPR, which is rather expensive. Through membership in Sällskapet för Parapsykologisk Forskning (SPF) (address in 1970: Box 206, 182 52 Djursholm 2), Swedes can support parapsychological work in Sweden and may borrow current periodicals. Several of the above-mentioned periodicals also appear in university libraries.

Only two of the more popular periodicals will be mentioned here. *Psychic,* published in San Francisco, appears six times a year, and includes more popularly written articles on parapsychological research, interviews with parapsychologists and psychics and other matters of varying merit.

The periodical *Sökaren* (Box 3063, 103 61 Stockholm 3) contains both ambitious original articles and accounts of articles in foreign parapsychological and other periodicals. These accounts and references are included primarily as a service for readers who have difficulty obtaining or reading foreign literature.

Articles in periodicals are referred to here in the usual way: by volume, year, and page numbers. Medical periodicals are abbreviated mostly following the *Index Medicus.* To illustrate controversial subject matter more comprehensively from different viewpoints, some special book reviews (marked "R") have also been included, as well as contributions to discussions (marked "D"). As a rule, only the author, publication, and page number of these have been given. This bibliography and the notes include works accessible to me up to the autumn of 1970, when this manuscript was completed, with some later additions.

The notes here are divided into chapters and follow the numbers in the text, with the exception of a few last-minute references. In the case of references to earlier chapters and earlier notes, only the author's name and the earlier reference number are given.

Parapsychological literature is extensive and difficult to survey and cover. So that the reader interested in finding suitable introductory literature can do so more easily, I have indicated these works with an asterisk (*). These include books which summarize discussions or give a more complete survey of a particular area with further references opening new fields of research, or works which for some other reason seem to be especially valuable to read as source material. This selection is, of course, completely subjective, but still, hopefully, may be of some assistance.

An individual with no access to the resources of a parapsychological institute has neither means to buy nor time to read everything published in parapsychology and related fields. In Sweden, months pass before one hears about many books and articles published in the United States, for example. More time may go by before one can get hold of these works. Parapsychological research is often not included in the indices of scientific literature, and, therefore, beyond those references which appear in the standard periodicals, one may only hear of new work quite by chance. Valuable work is also published in Russian, French, and other languages. It is very possible that the reader is familiar with works I should have mentioned in the presentation of my argument. In that case, I would be most grateful to hear of them. My address is: Dr. Nils O. Jacobson, Vårvädersvägen 4 G, S-222 27 Lund, Sweden.

Chapter 1. Four Ways of Looking at Death

1. A series of articles appeared in *Svenska Dagbladet* in 1967 on the attitude toward death and the difficulty of talking about it. These articles were collected in a book: *Tala om döden*. Stockholm: Verbum, 1967.

Chapter 2. What Is Parapsychology?

1. For a more current definition of paranormal phenomena: Broad, C. D. *Parapsykologi och filosofi*. Issued by SPF no. 8, 1962.
2. *Lilla Uppslagsboken*. Second edition, Malmö, vol. 7, 1966.
3. *Introduction to Parapsychology*. New York: PF, 1969.

4–11: A selection of books of parapsychology:

4. Bjerre, Poul. *Spökerier*. Centrum, 1947. Lively accounts of the author's investigations of certain phenomena thought to be caused by "spirits."
5. Björkhem, John. *Det ockulta problemet*. Third edition. Lindblads, 1954. Describes, among other things, some of the author's own investigations of psychics.
6. Qvarnström, Birger. *Parapsykologi*. Natur och Kultur, 1959. A survey of the history of parapsychology up to the Forties, with emphasis on investigations of psychics and others during the first part of the twentieth century.
7. Tyrrell, G. N. M. *The Personality of Man*. Penguin Books, 1948. In the Swedish edition published by Prisma in 1963, H. Bender adds a postscript which brings the book up-to-date as of *ca.* 1960. Tyrrell, who was a distinguished researcher and spokesman in SPR, gives a lucid and systematic survey of the areas of research within parapsychology at that time.
8. *Heywood, Rosalind. *The Sixth Sense*. London: Chatto & Windus, 1959. The author is a well-known psychic and an active member of SPR. Among other things, this book discusses the development of SPR, the cross-correspondences, psychic phenomena, and the question of life after death; a good synopsis and easy to read.
9. *Schjelderup, Harald. *Den dolda människan*. Orion/Forum, 1962 (first edition, 1961). The author, a psychoanalyst, discusses the study of the unconscious and also gives a short history of the beginnings of parapsychology.
10. *Holmberg, Olle. *Den osannolika verkligheten*. Second edition. Aldus, 1970 (first edition, 1968). Personal experiences of psychics; also about Richet and Rhine.
11. (a) Svanqvist, Alfred. *Orimligt—men sant* (1957) and *Det eviga nuet* (1960). Both published by Excelsior. Spiritualistically oriented but without exaggeration. Describes famous seances and spontaneous cases around the turn of the century. (b) Lange,

Birgit. *Jordskred?* Sökarens förlag, 1969. Accounts from foreign literature of automatic writing, out-of-the-body experiences, and research on reincarnation.

12. *Pratt, J. G. *Parapsychology: An Insider's View of ESP.* New York: Dutton, 1966 (first edition, 1964). A personal description of the development of parapsychology by one of its pioneers.

13. Rhine, J. B. and Pratt, J. G. "A review of the Pearce–Pratt distance series of ESP tests." *JP* 18 (1954): 165–77.

14. Soal, S. G. and Bateman, F. *Modern Experiments in Telepathy.* London: Faber & Faber, 1954. A summary appears in Broad, C. D. Dr. *Soal's forskning i telepati och framtidsförnimmelse.* Issued by SPF no. 1, 1950.

15. McMahan, M. E. A. "An Experiment in pure telepathy." *JP* 10 (1946): 224–42.

16. Tyrrell, G. N. M. "Further research in ESP." *PSPR* 44 (1936): 99–168. See also Heywood 2:8, pp. 138 ff.

17. A summary of experimental parapsychological work up to 1940 appears in Pratt, J. G. et al. *Extra-sensory Perception after Sixty Years.* Boston: Bruce Humphries, 1966 (first edition, 1940). The years 1940–1965 are treated by Rao, K. R. *Experimental Parapsychology.* Springfield, Ill.: Thomas, 1966. This includes 1,251 notes.

18. Examples of periodicals which have devoted whole issues to parapsychological work: (a) *Int. J. Neuropsychiat.,* vol. 2, no. 5, Oct. 1966; (b) *Corr. Psych. & J. Soc. Ther.,* vol. 12, no. 2, March 1966; (c) *J. Amer. Soc. Psychosom. Dent.* vol. 14, no. 4, Oct. 1968; (d) *Psychoan. Rev.,* vol. 56, no. 1, 1969 (R of this: *JASPR* 64 [1970]: 121–24).

Chapter 3. Clairvoyance and Psychometry

1. Ryzl, M. and Ryzlova, J. "A case of high-scoring ESP performance in the hypnotic state." *JP* 26 (1962): 153–71.

2. Blom, J. G. and Pratt, J. G. "A second confirmatory experiment with Pavel Stepanek as a 'borrowed' subject." *JASPR* 62 (1968): 28–45. Postscript: *JASPR* 63 (1969): 207–9. Errata: *JASPR* 65 (1971): 65, 87.

3. Pratt, J. G. "Further significant ESP results from Pavel Stepanek and findings bearing upon the focusing effect." *JASPR* 61 (1967): 95–119.

4. Pratt, J. G. et al. "A transitional period of research in the focusing effect: from confirmation toward explanation." *JASPR* 63 (1969): 21–37.

5. Pratt, J. G. et al. "Identification of concealed randomized objects through acquired response habits of stimulus and word association." *Nature* 220 (Oct. 5, 1968): 89–91. This article led to a lively discussion of parapsychology in *Nature* and other periodicals; see further references 7:9.

6. Pratt, J. G. and Keil, H. "The focusing effect as patterned behavior based on habitual object-word associations." *JASPR* 63 (1969): 314–37. See also Keil, H. "A wider conceptual framework for the Stepanek focusing effect." *JASPR* 65 (1971): 75–82.

7. *Roll, W. G. "Pagenstecher's contribution to parapsychology." *JASPR* 61 (1967): 219–40.

8. West, D. J. and Fisk, G. W. "A dual ESP experiment with clock cards." *JSPR* 37 (1953): 185–89.

9. (a) LeShan, L. "The vanished man—a psychometry experiment with Mrs. Eileen J. Garrett." *JASPR* 62 (1968): 46–62; (b) Tenhaeff, W. H. C. and van Woudenberg, G. D. H. "Praktische Erfolgen von Sensitiven." *ZPG* 7 (1964): 159–73. Reference in Qvarnström, B. "Dikt och sanning i parapsykologin." *Sökaren* no. 4, 1970.

10. Åkerblom, Lilly. *Bortom mänsklig horisont.* Stilförlaget, 1966, pp. 103–8.

11. Police commissioner A. S., Vasa. Letters May–June 1970.

12. Tromp, S. W. "Review of the possible physiological causes of dowsing." *IJP* 10 (1968): 363–92. Refer to Schwarz, B. E. "Physiological aspects of Henry Gross's dowsing." *Parapsychology* 4:2 (1962–1963): 72–86.

13. Nash, C. B. "Cutaneous perception of colour." *JASPR* 63 (1969): 83–87. Nash, C. B. "Cutaneous perception of colour with a head box." *JASPR* 65 (1971): 83–87.

Chapter 4. Telepathy

1. As I said in the Forward, this phrase does not mean that I consider it a closed case or that it has been proven that what is described in this and the following chapters *are* telepathic, precognitive, etc.

2. Moss, T. and Gengerelli, J. A. "Telepathy and emotional stimuli: a controlled experiment." *J. Abnorm. Soc. Psychol.* 72 (1967): 341–48.

3. Moss, T. and Gengerelli, J. A. "ESP effects generated by affective states." *JP* 32 (1968): 90–100.

4. Moss, T. "ESP effects on 'artists' contrasted with non-artists." *JP* 33 (1969): 57–69.

5. Moss, T. "Long-distance ESP: a controlled experiment." Papers presented for the 11th annual convention of the Parapsychological Association, Freiburg, 1968, 156–76. A summary appeared in *PA* 1968.

6. Electroencephalograph: contacts are fastened to the head and the minute variations in electrical voltage related to different levels of activity in the brain are intensified and registered on a chart. The process is painless.

7. *Krippner, S. "Experiments in telepathy." *J. Amer. Soc. Psychosom. Dent. Med.* 15 (1968): 158–63.

8. *Ullman, M., Krippner, S., and Feldstein, S. "Experimentally induced telepathic dreams: Two studies using EEG-REM monitoring technique." *Int. J. Neuropsychiat.* 2 (1966): 420–38. Also *Ullman, M. "An experimental study of the telepathic dream." *Corr. Psych.* 12 (1966): 115–41.

9. Ullman, M. and Krippner, S. *Dream Studies and Telepathy, an Experimental Approach. Parapsychological Monographs* no. 12. New York: PF, 1970.

10. *Vaughan, Alan. "A dream grows in Brooklyn." *Psychic* 1:4 (1970): 40–46.

11. Krippner, S. "Electrophysiological studies of ESP in dreams: Sex differences in 74 telepathy sessions." *JASPR* 64 (1970): 277–85.

12. Krippner, S. et al. "A long distance 'sensory bombardment' study of ESP in dreams." *JASPR* 65 (1971): 468–75.

13. Vaughan, A. "Psychenauts of inner space." *Psychic* 1:6 (1970): 8–13.

14. *Servadio, E. "The psychodynamic approach to parapsychological problems." *Psychother. Psychosom.* 15 (1967): 245–59.

15. Schwarz, B. E. "Built-in controls and postulates for the telepathic event." *Corr. Psych.* 12 (1966): 64–82.

16. Eisenbud, J. "Chronologically extraordinary psi-correspondences in the psychoanalytic setting." *Psychoan. Rev.* 56 (1969): 9–27.

17. Meerlo, J. A. M. "Sympathy and telepathy: a model for the

psychodynamic research in parapsychology." *IJP* 10 (1968): 57–84.

18. Vasiliev, L. L. *Experiments in Mental Suggestion.* Church Crook-ham, Hampshire: Study of Mental Images Publications, 1963 (original Russian edition, 1963).

19. Weiler, R. B. "Apparent telepathy in psychotherapy." *Psychiat. Quart.* 41 (1967): 448–73.

20. A basic, very significant and wide-ranging study in depth of im-pressions of type 3 is *Stevenson, I. "Telepathic impressions: a review and report of 35 new cases." *PASPR* 29 (1970): 1–198.

21. See Soal 2:14 and McMahan 2:15.

Chapter 5. Precognition

1. Carington, W. "Experiment on the paranormal cognition of drawings." *PSPR* 46 (1940–1941): 24–151 and 277–344.

2. Schmidt, H. "Precognition of a quantum process." *JP* 33 (1969): 99–108. Included again in Haraldsson, E. "Subject selection in a machine precognition test." *JP* 34 (1970): 182–91.

3. Schmidt, H. "Quantum processes predicted?" *New Scientist* 44 (Oct. 16, 1969): 114–15.

4. *Krippner, S. "The paranormal dream and man's pliable future." *Psychoan. Rev.* 56 (1969): 28–43.

5. Jung, C. G. et al. *Man and His Symbols.* New York: Doubleday & Co., 1968, pp. 69–75. Several examples are given in Ma-honey, Maria F. *The Meaning in Dreams and Dreaming.* New York: Citadel Press, 1966, chapters 1 and 16.

6. *A personal essay about the problem of time that is well worth reading is Priestley, J. B. *Man and Time.* New York: Double-day, 1964. Also in paperback, Dell, Laurel Edition. On the dreams, pp. 198 and 227. On Dunne's concept of time, p. 242. R: *JSPR* 43 (1965): 31–39.

7. *Stevenson, I. "Precognition of disasters." *JASPR* 64 (1970): 187–210.

8. Jung, C. G. *Memories, Dreams and Reflections.* New York: Pan-theon, 1961, pp. 175–76. Original title: *Erinnerungen, Traüme, Gedanken.*

9. Broad, C. D. "The notion of precognition." *IJP* 10 (1968): 165–96.

10. Garnett, A. C. "Matter, mind and precognition." *JP* 29 (1965): 19–26. D: *JP* 29 (1965): 185–99.

11. Struckmeyer, F. R. "Precognition and the 'intervention paradox.' " *JASPR* 64 (1970): 320–26.
12. See Chapter 4, Note 15.
13. O'Neill, P. E. "A bookmaker's nightmare." *Fate* magazine 20:8 (Aug. 1967): 45–54.
14. Brier, R. M. and Tyminski, W. V. "Psi application: Part I: A preliminary attempt." *JP* 34 (1970): 1–25.
15. Barker, J. C. "Premonitions of the Aberfan disaster." *JSPR* 44 (1967): 169–81.
16. Nelson, R. D. "The central premonitions registry." *Psychic* 1:5 (1970): 27–30.

Chapter 6. Psychokinesis

1. Bender, H. "Der Rosenheimer Spuk—ein Fall spontaner Psychokinesie." *ZPG* 11 (1968): 104–12.
2. Karger, F. and Zicha, G. "Physikalische Untersuchung des Spukfalles in Rosenheim 1967." *ZPG* 11 (1968): 113–31.
3. Pratt 2:12, p. 145.
4. In the U. S., W. G. Roll has been the principal investigator of RSPK cases: (a) "Some physical and psychological aspects of a series of poltergeist phenomena." *JASPR* 62 (1968): 263–308; (b) "The Newark disturbances." *JASPR* 63 (1969): 123–74; (c) "Poltergeist phenomena and interpersonal relations." *JASPR* 64 (1970): 66–99.
5. *Bender, H. "Neue Entwicklungen in der Spukforschung." *ZPG* 12:1 (1970): 1–18. Popularly presented by Vaughan, A. "Poltergeist investigations in Germany." *Psychic* 1:5 (1970): 9–13. The boy in Bremen is also described by Mischo, J. et al. "A psychokinetic effect personally observed (The 'Bremen boy'). *PA* 1968, pp. 393–94 (see 4:5). Concerning the personality of RSPK psychics, see Mischo, J. "Personality structure of psychokinetic mediums." *PA* 1968, pp. 388–92. The German version: *ZPG* 12:1 (1970): 19–25.
6. Brookes-Smith, C. and Hunt, D. W. "Some experiments in psychokinesis." *JSPR* 45 (1970): 265–81. This article is a good introduction for those who would like to make their own experiments with PK. A person may start with "table-rapping," but as soon as tangible results are received, this should be abandoned (for otherwise uncontrollable and risky phenomena may occur) and instead it would be preferable to work with a PK apparatus

of the simple sort which is shown on page 274. Such a device can be easily constructed. The object should be to demonstrate results with it under the objective, critical control of outside observers.

7. McConnell, R. A. and Forwald, H. "Psychokinetic placement I–III." *JP* 31 (1967): 51–69 and 198–213, also *JP* 32 (1968): 9–38. On Forwald, see Holmberg 2:10, 176–77. In addition: Forwald, H. *Mind, Matter and Gravitation, a Theoretical and Experimental Study.* Parapsychological Monographs no. 11. New York: *PF,* 1969; Schmidt, H. "A PK test with electronic equipment." *JP* 34 (1970): 175–81.

8. Barry, J. "General and comparative study of the psychokinetic effect on a fungus culture." *JP* 32 (1968): 237–43.

9. *Grad, B. "The 'laying on of hands': Implications for psychotherapy, gentling, and the placebo effect." *JASPR* 61 (1967): 286–305. Shortened version with the same title in *Corr. Psych.* 12 (1966): 192–203.

10. Elgvin, G. H. and Onetto, B. *Acta. Psiquat. Psicol. Amer. Lat.* 14 (1968): 47. Ref. in *JSPR* 44 (1968): 428.

11. Smith, Sister J. "Paranormal effects on enzyme activity." *PA* 1968 (see 4:5), pp. 275–94.

12. Johnson, M. and Jacobson, N. O. Unpublished material, 1969.

13. Bender, H. " 'Wunderheilungen' im affektiven Field." *ZPG* 7 (1964): 7–24.

14. Sherman, H. *"Wonder Healers" of the Philippines.* Los Angeles: De Vorss & Co., 1967, a popular presentation which was reviewed in: R: *JSPR* 44 (1968): 295–98. On frauds in America see: Rogo, D. Scott and Bayless, R. *JSPR* 44 (1968): 426–28.

15. Puharich, H. K. "The work of the Brazilian healer, Arigo" in *The Varieties of Healing Experience.* Los Altos, California: The Academy of Parapsychology and Medicine, 1972, pp. 45–54.

16. *Lilla Uppslagsboken.* Second edition, Malmö, 1966, vol. 6.

17. On walking on live coals and magic in Polynesia, see Long, Max Freedom. *The Secret Science behind Miracles.* Vista, Calif.: Huna Research Publ., 1954.

18. David-Neel, Alexandra. *Magic and Mystery in Tibet.* London: Souvenir Press, 1961.

19. Brockhaus, E. "Möglichkeiten und Grenzen der Erforschung paranormaler Phänomene in Westafrika." *Neue Wissenschaft* 16 (1968): 27–36.

20. On voodoo-death and "dying of fright," see (a) Cannon, W. B. " 'Voodoo' death." *Psychosom. Med.* 19 (1957): 182–98; (b)

Mathis, J. L. "A sophisticated version of voodoo death." *Psychosom. Med.* 26 (1964): 104–7; (c) *Brit. Med. J.* (1965): 363, 591, 700–1, 821, 876, 1004; (d) Barker, J. C. *Scared to Death: An Examination of Fear, Its Causes and Effects.* London: F. Muller, 1968. R: *JSPR* 45 (1969): 17–21 and *JASPR* 64 (1970): 347–50.

21. *Christiansen, J. *Kavadi—en rejse til Østens mystik.* Spectrum, 1964.

22. Some works on Serios: (a) Eisenbud, J. *The World of Ted Serios.* New York: W. Morrow, 1967. A good summary is presented in *Roll, W. G., R: *JASPR* 62 (1968): 193–216. Reference in *Sökaren* 1/69: "Kan tankar fotograferas?"; (b) Stevenson, I. and Pratt, J. G. "Exploratory investigations of the psychic photography of Ted Serios." *JASPR* 62 (1968): 103–29; (c) Stevenson, I. and Pratt, J. G. "Further investigations of the psychic photography of Ted Serios." *JASPR* 63 (1969): 352–64; (d) Eisenbud, J. et al. "An archeological 'tour de force' with Ted Serios." *JASPR* 64 (1970): 40–51; (e) Eisenbud, J. et al. "Two camera and television experiments with Ted Serios." *JASPR* 64 (1970): 261–76.

23. Thorlin, Claude. "Andefotografering." *Sökaren* 6/69. See also *Arbetet,* April 25, 1969, p. 7.

24. Patterson, T. *100 Years of Spirit Photography.* London: Regency Press, 1965.

25. General articles on psychic photography: Rogo, D. S. "Photographs by the mind." *Psychic* 1:5 (1970): 40–46. Critical: Chari, C. T. K. "Some disputable phenomena allied to thoughtography." *JASPR* 63 (1969): 273–86. On a psychoanalytical case connected with psychic photography: Schwarz, B. E. "Telepathy and pseudotelekinesis in psychotherapy." *J. Amer. Soc. Psychosom. Dent. Med.* 15:4 (1968): 144–54. Reference to a Swedish doctor's experience: *Sökaren,* June 1968, p. 11.

26. Barber, T. X. "Death by suggestion, a critical note." *Psychosom. Med.* 23 (1961): 153–55. See also Stevenson, I. 4:20, pp. 128–32. G. Zorab recounts a remarkable case of predicted death: *JSPR* 45 (1969): 141–44.

Chapter 7. Parapsychology—Fraud or Science?

1. This may occur even later. See, for example: v. Fieandt, Kai. "Om vissa felkällor inom parapsykologin." *Nord. Psykol.* 21

(1969): 277–82. A summary of criticism of parapsychology: Ransom, C. "Recent criticisms of parapsychology: a review." *JASPR* 65 (1971): 289–307.

2. Price, G. R. "Science and the supernatural." *Science* 122 (1955): 259–67. D: 123 (1956): 9–19. Summary and further additions: "The controversy in *Science* over ESP." *JP* 19 (1956): 236–71.

3. Hansel, C. E. M. *ESP—A Scientific Evaluation.* New York: Scribner's, 1966.

4. Slater, E. Review. *Brit. J. Psychiat.* 114 (1968): 653–72. D: 114 (1968): 1471–80 and 115 (1969): 743–45.

5. Stevens, S. S. "The market for miracles." *Contemp. Psychol.* 12 (1967): 1–3. D: 13 (1968): 41. See also *McConnell, R. A. "ESP and credibility in science." *Amer. Psychologist* 24 (1969): 531–38.

6. Stevenson, I. "An antagonist's view of parapsychology." *JASPR* 61 (1967): 254–67.

7. Medhurst, R. G. "The fraudulent experimenter: Professor Hansel's case against psychical research." *JSPR* 44 (1968): 217–32. D: 44 (1968): 299–312 and 422–24.

8. Schmidt, H. "Clairvoyance test with a machine." *JP* 33 (1969): 300–7.

9. The article in *Nature* on Stepanek (Pratt 3:5) started a year-long dispute: *Nature,* Oct. 26 and Nov. 23, 1968, Feb. 8, Feb. 15 and March 22, 1969, and also Jan. 24, 1970 (pp. 313 and 394). With reference to the *Nature* article, J. Beloff wrote "ESP —proof from Prague?" *New Scientist* 40 (Oct. 10, 1968) 76–77, which gave rise to a new debate: *New Scientist,* Oct. 24, Nov. 14, Nov. 21, Nov. 28, Dec. 12, Dec. 26, 1968 and Jan. 9, Feb. 13, p. 192, March 20, p. 638, March 27, April 24, 1969.

10. Hansel 7:3, p. 235. Treated in *JSPR* 45 (1969): 91–92.

11. LeShan, L. "Some psychological hypotheses on the non-acceptance of parapsychology as a science." *IJP* 8 (1966): 367–85.

12. From a large number of works on ESP and personality, here are some by the pioneer in the field, Schmeidler, G. (a) *"The influence of attitude on ESP scores." *Int. J. Neuropsychiat.* 2 (1966): 387–97; (b) *"Two horns of a dilemma in relating ESP to personality." *Corr. Psych.* 12 (1966): 98–114; (c) "ESP breakthroughs: paranormal effects in real life." *JASPR* 61 (1967): 306–25; (d) with LeShan, L. "An aspect of body image related to ESP scores." *JASPR* 64 (1970): 211–18.

13. Eysenck, H. J. "Personality and ESP." *JSPR* 44 (1967): 55–71.
14. (a) Dean, E. D. "Plethysmograph recordings as ESP responses." *Int. J. Neuropsychiat.* 2 (1966): 439–46; (b) Dean, E. D. and Nash, C. B. "Coincident plethysmograph results under controlled conditions." *JSPR* 44 (1967): 1–14.
15. A survey appears in Cadoret, R. J. "Physiology and ESP." *Corr. Psych.* 12 (1966): 164–78.
16. (a) Dean's results are supported by Esser, A. H. et al. "Preliminary report: Physiological concomitants of 'communication' between isolated subjects." *IJP* 9 (1967): 53–59. Negative results are reported by (b) Sanjar, M. "A study of coincident autonomic activity in closely related persons." *JASPR* 63 (1969): 88–94. See also *Dean, E. D. "A procedural postscript." *JASPR* 64 (1970): 237–40. Negative results also in (c) Beloff, J., Cowles, M., and Bate, D. "Autonomic reactions to emotive stimuli under sensory and extrasensory conditions of presentation." *JASPR* 64 (1970): 313–19. In both (b) and (c) the method differed from that of Dean.
17. Barker, J. C. "The pre-disaster syndrome." *JAMA* 201 (1967): 141–42.
18. Mentioned in Barker, J. C. "Psyche Submerged." *Lancet* Dec. 24, 1966, p. 1414. See also Stevenson, I. 4:20, pp. 108–28 and Jung, C. G. 5:8, pp. 135–36.
19. Pratt, J. G. 2:12, pp. 78–98.
20. Fahler, J. "Does hypnosis increase psychic powers?" *Tomorrow* 6:4 (1958): 71–80.
21. Lorenz, R., personal communication, 1968. Poul Bjerre also succeeded; *vide* 2:4, pp. 130–31.
22. "Sensibilitetens exteriorisering eller känselsinnets utflyttande. Efteråt –." *Tidskrift för Spiritism och dermed Beslägtade Ämnen.* no. 60 (May 1896): 65–68.
23. LeShan, L. "Parapsychology and the concept of the repeatable experiment." *IJP* 8 (1966): 133–45.

*Chapter 8. In the World of the Dream
and Out-of-the-Body*

1. Jung 5:8, pp. 220–23.
2. Lukianowicz, N. " 'Body image' disturbances in psychiatric disorders." *Brit. J. Psychiat.* 113 (1967): 31–47.

3. *Hart, H. "ESP projection: Spontaneous cases and the experimental method." *PSPR* 48 (1954): 121–46.

4. Here a "psychically healthy" person refers to one who feels healthy and can live together with others and function in his milieu without having to harm, tyrannize, or act passively toward others. Whether someone with a certain behavior is thought healthy or ill depends largely on the dominant set of values presently operative in that place. The concept of psychic illness and health is therefore actually open to dispute. For a more detailed and thorough discussion of this see, for example, Löfgren, B. *Alkoholismen, människan och samhället.* Aldus/Bonniers, 1970, pp. 34–50.

5. *Tart, C. T. Review of Green 8:10 and 8:11. *JASPR* 64 (1970): 219–26.

6. Muldoon, S. J. and Carrington, H. *The Projection of the Astral Body.* London: Rider, 1929.

7. Fox, Oliver. *Astral Projection.* New York: University Books, 1962.

8. Lobsang Rampa, T. *You—Forever.* London: Corgi Books, 1965, pp. 65–91.

9. Green, C. E. "Ecsomatic experiences and related phenomena." *JSPR* 44 (1967): 111–31.

10. Green, C. E. *Out-of-the-Body Experiences.* Oxford, Institute of Psychophysiological Research, 1968.

11. Green, C. E. *Lucid Dreams.* London: Hamilton, 1968. R: *JSPR* 45 (1969): 21–25.

12. Fridell, Carri. *Astrala upplevelser.* SSF's writing series, no. 17.

13. Gilmark, Astrid. *Jag vet.* Nybloms, 1965, pp. 105–8.

14. On this, see Christiansen 6:21.

15. A great number of accounts of separation have been collected by Robert Crookall and described in several books. Crookall uses the expression "Soul Body" for the separated body. For a short synopsis of Crookall's studies of separation, see Lange 2:11, pp. 47–72. On the silver cord and the circumstances of temporary and definite separations, see *Crookall, R. *Intimations of Immortality.* London: James Clarke, 1965. Refer to Ecclesiastes 12: 6–7.

16. See, for example, Crookall, R. "Out-of-the-body experiences and cultural traditions." *JSPR* 44 (1968): 358–62, and also 8:15. Plutarch describes a typical case of separation, ref. 8:15, p. 7. See also 2 Corinthians 12: 1–4 in reference to case 29. Two

attempts to find words for what is fundamentally the same experience?

17. Tart, C. T. (a) "A psychophysiological study of out-of-the-body experiences in a selected subject." *JASPR* 62 (1968): 28–45; (b) "A second psychophysiological study of out-of-the-body experiences in a gifted subject." *IJP* 9 (1967): 251–58.

18. Tart, C. T. "The control of nocturnal dreaming by means of posthypnotic suggestion." *IJP* 9 (1967): 184–89.

19. Whiteman, J. H. M. "The process of separation and return in experiences fully 'out of the body.'" *PSPR* 50 (1956): 240–74.

20. Freud, S. *The Interpretation of Dreams.* First edition, 1900. New York: Avon, 1970.

Chapter 9. Ghosts and Apparitions

1. Hart's expression "the appearer," for the person who experiences the separation, means more precisely, "he who manifests himself." For simplicity's sake, we will consistently use the term "projector" even in cases in which the projection is not conscious or in which the projector is dead. Louisa Rhine uses the word "agent," for, according to her, the phenomenon of ESP projection is nothing other than a form of ordinary telepathic contact.

2. Tyrrell, G. N. M. *Apparitions.* New York: Collier, 1963, revised edition (first edition, 1942).

3. Hart, H. "Six theories about apparitions." *PSPR* 50 (1956): 153–239.

4. The case is cited by G. Murphy in Feifel, H. ed. *The Meaning of Death.* New York: McGraw-Hill, 1969, pp. 317–40. See also *JASPR* 39 (1945): 113–25.

5. Hart, H. *Toward a New Philosophical Basis for Parapsychological Phenomena.* Parapsychological Monographs no. 6. New York: PF, 1965.

6. *Hart, H. *The Enigma of Survival.* Springfield, Ill.: Thomas, 1959.

7. Rhine, Louisa E. "Hallucinatory psi experiences. I: An introductory survey." *JP* 20 (1956): 233–56; "II: The initiative of the percipient in hallucinations of the living, the dying and the dead." *JP* 21 (1957): 13–46; "III: The intuition of the agent and the dramatizing tendency of the percipient." *JP* 21 (1957): 186–226. D: 21 (1957): 74–76 and 227–37.

8. *H. Hart summarized his results briefly and succinctly in "Scientific survival research." *IJP* 9 (1967): 43–52. Also see 8:3.
9. This opinion is put forth by Qvarnström 2:6, pp. 78–80. Refer also to Slomann, A. "Några fall av dubbelgångarupplevelse och bilokation." *Sökaren* 3–4, 1969.
10. Osis, K. *Deathbed Observations by Physicians and Nurses*. Parapsychological Monographs no. 3. New York: PF, 1961.
11. Moss, T. and Schmeidler, G. "Quantitative investigations of a 'haunted house' with sensitives and a control group." *JASPR* 62 (1968): 399–410.
12. Ousley, S. G. J. *Science of the Aura*. London: Fowler, 1960 (first edition, 1949).
13. Kilner, Walter J. *The Human Aura*. New York: University Books, 1965 (first edition, 1911). Critical R: *JSPR* 44 (1967): 27–34.
14. Burr, H. S. and Northrop, F. S. C. (a) "Evidence for the existence of an electromagnetic field in living organisms." *Proc. Nat. Acad. Sc.* 25 (1939): 284; (b) "The electrodynamic theory of life." *Main Currents in Modern Thought* 19 (Oct. 1962): 4–10 (first published, 1935).
15. Muftic, M. K. *Research on the aura phenomenon I–II*. Hastings, Sussex: Metaphysical Research Group, 1960–1961.
16. Minto, W. L. "Measuring the human aura." *Exploring the Unknown*, Aug. 1960, pp. 94–98.
17. Reference in Bentley, W. P. "An approach to a theory of survival of personality." *JASPR* 59 (1965): 3–21.
18. MacDougall, D. *JASPR* May 1907. Reprinted in Carrington, H. *The Coming Science*. New York: Dodd & Mead, 1908, 1920, pp. 286–98.
19. An instrument for observing atomic particles. It is filled with saturated vapor which is condensed into visible streaks indicating the paths of the particles.
20. Watters, R. A. "Phantoms." *JASPR* 29:3 (1935): 68–81.
21. For a further discussion of this, see Carrington, H. *The Invisible World*. New York: Ackerman, 1946. "The intra-atomic quantity," pp. 94–104.
22. Rogo, D. Scott. "At the moment of death." *Fate* magazine, Feb. 1970. On Baraduc, see also Carrington, H. *The Problems of Psychical Research*. New York: Dodd & Mead, 1921, and in Carrington and Meader. *Death—Its Causes and Phenomena*. London: Rider, 1911.

23. For examples of such reports, see Crookall 8:15, pp. 23–26. See also *Sökaren,* July 1970.
24. Even if this chapter should have made it appear plausible that not all cases of "ghosts" are purely subjective visual illusions, nevertheless this may still be true of many of them. Cornell, A. D. and Gauld, A. "A 'ghost' on television." *JSPR* 45 (1969): 14ff. This article describes how twenty people independently saw a "ghost" on a television program which was about the investigation of a haunted house. But the "ghost" was a stain on the wall.
25. *Stevenson, I. and Rhine, L. E. *JP* 34 (1970): 143–63.

Chapter 10. Spiritualism and Spirits

1. Schjelderup 2:9, pp. 134–36.
2. Reference in Holmberg 2:10, p. 62.
3. The National Swedish Federation of Spiritualists (Svenska Spiritualisters Riksförbund) periodical, *Utan Gräns,* extra edition, 1970. For a brief survey of spiritualism, see Carleson, Rolf. "Spiritualism." *Sökaren,* Jan. 1968.
4. *Ducasse, C. J. *The Belief in a Life after Death.* Springfield, Ill.: Thomas, 1961. On materialization, see p. 166. Bjerre 2:4, p. 139. For dubious photographs of materializations, see *Sökaren,* July 1970. Quote from *Sydsvensk Dagbladet,* Nov. 22, 1970.
5. David-Neel 6:18. See also R: *JSPR* 44 (1967): 199–201 and D: 44 (1968): 369. Refer to Payne, P. D. and Bendit, L. J. *The Psychic Sense.* London: Faber & Faber, 1958 (first edition, 1943). (Also: The Theosophical Publishing House, Wheaton, Ill., 1967.) Faber edition, pp. 113–14: Payne and Bendit describe how a clairvoyant could see an apparition of a certain author take shape beside a lecturer who was discussing the author's life and poetry. The apparition faded away at the conclusion of the lecture.
6. On apports during RSPK phenomena, see Bender 6:5. On apports of people and other improbable occurrences, see Svanqvist in 1:12. Poul Bjerre discusses in "The case of Karin" (first published, 1905; reprinted in Bjerre 2:4) the nature of the spirit knockings in PK: he could produce knockings by giving Karin suggestions under hypnosis. Holmberg 2:10 mentions definite

"table rapping" as obviously a form of PK: note the picture on the cover of the book. Jung 5:8, p. 152, relates how, to the horror of Freud, he could demonstrate knockings apparently at will. On Jung, see also Slomann, A. "Freud, Jung und ockultismen." *Sökaren* 4–5, 1968. Also Johnson, M. "Parapsykologiska inslag hos C. G. Jung." *Sökaren,* June 1969.

7. *Stevenson, I. "A communicator unknown to medium and sitters." *JASPR* 64 (1970): 53–65.

8. Nyberg, Helmer V. (a) *Samtal med osynlig.* Norstedts, 1967; (b) (with S. Hagliden) *Bortom—och här.* Läromedelsförlagen, 1968. On the author, see *Sökaren,* July 1970.

9. See Schjelderup 2:9, pp. 113ff., Heywood 2:8, pp. 102–106 and Qvarnström 2:6, pp. 208–13.

10. *Bender, H. *Parapsychologie.* Darmstadt: Wissenschaftliche Buchgesellschaft, 1966. See "Mediumistische Psychosen—Ein Beitrag zur Pathologie spiritistischer Praktiken," pp. 574–604.

11. See, for example, Mahoney 5:15, chapter 5.

12. Thigpen, C. H. and Cleckley, H. M. *The Three Faces of Eve.* New York: McGraw-Hill, 1957.

13. On persona, see Hart 9:5 and 9:6, chapter 13.

14. Yogananda, Paramahansa. *Autobiography of a Yogi.* Los Angeles: Self-Realisation Fellowship, 1946.

15. Björkhem 2:5, p. 108.

16. "Spiritualists cry fraud in mediums investigation." *Newsletter* 16:5 (1969): 24. "Tidning prövar medier." *Sökaren,* Sept. 1969. "Kan man tro på medier?" *Sökaren* 2–3, 1970.

17. For a similar known case, see Ellwood, G. F. "The Soal-Cooper-Davis communal 'I.' " *IJP* 10 (1968): 393–410.

18. *Broad, C. D. "Tre föredrag: (1) Parapsykologi och filosofi. (2) Femtio år av parapsykologisk forskning. (3) Några paradoxala mediumistiska fall." Issued by SPF no. 8, 1962. No. 3 also appears in *Sökaren,* April–May 1967.

19. Osis, K. "Linkage experiments with mediums." *JASPR* 60 (1966): 91–124.

20. Beer, Puck. *Anteckningar från en mötesplats.* Rundqvists, 1968.

21. *Pole, W. Tudor. *Private Dowding,* London: Spearman, 1966 (first edition, 1917).

22. On the cross-correspondences, see Heywood 2:8, pp. 65–102. Qvarnström 2:6, on the other hand, supports the telepathy hypothesis, pp. 258–98. See also Ducasse 10:4, pp. 186–90.

23. Cummins, Geraldine. *Swan on a Black Sea. A Study in Automatic Writing: the Cummins-Willet Scripts.* London: Routledge

3. Wickland, Carl A. *Thirty Years Among the Dead.* London: Spiritualist Press, Ltd., *ca.* 1923.
4. On possession as a symptom of illness, see Stanley, A. and Freed, R. S. "Spirit possession as illness in a north Indian village." *IJP* 8 (1966): 105–32.
5. The history of possession and utterances is covered in a weighty volume: Oesterrich, T. K. *Possession—Demoniacal and other, among Primitive Races, in Antiquity, the Middle Ages, and Modern Times.* New York: University Books, 1966 (first edition, 1921).

Chapter 12. The Voices from Space

1. Jürgenson, Friedrich. *Rösterna från rymden.* Saxon & Lindström, 1964.
2. Raudive, Konstantin. *Breakthrough.* New York: Taplinger, 1971.
3. *Svenska Dagbladet,* May 15, 1970. H. Bender, letter May 11, 1970. Bender, H. "Zur Analyse aussergewöhnlicher Stimmphänomene auf Tonband." *ZPG* 12 (1971): 226–38. See also *Sökarnen,* July 1970.
4. Raudive, K. "Röstfenomenet." *Seklet,* Jan. 1970.
5. These methods are described in greater detail in the English-language editions of Raudive's book, *Breakthrough* 12:2.
6. On Swedish taped voices, see also Thorlin, C. *Sökaren,* March–April 1969 and June 1969. See also Jürgenson, F. *Radio- och mikrofonkontakt med de döda.* Nybloms, 1968.

Chapter 13. Reincarnation?

1. Thouless, R. H. "A test of survival." *PSPR* 48 (1948–1949): 253–63 and 342–43.
2. Wood, T. E. "A further test for survival." *PSPR* 49 (1950): 105–106.
3. *Stevenson, I. "The combination lock test for survival." *JASPR* 62 (1968): 246–54.
4. See, for example, (a) Hyslop, J. "The Thompson-Gifford case." *IJP* 9 (1967): 108–24; (b) Tabori, C. "The case of Iris Farczady, an unsolved mystery." *IJP* 9 (1967): 223–26; (c) Smith,

& Kegan Paul, 1965. R: *IJP* 8 (1966): 483–84. The book
rise to a lively discussion in JSPR: (a) Edmunds, S. "An a
atist's scripts compared with some original writings by tl
leged communicator." 43 (1966): 263–67; (b) R: 43 (19
267–70; (c) Barrington, M. R. "How much could Miss
mins have known?" 43 (1966): 289–300; (d) D: 43 (19
378–82; and 44 (1967): 45–48, 164, 211. On Cummins
also Lange 2:11, pp. 19–46.

24. Stevenson, I. Review of Cummins, *JASPR* 61 (1967): 81

25. *Gauld, A. "The super-ESP hypothesis." *PSPR* 53 (19
226–46.

26. Three of the many examples of investigations of psychic
terial related to the survival hypothesis: (a) Stevenson, I. "
evidence on an important detail in the case of Abraham Fl
tine." *JASPR* 59 (1965): 47–55; (b) Zorab, G. "Experin
in extrasensory perception in connection with scientific in\
gation." *JSPR* 45 (1970): 211–220; (c) Pearce-Higgins, J
and Heywood, R. "The blue dress case." *JSPR* 45 (1970): 2
45.

27. (a) Stevenson, I. "The analysis of a mediumistic session l
new method." *JASPR* 62 (1968): 334–55; (b) Pratt, J. G.
the Evaluation of Verbal Material in Parapsychology. Para
chological Monographs no. 10. New York: PF, 1969.

28. On the investigation of psychics in general: (a) Roll, W.
"The contribution of studies of 'mediumship' to research on
vival after death." *JP* 24 (1960): 258–78; (b) *"Hints on
tings with mediums." London: SPR, 1965; (c) *Roll, W.
"Designs for tests with free response material." *JASPR*
(1962): 184–95; (d) Further development of statistical me
ods: Roll, W. G. and Burdick, D. S. "Statistical models for
assessment of verbal and other ESP responses." *JASPR*
(1969): 253–72.

Chapter 11. Possession?

1. Excerpts from Dr. W. F. Prince's paper "The Cure of T\
Cases of Paranoia," *Bulletin VI,* 1927, Boston Society for P;
chic Research.

2. Odencrants, Gerard. "A case of an obsessional type." *Psyck
Science* (Quarterly Journal IIPI) 18 (1939): 131–38.

S. "Wateska-fallet." *Sökaren,* June 1968. On the same case, see Ducasse 10:4, pp. 171–74.

5. On philosophers and reincarnation: Ducasse 10:4. See also Lönnerstrand, S. "Reinkarnationens mysterium." *Sökaren,* March 1968.

6. See, for example, Guirdham, A. *Religious aspects of ESP.* London: The Churches' Fellowship for Psychical and Spiritual Studies (21 pp., date missing).

7. Stevenson, I. "Cultural patterns in cases suggestive of reincarnation among Tlingit Indians of southeastern Alaska." *JASPR* 60 (1967): 229–43.

8. *Stevenson, I. *Twenty Cases Suggestive of Reincarnation. PASPR* 26 (1966): 1–362. Brief account, among others, of the case of Jasbir, in Lange 2:11, pp. 83–115.

9. R of *Twenty Cases:* Beloff, J. *JSPR* 44 (1967): 88–94. Chari, C. K. T. "New light on an old doctrine." *IJP* 9 (1967): 217–22. D: *IJP* 10 (1968): 103–107. See also *JASPR* 63 (1969): 309–12.

10. Some of the criticisms are commented on in *Story, F. and Stevenson, I. "A case of the reincarnation type in Ceylon." *JASPR* 61 (1967): 130–45. A case with the birthmark: Story, F. "Ett fall av återfödelse?" *Sökaren,* Feb. 1967.

11. See Gauld 10:25.

12. This viewpoint is put forth by U. Timm in *ZPG* 9 (1966): 155–56.

13. The quote is from Laurent, T., B. E. and T. C. "Parapsykologi, hypnos och suggestion." *Årsbok för Kristen Humanism* 31 (1969): 147–56, published by Gleerups. The authors seem to consider that all paranormal phenomena, or in any case all those they have themselves experienced, are caused by hypnosis, etc. The article is a R of Holmberg 2:10 and Lange 2:11. They present a very wide interpretation of the déjà vu concept. On déjà vu see, for example, *Schjelderup, H. *Psykologi.* Wahlström & Widstrand, 1966, or Strömgren, E. *Psykiatri.* København: Munksgaard, tenth edition, 1969.

14. Similar experiments are described, among others, by Schjelderup 2:9, pp. 92–98 and by Jacobson, N. O. "Reinkarnationsexperiment." *Sökaren,* Feb. 1964. John Björkhem provides a full, rich account in his *De hypnotiska hallucinationerna.* Gleerups, 1942. The information suggests that Björkhem should have been able to find correlations in his research between the accounts provided

by his subjects under hypnosis and actual conditions for people who had lived previously, therefore indicating reincarnation. Nevertheless, Björkhem did not publish any such results and in the article "Hypnos och personlighetsförvandling" (issued by SPF no. 7, 1959; republished in the memoirs: Björkhem, John. *Människan och makterna.* Verbum, 1966) he does not take a position on reincarnation. See also Ducasse 10:4, chapter 24.

15. Bernstein, Morey. *The Search for Bridey Murphy.* Revised edition with new material by W. J. Barker. New York: Lancer Books, 1968 (first edition, 1956). See also Ducasse, C. J. "How the case of 'The Search for Bridey Murphy' stands today." *JASPR* 54 (1960): 3–22 (also included in Ducasse 10:4). The case of Bridey Murphy and problems related to similar experiments are also discussed by Mason, A. A. *Hypnos för läkare och tändläkare. Natur och Kultur,* 1961, pp. 159–76.

16. Stevenson, I. "Cryptomnesia and plagiarism." *Brit. J. Psychiat.* 112 (1966): 521–22.

17. Several examples of memories related to former lives and their meaning for the percipient: Lindbohm, D., articles in *Sökaren* from May 1970, and the book *Jagets eld.* Sökarens förlag, 1971.

18. A summary of the possibilities and difficulties in this work is given by Stevenson, I. "The evidence for survival from claimed memories of former incarnations." *JASPR* 54 (1960): 51–71 and 95–117. This provides a short survey of the better-known cases published to date.

Chapter 14. Speaking Unknown Languages: Xenoglossy

1. "Ryska inkarnerad i Norge?" *Sökaren,* July 1968, p. 7. The case of Iris Farczady (Tabori 13:4) mentioned in *Sökaren,* July 1968, p. 1, is remarkably like case I. E.: there too a young woman altered personality and language after a period of loss of consciousness, in that case from Hungarian to Spanish. Genuine or fraud?

2. In greater detail: *Sökaren,* Oct. 1968, p. 16.

3. Kline, M. V., ed. *A Scientific Report on "The Search for Bridey Murphy."* New York: Julian Press, 1956, pp. xvi–xviii. This book was published as a scathing criticism of the book on Bridey Murphy (Bernstein 13:13). However, this criticism was in some ways rather poorly conceived. See, for example, Ducasse 13:13.

4. Wood, F. H. *This Egyptian Miracle.* London: John M. Watkins,

second revised edition, 1955. A brief summary of this case appears in Ducasse 10:4, pp. 248–56.

5. See Qvarnström 2:6, pp. 239–45, for example.

6. Stevenson, I. "Responsive xenoglossy: A review and report of a case." *PASPR* 30, 1973. Also Univ. of Va. Press, 1973.

7. Shepherd 19:3, pp. 103–6. Compare with Case 40a.

Chapter 15. Altered States of Consciousness and ESP

1. This survey of states of consciousness is based in part on *Krippner, S. "Investigations of 'extrasensory' phenomena in dream and other altered states of consciousness." *J. Amer. Soc. Psychosom. Dent. Med.* 16 (1969): 7–14. Krippner considers that the trance state may be characterized by *absence* of continuous alpha waves on EEG, but other authors hold the opposite view. See Stokvis, B. and Langen, D. *Lehrbuch der Hypnose.* Basel: Karger, 1965. Others question the whole concept of "states of consciousness." T. X. Barker does not consider that hypnosis (trance) is a distinct, separate state. For a discussion on this, see Hilgard, E. R. "Altered states of awareness." *J. Nerv. Ment. Dis.* 149 (1969): 68–79. Hypnosis has been described and defined both as a sleeping and a waking state: see Mason 13:15, chapter 3.

2. Thirty-five articles on altered states of consciousness may be found collected in *Tart, C. T. (ed.) *Altered States of Consciousness.* New York: Wiley, 1969.

3. Bertini, M., Lewis, H. B., and Witkin, H. A. "Some preliminary observations with an experimental procedure for the study of hypnagogic and related phenomena." *Arch. Psycol. Neurol. Psychiat.* 6 (1964): 493–534. Also in Tart 15:2.

4. Vogel, G., Foulkes, D., and Trosman, H. "Ego functions and dreaming during sleep onset." *Arch. Gen. Psychiat.* 14 (1966): 238–48. Also in Tart 15:2.

5. van Eeden, F. "A study of dreams." *PSPR* 26 (1913): 431–61. Also in Tart 15:2.

6. Regression can, for example, be produced as a lead-in to hypnosis experiments of the sort mentioned in 13:14.

7. Underhill, Evelyn. *Mysticism.* London: Methuen, 1957 (first edition, 1911), pp. 358–79.

8. Refer to Seligmann, C. G. "An Egyptian holy man." *Lancet,* March 18, 1911, p. 755.

9. *Schwarz, B. E. "Ordeal by serpents, fire, and strychnin." *Psychiat. Quart.* 34 (1960): 405–29. Qvarnström 2:6, chapter 6, gives examples of artistic and scientific creativity under inspiration.

10. Aaronson, B. S. "Hypnosis, depth perception and the psychedelic experience." Tart 15:2, pp. 263–70. See also by the same author: "Hypnotic alterations of space and time." *IJP* 10 (1968): 5–26.

11. Tart, C. T. "Psychedelic experiences associated with a novel hypnotic procedure, mutual hypnosis." Tart 15:2, pp. 291–308.

12. *Deikman, A. J. "Experimental meditation." *J. Nerv. Ment. Dis.* 136 (1963): 329–43. Also in Tart 15:2.

13. Deikman, A. J. "Implication of experimentally induced contemplative meditation." *J. Nerv. Ment. Dis.* 142 (1966): 101–16.

14. Masters, R. E. L. and Houston, J. *The Varieties of Psychedelic Experience.* New York: Holt, Rinehart & Winston, 1966.

15. Ehrenwald, J. "Parapsychology: exoneration of the occult?" *Corr. Psych.* 12 (1966): 142–51.

16. Ehrenwald, J. "Human personality and the nature of psi phenomena." *JASPR* 62 (1968): 366–80.

17. Smythies, J. and Beloff, J. "The influence of stereotactic surgery on ESP." *JSPR* 43 (1965): 20–24.

18. Thouless, R. H. and Weisner, B. P. "The psi process in the normal and paranormal psychology." *PSPR* 48 (1947): 177–96.

19. *Roll, W. G. "ESP and memory." *Int. J. Neuropsychiat.* 2 (1966): 505–22.

20. Jaffé, A. "C. G. Jung and parapsychology." *IJP* 10 (1968): 37–56.

21. *Honorton, C. and Krippner, S. "Hypnosis and ESP: A review of the experimental literature." *JASPR* 63 (1969): 214–52.

22. Remarkable results described by *Levinson, L. E. "Hypnosis: The key to unlocking latent psi faculties." *IJP* 10 (1968): 117–48.

23. See Tart 8:15 and 8:16, Hart 8:3 and 9:5.

24. van de Castle, R. L. "The facilitation of ESP through hypnosis." *Amer. J. Clin. Hypnosis.* 12 (1969): 37–56.

25. Kasamatsu, A. and Hirai, T. "An EEG study on the Zen meditation." *Fol. Psychiat. Neurol. Japonica.* 20 (1966): 315–66. Also in Tart 15:2.

26. Anand, B. K., Chhina, G. S., and Singh, B. "Some aspects of EEG studies in Yogis." *Electroenceph. Clin. Neurophysiol.* 13 (1961): 452–56. Also in Tart 15:2. It would normally cause a person intense pain within a minute if he were to hold his hand

in 0° Centigrade water. Hilgard 15:1 describes similar experiments.

27. Wallace, R. K. "Physiological effects of transcendental meditation." *Science* 167 (1970): 1751–54. Also Allison, J. "Respiratory changes during transcendental meditation." *Lancet,* April 18, 1970. These studies describe profound physiological alterations during meditation, according to Maharishi, a "purely mental" technique.

28. Schmeidler, G. "High ESP scores after a Swami's brief instruction in meditation and breathing." *JASPR* 64 (1970): 100–103.

29. Fredericks, G. "An experimental evaluation of a class in psychic development." *Newsletter* 16:6 (1969): 6–11.

30. *Honorton, C., Davidson, R., Bindler, P. "Feedback-augmented EEG Alpha, shifts in subjective state, and ESP card-guessing performance." *JASPR* 65 (1971): 308–23. There is great interest in the "alpha state," and many works have been published during the last two years. This article provides a survey as of now of the studies in "bio-feedback" in relation to ESP.

31. Kamiya, J. "Operant control of the EEG alpha rhythm and some of its reported effects on consciousness." Tart 15:2, pp. 507–17.

32. v. Asperen, S. R., Barkema, P. R., Kappers, J. "Is it possible to induce ESP with psilocybin?" *Int. J. Neuropsychiat.* 2 (1966): 447–73.

33. Puharich, K. H. "Electrical field reinforcement of ESP." *Int. J. Neuropsychiat.* 2 (1966): 474–86. Also in *IJP* 9 (1967): 175–83.

34. Pozwolski, A. "Telepathy an electromagnetic theory." *JSPR* 43 (1965): 1–5.

35. Osis, K. and Turner, M. E., Jr., "Distance and ESP: a transcontinental experiment." *PASPR* 27 (1968): 1–48. They found that distance does seem to have a certain influence on the ability to demonstrate ESP. Refer to Moss 4:5.

36. Tart, C. T. "Models for the explanation of ESP." *Int. J. Neuropsychiat.* 2 (1966): 488–504.

37. Murphy, G. "Are there any solid facts in psychical research?" *JASPR* 64 (1970): 3–17.

38. This is discussed by Bender 6:5.

39. A comprehensive attempt to study different methods of meditation and their effect on ESP has recently been reported, but it is much too complex to be included here. Osis, K. and Bokert, E. "ESP and changed states of consciousness induced by meditation." *JASPR* 65 (1971): 17–65.

Chapter 16. Consciousness, the Brain and Death

1. *Ducasse, 10:4, pp. 39–118. For a critical appraisal of Ducasse's work, see Beloff, J., Chari, C. T. K., and Price, H. H. "Three essays in honor of C. J. Ducasse." *JASPR* 64 (1970): 327–42.
2. Wheatley, J. M. O. "The question of survival: Some logical reflections." *JASPR* 59 (1965): 202–10. See also Binkely, R. "Philosophy and the survival hypothesis." *JASPR* 60 (1966): 27–31.
3. Cheek, D. B. "Unconscious perception of meaningful sounds during surgical anesthesia as revealed under hypnosis." *Amer. J. Clin. Hypn.* 1 (1959): 101–113. See also an instructive case in LeCron, L. M. *Self-Hypnotism.* Englewood Cliffs, N.J.: Prentice-Hall, 1964, pp. 82–83.
4. The word "mind" is given here as "psyche" to indicate all the psychic activities of a person.
5. Epiphenomenalism is discussed in Schaffer, J. A. *Philosophy of Mind.* Englewood Cliffs, N.J.: Prentice-Hall, 1968. His argument, at least to me, does not seem as convincing as that of Ducasse.
6. Burt, C. "Parapsychology and its implications." *Int. J. Neuropsychiat.* 2 (1966): 363–77.
7. *Burt, C. "Brain and consciousness." *Brit. J. Psychol.* 59 (1968): 55–69. This gives a summary of the current debate on the brain-consciousness problem. See also Ahlberg, Alf. "Vision och verklighet." *Sökaren,* July 1970. J. P. Powell protests against Burt (*Bull. Br. Psychol. Soc.* 22 (1969): 27–28). Powell favors the theory of identity.
8. The idea of survival may also be attacked philosophically from a concept-analyzing, semantic point of view. Mats Furberg intends, in *Tankar om döden* (Aldus, 1970) to demonstrate that the question of immortality, from purely conceptual, fundamental reasons, *cannot* have any refutation which is true. His argument is commented on in the review of his work in *Sökaren,* March 1971.

Chapter 17. The Mystical Experience and the Psychic Field

1. Dean, S. R. "Beyond the unconscious: the ultraconscious." *Amer. J. Psychiat.* 122:1 (1965): 471. D: 122:2 (1966): 953–54 and 1317.

2. Bowers, M. B. and Freedman, D. X. " 'Psychedelic' experiences in acute psychoses." *Arch. Gen. Psych.* 15 (1966): 240–48. Also in Tart 15:2. See also Jacobs, Hans. *Djuppsykologi och yogalära.* Stockholm: Rabén & Sjögren, 1963, pp. 176–84. A study of mystical experiences in relation to age and social class has been made by Douglas-Smith, B. "An empirical study of religious mysticism." *Brit. J. Psychiat.* 118 (1971): 549–54. He considers that these experiences occur primarily unrelated to ordinary psychiatric diagnoses, to people of good intelligence and in the higher social strata.
3. Pahnke, W. N. "Drugs and mysticism." *IJP* 8 (1966): 295–320.
4. Cooper, L. and Erickson, M. *Time Distortion and Hypnosis.* Baltimore: Williams & Wilkins, 1954.
5. *Pahnke, W. H. and Richards, W. A. "Implications of LSD and experimental mysticism." *J. Religion and Health* 5 (1966): 175–208. Also in Tart 15:2.
6. *Edsman, C. M. "Mystiker i Vällingby." Sveriges Radio, 1968, pp. 90–108. Compare with Pahnke 17:5.
7. Maslow, A. H. "Cognition of being in the peak experience." *J. Genetic Psychol.* 94 (1959): 43–66.
8. Deikman, A. J. "Deautomatization and the mystic experience." *Psychiatry* 29 (1966): 324–38. Also in Tart 15:2. The outward-directed and the assimilating receptive attitudes toward the outside world are described by Deikman in *"Bimodal consciousness," *Arch. Gen. Psychiat.* 25 (1971): 481–89.
9. James, William. *The Varieties of Religious Experience.* New York: Modern Library, 1929, pp. 422–28.
10. *LeShan, Lawrence. *Toward a General Theory of the Paranormal: A Report of Work in Progress.* Parapsychological Monographs no. 9. New York: PF, 1969. R: *JASPR* 64 (1970): 343–47 and *JSPR* 45 (1970): 247–49. See also *Sökaren,* July 1970. LeShan compares the world picture which mystics describe with that proposed by present-day prominent men in physics and finds amazing similarities. Arthur Koestler also attempts to make a synthesis of physics and parapsychology in his *The Roots of Coincidence.* New York: Random House, 1972. This book includes a very stimulating discussion of discoveries in physics and parapsychology and their consequences for our world view.
11. Discussed by Burt 16:6. See also Ahlberg 16:7.
12. Different qualities and aspects of psychicness are discussed more thoroughly by Bendit 10:5. The psychic storm, p. 152.

13. Discussed by Murphy 15:37.
14. *Morris, R. L. "Psi and animal behavior: A survey." *JASPR* 64 (1970): 242–60. See also Pratt 2:12, pp. 206–71.
15. Backster, C. "Evidence of a primary perception in plant life." *IJP* 10 (1968): 329–48.
16. See, for example, Barry 6:8.
17. Edsman 17:6, pp. 48–50. See also *Sökaren,* June 1970.
18. *Bucke, Richard M. *Cosmic Consciousness.* New York: Dutton, 1968 (first edition, 1901). Bucke describes his experience in the third person, pp. 9–10. The quotation here is from James 17:9, p. 399. On Bucke, see also *Sökaren,* April 1970.
19. Edsman 17:6, pp. 104–105.
20. *Martinus. *Omkring min missions fødsel.* København: Martinus Institut, 1942, pp. 52–66. The last section is from *Livets Bog,* del I, p. 22, published by the Martinus Institut in 1932.
21. Some experiments are mentioned by LeShan 17:10, pp. 97–101.
22. "The schizophrenic patient's so-frequent delusion of being magically 'influenced' by outside forces (radar, electricity, or what not) is rooted partially in the fact of his responding to unconscious processes in persons about him—persons who, being unaware of these processes, will not and can not help him to realize that the 'influence' comes from a non-magical interpersonal source." Searles, H. F. "The schizophrenic's vulnerability to the therapist's unconscious processes." *J. Nerv. Ment. Dis.* 127 (1958): 247–62.
23. This obviously does not concern the first version, which came spontaneously and unexpectedly, but only the second vision and the subsequent intuitive experiences.
24. The term "cosmic flash" was first used by Martinus, to the best of my knowledge.

Chapter 18. How Can Life After Death Be Pictured?

1. Ducasse 10:4, pp. 121–31.
2. Broad, C. D. *Personal Identity and Survival.* London: SPR, 1958. Quote from Ducasse 18:1.
3. Price, H. H. "Survival and the idea of 'another world.' " *PSPR* 50 (1953): 1–25.
4. *Stevenson, I. "Some implications of parapsychological research on survival after death." *PASPR* 28 (1969): 18–35. D: *JASPR* 64 (1970): 231–36.

5. *Whiteman, J. H. M. "Evidence of survival from 'other world' experiences." *JASPR* 59 (1965): 160–66. See also Hart 9:6, pp. 232–45. Compare Case 30.
6. Wolff, H. G. and Curran, D. "Nature of delirium and allied states." *Arch. Neurol. Psychiat.* (1935): 1175–1215.
7. Thurmond, C. J. "Last thoughts before drowning." *J. Abnorm. Soc. Psychol.* 38 (1943): 165–84.
8. Evans-Wentz, W. Y. (ed.) *The Tibetan Book of the Dead.* New York: Oxford University Press, 1960 (first edition, 1927).
9. *Stevenson, I. "Some psychological principles relevant to research in survival." *JASPR* 59 (1965): 318–37.

Chapter 19. A Contemporary Mystic's Description of Life After Death

1. *Theosophy—what's it all about?* London: Theosophical Publishing House, 1967, chapter 5.
2. Steiner, Rudolf. *An Outline of Occult Science.* New York: Anthroposophical Press, 1922.
3. Shepherd, A. P. *A Scientist of the Invisible.* London: Hodder & Stoughton, 1954.
4. *Lilla Focus,* 1961.
5. The account is based on (a) *Martinus. *Vejen til paradis I–II.* København: Forlaget Kosmos, 1965, together with a lecture by Martinus; (b) Bruus-Jensen, Per. *Korrespondancekursus i Martinus Kosmologi.* København: Martinus Institut (in the course of publication), chapter 9: "Det levende vaesen og doden," pp. 571–674.
6. Herbert Tingsten, in *Notiser om liv och död* (Nordstedts, 1967) expresses, in a chapter called "Bön och vidskeplese," an atheist's concept of prayer as a last resort in a desperate situation, as an expression of desperation. He concedes that prayers can involve "a flash of belief, that I for that instant imagined that some little outlook exists so that the game can succeed. Perhaps there exists in prayer a trace of the baroque thought: 'When I, who deny you, pray, you must pull yourself together up there and exist.'" The book also gives expression of the fear of death in the sense of fear of death equalling fear of annihilation rather than of dying itself. Intense fear of death is also expressed in Furberg 16:8 and in Eriksson, Jörgen. *Revolt i huvet.* Bonniers, 1971. Ingemar

Hedenius analyzes an atheist's attitude toward death in two contributions to *Tala om döden* 1:1.

7. Martinus. *Vejen til paradis I,* p. 66.
8. Compare Matthew 22:1, 11–13.
9. Per Bruus-Jensen, personal communication, 1969, original source unknown.
10. Hart 9:6, p. 233, lists sixty-three books which discuss the existence of life after death and its nature, as described by communicators. Here are only a few examples: (a) Scultorp, F. C. *Livet i andevärlden.* Excelsior, 1962, describes life in the first sphere, which the author says he has experienced during separations; (b) Pole, W. T. 10:21. *Private Dowding* is fundamentally a striking illustration of Martinus' account; (c) the following two novels: Fridegård, Jan. *Torntuppen* (Stockholm, 1941) and Vallius, Eva. *Sjukhuset Det stora lugnet.* (Helsingfors, 1938) provide spiritualistically inspired descriptions of the first sphere; (d) Lange, Birgit. "Dom efter döden?" *Sökaren,* Sept. 1968, refers to literature in English on the state after death.
11. On communicators' views of reincarnation, see Ducasse 10:4, pp. 234–40.
12. *De fyra evangelierna på vår tids språk.* EFS förlaget, 1964.

Chapter 20. The Conception of Death and Life

1. LeShan 17:10, pp. 72–89.
2. Discussed in greater detail by Stevenson 18:4.
3. See, for example, Gerholm, T. R. and Hof, H. "Naturvetenskap och mystik." Årsbok för Kristen Humanism 31 (1969): 73–83.
4. The question is illustrated by J. Helander in "Om döden som livets spegel" in Sundström, J. C. (ed.) *Att åldras i Sverige.* Prisma, 1970, pp. 90–98.
5. Rumi, Jalaluddin, *The Mathnawi,* R. A. Nicholson, translator (London: Cambridge University Press, 1926). (A new translation by R. A. Nicholson, 1972, has been published by Luzac and Co., 46 Great Russell Street, London, W.C.)

Sources for the Quotations under the Chapter Headings

1. Quoted in Tingsten 19:6.
2. & 8. Quoted in LeShan 17:10. F. W. H. Myers was one of the

pioneers of parapsychology and, among other things, the author of the impressive book *Human Personality and Its Survival of Bodily Death,* written in 1903.

7. Quoted in *Sökaren,* April 1970.

9. & 15. *Om vår erkjennelses grunnlag.* Oslo: Servolibris, 1963.

10. Quoted in Ahlberg 16:7.

13. Offerhymn; Kärlek i tjugonde seklet, 1933.

14. *Morning of the Magicians.* New York: Harper & Row, 1967.

16. & 17. Filosofiens virkelighet. Oslo, 1964.

18. Själamässa; I en främmande stad, 1927.

19. *Livets Bog* I, p. 183.

20. *Tanker i tiden.* Oslo, 1961.

Translator's note: The most complete and comprehensive bibliography of works on, and related to, parapsychology is White, Rhea A. and Dale, Laura A., *Parapsychology: Sources of Information.* Metuchen, N.J.: Scarecrow Press, 1973.

Glossary

Only the most frequently used words and terms are included here; others are listed in the Index. Words are defined when they are first mentioned in the text.

agent The person about whom the percipient experiences something; "the sender" in a telepathic contact.

apparition A hallucination in which the percipient perceives a person' (or object) as being present near him, although the person in question is not actually there. Otherwise, the surroundings are experienced normally.

automatic activities Those activities which can be carried on without the help of normal consciousness, for example, automatic writing.

clairaudience The experience of receiving paranormal information through auditory impressions.

clairvoyance Supersensory perception or impression of occurrences related to objects and events.

communicator A personality which manifests itself or communicates through a medium.

cryptomnesia Something which has been observed or experienced without the person having been fully conscious of it, and which he has totally forgotten. But the impression exists in him, registered unconsciously and thus may later give rise to "false recognition" and what appears to be paranormal knowledge.

dissociation The splintering of a certain part of the psyche, which may then function more or less independently and even behave in a contradictory manner to the psyche as a whole.

ESP Abbreviation of *extrasensory perception,* includes telepathy, clairvoyance, clairaudience, pre- and retro-cognition; that is, all experiences or reactions to objects, events, states, or appearances which take place without the intermediary of the senses.

ESP-cards Five different cards each with a picture on it: a star, circle, square, cross, or wavy lines. A standard pack includes five of each picture.

ESP-projection, complete (1) A person (the projector, the agent) experiences a separation to another place, and (2) a percipient in that other place at the same time observes an apparition of the projector.

etheric body A hypothetical "double" of the physical body. Also used of the body which is assumed during a separation. Sometimes called "astral body" or "soul body."

etheric double See "etheric body."

focusing The ability during an ESP experiment to "concentrate" ESP on a certain object. Example: a person who often guesses correctly when a certain card is presented to him but produces only chance level results with all the other cards.

lucid dream A dream in which the dreamer is conscious that he is dreaming and can influence the events in the dream.

materialization "Clad in matter." According to spiritualism, a medium gives off a hypothetical substance, ectoplasm, out of which shapes with human appearances are formed; these can move, talk, be seen, touched, and photographed.

medium "Middleman." According to spiritualism, a person who, as an intermediary, establishes contact with the spirit world. A more general meaning: a person who experiences paranormal phenomena.

memory-traces The equivalent for a person of "psi-traces" in an object.

object association A descriptive term for psychometry.

out-of-the-body experience The conscious experience of being outside your own physical body and of possibly being able to see it from without; also called separation.

paranormal phenomena Occurrences which do not fit our ordinary conception of cause and effect: "supernatural" occurrences.

parapsychology That branch of science which investigates paranormal phenomena.

percipient A person who experiences a paranormal occurrence; a subject whose ESP is investigated during an experiment.

persona The concept advanced by Hart to designate everything which can be observed of a *person*. When a person is described, it is his persona which is mentioned. (C. G. Jung uses the term persona in another sense.)

precognition Foreknowledge of future occurrences which cannot be deducted from present knowledge.

psi The general term designating a person's paranormal perception or ability to influence his surroundings. This includes both ESP and PK.

psi-field A hypothetical field around objects; can be influenced by events and occurrences which produce psi-traces in it.

psi-hallucinations Hallucinations which give paranormal information concerning conditions in the surrounding world.

psi-traces The hypothetical alteration of an object's psi-field. It is suggested that a medium perceives these psi-traces in psychometry.

psyche The general term for a person's total psychic capability and qualities.

psychic The capacity to be a medium or "sensitive," and able to experience ESP frequently.

psychodynamic A concept in psychoanalysis, usually indicating unconscious psychic mechanisms.

psychokinesis, PK Direct psychic influence on objects or living organisms, such as moving them from place to place, without physical or chemical influence.

psychometry The ability to make contact with an object, the "psychometric object," and to receive paranormal knowledge of persons or events with which the object has been associated. The word actually means "the measuring of the psyche" and is used with this meaning in psychological testing.

retrocognition Supernatural or paranormal knowledge of past occurrences.

RSPK Abbreviation of recurrent spontaneous psychokinesis.

separation *See* out-of-the-body experience.

shared dream Two people dream simultaneously of the same course of events in which both of them take part.

super-ESP A hypothetical, actively operating form of ESP.

telepathy "Distant knowledge." Supernatural or paranormal perception of another person's psychic state or activities.

trance A state of limited attentiveness and increased suggestibility.

xenoglossy The ability to express oneself in a foreign language without ever having learned or studied it.

Zener-cards *See* ESP-cards.

Index

The Author

NILS O. JACOBSON, M.D., is a psychiatrist practicing in Lund, Sweden. For a number of years he has been doing research in parapsychology and investigating the subject of death. Recently he has been studying the physiological and psychological effects of meditation.